T0385515

YEARS OF PLENTY, YEARS OF WANT

YEARS OF PLENTY, YEARS OF WANT

France and the Legacy of the Great War

Benjamin Franklin Martin

NIU PRESS / *DeKalb, IL*

Library of Congress Cataloging-in-Publication Data
Martin, Benjamin F., 1947–
  Years of plenty, years of want : France and the legacy of the
Great War / Benjamin Franklin Martin.
      pages cm
  Includes bibliographical references and index.
  ISBN 978 0 87580 468 2 (cloth) — ISBN 978 1 60909 080 7 (e
book)
  1. France—History—1914–1940. 2. France—Politics and
government—19140–1940. 3. France—Intellectual life—20th
century. 4. World War, 1914–1918—Influence. I. Title.
  DC389.M274 2013
  944.081'5—dc23

                      2012045343

*For
Amanda*

CONTENTS

PREFACE AND ACKNOWLEDGMENTS

When asked for advice about writing, my friend Courtlandt Dixon Barnes Bryan cited the famous injunction from J. D. Salinger's novella *Seymour: An Introduction*: ask yourself what story you most want to read and then dare to write it. In my case, the story has been the one that preoccupies me the most. Right now, I detect a whiff of the 1930s in the air: political polarization, economic collapse, general insecurity, recriminations, anger, fear. The impact of World War I made the 1920s a time of illusions, as if wishing hard enough could spare a recurrence. The 1930s proved that wishes do not come true. Everyone knows these main lines, but the details are what make history fascinating, poignant, and personal. For almost twenty years, I have been writing about France in the wake of the Great War, which became World War I when we had to start numbering them. For *France and the Après Guerre* (1999), I concentrated on the problems of the early 1920s that prevented the French leaders who defeated Germany from reaping the benefits of that victory. For *France in 1938* (2005), I turned to the economic, political, and foreign policy failures that brought a new generation of French leaders to Munich. Now in this book, I am examining a broader sweep from the early 1900s to 1939. I am concentrating on a few personalities and on literary portrayals of the period. As always, I write not just for scholars but for anyone who seeks out historical parallels, who shares my preoccupations.

In the Preface and Acknowledgments for *France and the Après Guerre*, I wrote that "my thinking remains profoundly influenced by a certain kind of education and by service as an army officer, revealed in my attitude toward loyalty, honor, courage, and betrayal." For me, the statement was a point of pride. For at least two of my reviewers, it implied a lack of objectivity toward historical figures whose sense of loyalty, honor, courage, and betrayal differed from mine. To benefit these and other detractors, I add here that I still have my army dog tags, which would have identified me for the purpose of memorial as "Episcopalian." I contribute annually to the Cheetah Conservation Fund, and I am proudly a Life Supporter of the Badger Trust, Ltd.

Amy Elizabeth Farranto convinced me to write this book. She is a superb editor whose reaction to its chapters as I sent them to her one by one speeded their completion and made their writing a joy. Her colleagues at Northern Illinois University Press all inspire the greatest confidence. At Corbis, Tim Davis and Donna Daley mined their extraordinary repository of images to locate the photographs that accompany the text. The staff at the Troy H. Middleton Library of Louisiana State University, and especially bibliographer Joseph Nicholson, acquired the books and newspapers I needed to consult. My research assistant at LSU, Kimberly Catherine Johnson, eagerly and tirelessly assembled material about the writers and novels discussed in chapter 4, "Shifting Ground"; she also prepared the index. To read the chapters, I enlisted three of my best former students—Katherine Louise Smith Patin, Tyler Caitlin Lott, and Paige Ivy Bowers—and three longtime friends—James Merlin Seidule, John Raymond Walser, and Nicolas Kariouk Pecquet du Bellay de Verton. Their comments have been beyond measure in worth: frequently challenging, sometimes confirming, always penetrating. Eugen Weber was my mentor and, with Jacqueline Suzanne Brument-Roth Weber, the truest of friends. They were my best supporters as I wrote five previous books. Although Eugen died in 2007, I have felt his spirit at my side with this one as well, and Jacqueline is ever my guide. Janis Kilduff Martin was my wife and remains my dearest companion.

YEARS OF PLENTY, YEARS OF WANT

Georges Clemenceau
© Bettmann/CORBIS

Joseph Caillaux
© Bettmann/CORBIS

Jean Jaurès
© Lebrecht Music
& Arts/CORBIS

Raymond Poincaré
© CORBIS

Albert de Mun
© Stefano Bianchetti/
CORBIS

Neville Chamberlain, Georges Bonnet, Edouard Daladier
© Hulton-Deutsch Collection/CORBIS

Roger Martin du Gard
© Bettmann/CORBIS

Henri Barbusse

Colette
© adoc-photos/CORBIS

Louis-Ferdinand Céline
© adoc-photos/CORBIS

Irène Némirovsky
© Stefano Bianchetti/CORBIS

Julien Green
© Bettmann/CORBIS

Joseph Caillaux
© Bettmann/CORBIS

Jean Jaurès
© Lebrecht Music
& Arts/CORBIS

July 1914

Summer 1914: at the end of June in Sarajevo, Bosnia, a Serbian-trained assassin shot dead the heir to the imperial throne of Austria-Hungary; at the beginning of August, the chanceries of the Great Powers exchanged declarations of war. Hell gaped open. The Great War, much predicted and much delayed, stalked forth. Blood and darkness enveloped Europe in the first cataclysm of what would become the century of catastrophe. A civilization constructed upon political, social, and economic revolutions broke apart. An abyss lay between what had been and what was to be.[1]

Rumors of war had circulated for almost a decade. In 1905 and 1911, Germany contested France's protectorate over Morocco. In 1906, 1912, and 1913, Austria-Hungary and Russia squared off over claims in the Balkans. France prevailed in Morocco through support from Great Britain. Austria-Hungary extended its control in the Balkans through support from Germany. These five crises originated from two fundamental alterations in the European power structure. The first was the long-term deterioration of the Ottoman Empire, whose writ once ran across North Africa, throughout the Middle East, and north into Hungary. Its retreat before nationalist revolts and the encroachment of the European Great Powers began in the late 1600s and, by the middle nineteenth century, threatened to become a rout. Great Britain, France, Italy, and later Germany jostled for empire in North Africa. Russia and Austria-Hungary competed for control of the Balkans. The second transformation was the sudden emergence of Germany as a Great Power. Prussia unified the disparate German states under its rule by defeating the two previously dominant land powers in continental Europe, Austria-Hungary in 1866 and France in 1871. Diminished, France sought compensation through an overseas empire, Austria-Hungary through extension of power over Slavic regions rebelling against the Ottomans.

During the nearly five decades that preceded the Great War, Europeans fought almost continually—but not against each other except in the Austro-Prussian and Franco-Prussian wars, which were brief and contained. Thanks to the Industrial Revolution, they possessed modern weapons and modern transportation (supremely summed up in the "gunboat"), which made British and French colonial wars in Africa or Asia, and Russia's war against the Ottomans in 1877–78, triumphal processions. Europeans, leaders and peoples, simply had no conception of general war among Great Powers. By 1914, modern weaponry was a synonym for "lethality": machine guns, rapid-firing highly accurate artillery, massively armed battleships, military aircraft, and poison gas. Each Great Power expanded its standing army, with both France and Germany having roughly 7 percent of their adult males in uniform. The greatest innovation of the period was the formation of peacetime alliances—previously, they had been concluded during war or in anticipation of it. The greatest humiliation France suffered from defeat by Prussia in 1871 was the loss of two eastern provinces, Alsace and Lorraine, to the new Germany. Its chancellor and the genius behind German unification, Otto von Bismarck, recognized that France would be a permanent enemy and reconciled with Austria-Hungary by emphasizing the threat to both from Russia. The result was the 1879 Dual Alliance, which became the Triple Alliance in 1882 through the inclusion of Italy. Because Bismarck believed that the most serious threat to Germany lay in any new general war, the alliance promised assistance only if a member were attacked.

Confronted by this coalition of Great Powers in central Europe, French diplomacy worked to encircle it. The first step was a defensive pact with Russia in 1894, a triumph of expediency: reactionary

Russian tsardom allied with republican France because Germany was the danger each feared the most. The second was an agreement with Great Britain, the Entente Cordiale (Friendly Understanding) in 1904, which settled all disputes between the world's two largest empires—and would lead afterward to semiformal pledges of mutual defense in a war against Germany. The third, almost simultaneously, was a détente with Italy, estranging it from the Triple Alliance. Never mind that what was increasingly called the "Triple Entente" also provided certain support only if a member were attacked, the European Great Powers had divided themselves into competing blocs.

The inevitable conclusion was that a war between two might easily become a war among all. Certainly Germany thought so, its military general staff now forced to plan for war on both the eastern and western frontiers. With boldness crossing over to grave risk, its leaders decided against fighting two wars simultaneously and for fighting two wars consecutively. Called the Schlieffen Plan after its formulator—General Count Alfred von Schlieffen, chief of the general staff from 1891 until 1905—it relied on the differences in mobilization time and population. With their modern, dense rail networks, both France and Germany could assemble and equip their armies within two weeks, but Russia, vast and underdeveloped, required six weeks or more. The French population was c. 40 million, the German c. 64 million, the Russian c. 165 million. The Schlieffen Plan called for a sudden attack on France at the outset of any war by almost all of Germany's military might, destroying the smaller French army within six weeks. German forces would then turn to face the Russians, who were more numerous but had inferior weaponry and training.

How to deal with these foreign policy, diplomatic, and military issues became the essential political debate in France beginning in the summer of 1911. Seven years earlier through the Entente Cordiale, British and French leaders had ended their competition in North Africa by granting Great Britain a free hand in Egypt, France a free hand in Morocco. Spain asserted rights to northwestern Morocco but had little means of backing them up. When Germany contested France's free hand in 1905, Great Britain sided firmly with its new imperial partner. Since then, the French had used Morocco's sultan,

Moulay Hafid, as a puppet as they pursued greater commercial interests and increasingly exercised police powers. This intervention
stimulated a nationalist revolt that swept through the country, be-
sieging Hafid and the European colony in Fez. The dispatch of French
troops relieved the city on 21 May 1911 and made clear how close
France was to imposing its will through a protectorate. Six weeks
later on 1 July, the German destroyer *Panther* dropped anchor in
the Moroccan Atlantic port of Agadir and was soon after replaced
by the much larger and more powerful cruiser *Berlin*. The claim of
protecting German merchants was absurd because none were within
two hundred miles of Agadir. Instead, Germany was making a heavy-
handed bid for some piece of the Moroccan action.

France's prime minister was Joseph Caillaux, who had been elevated from his position as minister of finance by a freak accident at
the Paris Air Show that severely injured the prime minister, Ernest
Monis, and killed the minister of war, Maurice Berteaux. Caillaux
was a millionaire who sat with the center-left Radical party and was
well-known for his proposal to replace France's old system of indirect taxes (both inelastic and hard to estimate) with a single levy on
all income. He became prime minister on 28 June, only two days before the *Panthersprung*, the "Leap of the *Panther*." The minister of
foreign affairs, Justin de Selves, was all for sending a French vessel
as a counter, but Caillaux quashed any bellicose response. Although
he had no experience in diplomacy, he had long believed that France
should seek an accommodation with Germany, which had now far
surpassed Great Britain as the industrial and commercial powerhouse
in Europe, even if the cost was a certain subservience. By mid-July,
Germany offered to recognize a French protectorate over Morocco
in return for "compensation," meaning France's possessions in the
Congo region of central Africa. To de Selves, the German demand
was extortion. The British agreed, with David Lloyd George, the influential chancellor of the exchequer, delivering a speech at the Mansion House on 21 July 1911 making clear Great Britain's support for
France and declaring that peace without honor was no peace.

Because de Selves was intransigent, Caillaux negotiated behind
his back with Baron Oskar von der Lancken-Wakenitz, a counselor

at the German embassy in Paris. France's foreign ministry, the Quai d'Orsay, was aware of the duplicity because French intelligence had broken the German diplomatic code. Jules Cambon, the ambassador to Berlin, and Maurice Paléologue, the secretary general of the ministry, cautiously filed away the deciphered telegrams, the so-called Greens (*documents verts*) from the colored diagonal bar in the margin. On 4 November, Caillaux announced that he had ended the crisis by signing the Treaty of Fez: Germany accepted a French protectorate; France ceded some 120,000 square miles of the French Congo linking the German Cameroons to the Congo and Ubangi Rivers. An explosion of indignation followed among the French public. In the lower house of the legislature, the Chamber of Deputies, only the fear of immediate war stemmed a revolt against the treaty, and even then, on 21 December a quarter of the deputies preferred to abstain rather than vote to endorse it. Before the turn of the upper house, the Senate, discreet whispers from the Quai d'Orsay alerted its most ferocious nationalist, Georges Clemenceau. When Caillaux and de Selves appeared before the Senate's foreign affairs committee on 12 January 1912, Caillaux formally denied conducting any unofficial negotiations. Clemenceau then asked de Selves for confirmation, but the foreign minister refused to reply and resigned. Caillaux resigned as well, two days later.

The episode and its revelations were a significant shock to the French public and their political system. The moment cried out for a leader with a reputation for energy, honesty, and patriotism. Count Albert de Mun, leader of the Catholic conservatives, captured the mood in his column for the newspaper *L'Echo de Paris*: "Antimilitarism and pacifism had grown like poisonous plants in a fen when suddenly the coup of Agadir struck the torpid hearts of France and in a moment her sons saw in one another's eyes their ancestral heritage. Among them ran the cry, like an electric shock, Enough!" The answer to "Enough!" was Raymond Poincaré, a brilliant attorney renowned for his assiduous attention to detail, cultured, literate, elected, like de Mun, to the Académie française, but most of all, possessed of an austere patriotism, and unwilling to forgive the Germans for seizing his native Lorraine. As the new prime minister, Poincaré pushed the

Treaty of Fez through the Senate but called it a disgrace. Clemenceau declared that Caillaux had misunderstood his patriotic duty when dealing with the Germans.[2]

A sense of national revival was in the air. Poincaré took the Quai d'Orsay for himself and sharpened the tone of French foreign policy. He accelerated the takeover in Morocco and appointed General Hubert Lyautey, recommended by de Mun, as its governor. In August 1912, he traveled to St. Petersburg to strengthen alliance ties with Russia. When the union of French schoolteachers voted to endorse the spread of antimilitarist propaganda among army recruits, he angrily ordered its dissolution. His minister of war, Alexandre Millerand, restored the military tattoo in Paris and named General Joseph Joffre, known for his toughness and nerve, as commander of military forces. Alarmed by German bluster over Morocco, Great Britain's military leaders quietly expanded the meaning of the Entente Cordiale if war with Germany came. The navies would split responsibilities, France taking the Mediterranean, Great Britain the north Atlantic, and the British army would send its Expeditionary Force to join the French army near the border with Belgium. War in the Balkans, beginning in 1912 and continuing into 1913, heightened tensions in general. De Mun wrote, again in the conservative newspaper *L'Echo de Paris*, "There are, in the history of a people, decisive hours. We touch one of those hours. . . . No one in Europe wants war, and yet it moves closer and closer, despite intentions, fears, exertions, and resolutions, led by the blind force of situations and events."[3]

At decisive hours, strong leadership is compelling. In the structure of France's Third Republic, the office of president was a ceremonial figurehead, elected to a seven-year term by the Chamber of Deputies and the Senate sitting together for the vote as the National Assembly. The political left especially feared the threat of a strong executive to legislative independence, citing Napoleon I and Napoleon III. Poincaré believed that he could transform the office into a center of power without jeopardizing republican traditions. The term of President Armand Fallières expired in January 1913, and Poincaré declared his candidacy. For ideology and for his treatment of Caillaux, the left, Radicals and Socialists, opposed him. He had many supporters among the center—and for the rest, he would need the right, whose allegiance to republican principles the left doubted. Clemenceau's Jacobin heritage meant that he worshiped at two altars, rude nationalism and legislative predominance: Poincaré could be prime minister but not president. On 17 January 1913, the votes of the conservatives, delivered by de Mun, were sufficient to sweep away tradition—proof of how much the issues made stark by the Agadir crisis had come to dominate life.

Poincaré sought the presidency to argue for a significant national sacrifice. In 1912, Germany had begun expanding the size of its standing army to c. 860,000 men, nearly double that of the French army at 480,000. With a population one and a half times greater than France, the Germans could add to their forces merely by expanding the draft. Already requiring two years of military service from every male at the age of twenty-one, France could match them only by adding a third year to the conscription term. Doing so would increase the number of draftees by 50 percent and the army as a whole by 30 percent, raising the total to c. 625,000, certainly better odds. But asking young men to serve an additional year, to take them from families, farms, businesses, and schools, would be a severe test of revived patriotism—and expensive. Poincaré's term was seven years, but he suspected that he had less than three in which to prepare France for war.

Two of his closest political supporters, moderates Aristide Briand and Louis Barthou, were his choices to guide three-year service through the legislature. The opposition came from the left, led by Caillaux among the Radicals and Jean Jaurès among the Socialists. They had first worked together opposing Poincaré's election and now had a score to settle. Caillaux burned with resentment over his humiliation a year earlier, and he joined his anger to the argument that France should regard Germany with friendship instead of hostility. Jaurès rejected traditional military conceptions, favoring instead a "nation in arms," which his 1910 book *L'Armée nouvelle* (The new army) described: every Frenchman would keep a rifle above the mantel to take down if war came. He thought war between France and Germany unlikely, even impossible—not because their ruling classes would keep the peace to maintain their profits but because their working classes would join hands across the border to threaten a general strike. Poincaré exerted his influence to the maximum, reviving the allegation that he sought an extension of presidential power. He used up political favors, reducing his leverage in the future. He relied on a majority including so much of the right that his centrist allies were uncomfortable, but he won the passage of three-year service in December 1913. With an additional provision: the enormous new expenses could not be covered by the traditional indirect taxes, which forced Poincaré and his allies to accept some form of tax on income, the details to be worked out later, and during the interim, the return of Caillaux to the ministry of finance.

This result set the stakes in the elections some five months later in April and May 1914 for the Chamber of Deputies. Victory for the center-right and right meant maintenance of the three-year service law and a watered-down income tax. Victory for the center-left and left meant possible reversal of the service law and a progressive income tax. Against this risk, Poincaré, Briand, and Barthou took a fateful decision. At their instigation, Gaston Calmette, editor of *Le Figaro*, the Parisian daily of the French bourgeoisie, began a series of vituperative editorials against Caillaux. Calmette's aim was not just to damage Caillaux politically but to ruin him personally. For that purpose, he used every resource to gain possession of three highly incriminating documents. First, he had copies of the Quai d'Orsay Greens, proving Caillaux's secret contacts with the Germans. Poincaré explicitly denied him permission to use them, because the Germans would then learn that their code had been broken. Calmette could, however, hint that he had proof of Caillaux's "treason." Second, he had a copy of the Fabre memorandum, which confirmed Caillaux's illicit use of political influence. In March 1911, Caillaux, as minister of finance, had pressured Victor Fabre, attorney general for the Paris region since 1906, to grant an exceptional postponement in the appeals court hearing on the fraud conviction of financier Henri Rochette. Subsequently, Rochette mounted new swindles and then fled the country. Feeling ill-used, Fabre wrote down his version of events, which he gave to Briand, then minister of justice, who in turn passed it to his successor, Barthou. The Fabre memorandum could be highly damaging, but so could its suppression, and so when Barthou gave Calmette a copy, he did so with the warning that it could be "used" but not "published" until he gave permission. Third, Calmette had a personal letter written by Caillaux to his first wife, Berthe-Eva Gueydan, before her divorce from Jules Dupré. Other newspapers might traffic in such an intimacy, but never *Le Figaro*. Calmette considered making an exception to destroy Caillaux.[4]

The first editorials appeared at the beginning of January 1914, shortly after the passage of three-year service and the promise of an income tax. Calmette recounted stories alleging Caillaux's involvement in various financial conspiracies but lost his readers in the maze of numbers. He shifted to an attack on the income tax at the end of the month, arguing that progressivity was discrimination against the successful and that requiring revelation of income amounted to an "inquisition." In mid-February, the attack turned to the Agadir crisis, with the reminder that de Selves had refused to back up Caillaux's disavowal of secret contacts. To this cascade of vitriol, Caillaux issued calm denials, in recognition that by striking back he would admit a wound. Then, on 10 March, Calmette described Caillaux's intervention in the Rochette case. Two days later, he revealed that the details came from a document prepared by the Paris attorney general, but the impact was blunted by Barthou's continued refusal to permit its publication. And so, on the day after, 13 March, the facsimile of a letter filled *Le Figaro*'s front page, a letter from July 1901 by Joseph Caillaux, then minister of finance for the first time, to his mistress, Berthe Gueydan Dupré, whose husband was the administrative assistant to a fellow cabinet member. Caillaux boasted of political duplicity, declared that he had "rendered a true service to my country," and signed himself, "Ton Jo"—her nickname for him in bed.[5]

Thus far, Calmette had meant to damage what remained of Caillaux's reputation for political integrity, and he had succeeded: the Chamber of Deputies announced plans to investigate the Rochette case. Now, by reproducing this "Ton Jo" letter for all to see, he meant to humiliate, to provoke him in the final weeks before the election. Perhaps Caillaux would threaten violence or challenge him to a duel.

Calmette did not reckon its effect upon Henriette Caillaux, coming after the cumulative effect of virulent attacks for the last two and a half months. The letter did not touch her, but she believed that its source could only be Gueydan. She knew Gueydan had other letters, letters that did indeed concern her, letters Joseph Caillaux had written to her in 1909 when she was his mistress and he was still married to Gueydan. If Gueydan had given the "Ton Jo" to Calmette, she might have given the others as well. Henriette Caillaux saw her social life and reputation in tatters. The law code denied prior restraint: a suit for defamation could not be initiated until after an offending item appeared in print. On 16 March 1914, Joseph Caillaux told Poincaré that if Calmette published anything reflecting on the conduct of his wife, "I'll kill him!" Henriette Caillaux was beyond threats. That afternoon, she purchased a caliber .32 Browning automatic pistol, then went to the offices of *Le Figaro*, where she shot at Calmette six times, hitting him with four bullets. He died six hours later, his final words before losing consciousness, "What I did, tell them, I did without hatred."[6]

The French political world was in shock. The initial judgment held that Calmette had paid with his life for the destruction of the Caillaux family. Henriette Caillaux sat in Saint Lazare prison, accused of premeditated murder. Joseph Caillaux resigned as minister of finance. Before the Chamber of Deputies, Barthou read aloud the Fabre memorandum, and a committee began an investigation into "abusive encroachments of the executive on the judiciary" with special attention to the Rochette case. Soon enough, however, that initial judgment came under doubt. Caillaux had been prime minister once, minister of finance three times, and since October 1913 was president of the Radical party. He had powerful allies, who now rallied to his defense. Jaurès contrived to chair the Chamber's committee of inquiry, declared it complete after eight days of testimony, and forced through a report that laid all the blame on Fabre for bending to political pressure—or for complaining about it. *Le Figaro* noted two escapes: Rochette to Greece, Caillaux from sanction. At Saint Lazare, Henriette Caillaux had special privileges: a well-scrubbed cell, a new stove and lamp, another prisoner assigned as her maid, and a foot rug, a gift from the warden himself. More serious, the Paris prosecutorial office displayed none of the aggressiveness that it usually adopted in capital crimes. Examining magistrate Henri Boucard dismissed her claim of meaning only to wound Calmette but accepted her assertion of acting to prevent the publication of intimate letters. She could then mount her defense on the basis of protecting her honor. Finally, the legislative elections on 26 April and 10 May produced an ambiguous result, with only the Socialists gaining seats. The new prime minister was René Viviani, a centrist Radical who excluded Caillaux from the cabinet and took the ministry of foreign affairs for himself. He also promised the retention of three-year service "until European conditions allow a revision." His declaration came after Paléologue warned that the Quai d'Orsay considered war to be a distinct possibility.[7]

The foreign ministry of Austria-Hungary also believed hostilities likely. The Balkan Wars of 1912 and 1913 completed the rout of the Ottoman Empire that had begun in earnest after a disastrous defeat by Russia in 1878. Three Ottoman possessions in the Balkans, Serbia, Montenegro, and Romania, won their independence. Two others, Bosnia and Herzegovina, came under military occupation by Austria-Hungary. Serbia especially had exalted aspirations, whether simply for "Greater Serbian" domination within the Balkan peninsula or for a "South-Slav" federation encompassing all who shared the Serbo-Croatian language, which would require the destruction first of the Ottoman Empire and then of the Austro-Hungarian. These grandiose—and bellicose—dreams would have been preposterous but for the Serbian cultural and religious links to Russia, which endorsed pan-Slavism as a means of extending its influence.

Whether Serbian or Russian, such aggrandizement meant acute danger for Austria-Hungary. Its leaders correctly understood that Serbia was the crux of the problem, for Russia would not act unilaterally. Assuaging the Serbs was the approach of Franz Josef, then eighty-three years old, who had been emperor since 1848. As chief witness to the humiliations endured by the empire of the Habsburgs, once suzerain of Europe—the loss of Italian hegemony in 1859, the loss of German hegemony in 1866—he feared any new war. Subduing the Serbs was the approach of foreign minister Lexa von Aehrenthal and army chief of staff Conrad von Hötzendorf, who also feared war but believed it inevitable. Embracing the *Schlamperei* (muddling) that so often characterized government in Vienna, Austria-Hungary pursued both policies simultaneously. In 1908, it formally annexed Bosnia and Herzegovina, ending the thirty-year fiction that military occupation did not mean possession, and placed them further out of Serbia's reach. Russia protested vehemently, complaining that Austria-Hungary had violated agreements signed at the Congress of Berlin in 1878 after the Russian victory over the Ottomans. At that moment, Germany took a momentous step. In signing the Dual Alliance, Bismarck had always insisted that Austria-Hungary was on its own in any collision with Russia involving the Balkans. He had famously declared that, for Germany, the entire peninsula was "not worth the bones of a single Pomeranian Grenadier." But Bismarck had been dead for ten years, and after Germany's new leaders, Kaiser Wilhelm II and Chancellor Bernhard von Bülow, made clear to Russia that any attack on Austria-Hungary would entail a German response, Russia decided to accept the annexation. In the Balkan Wars of 1912 and 1913, Serbia dominated the fighting and expected significant territorial gains, one of them a foothold to its west along the Adriatic coast, giving it ports on the Mediterranean Sea. Unwilling to countenance such an accession for Serbia, Austria-Hungary set up the region as an independent Albania. Once again the Russians protested, and once again Germany compelled their acquiescence. For Serbia, the time had come to act alone.

By 1914, Austria-Hungary had ruled Bosnia and Herzegovina for thirty-six years. However much it brought roads, railroads, schools, improved hygiene—all the benefits of improved administration—its imperialism was perceived as oppression. Bosnian nationalists naturally warmed to Serbia, which had once suffered like them under the Ottomans and now appeared to be the best chance of escaping the Habsburgs. Some of their youth became radicalized and crossed into Serbia, where a few were recruited to a secret group run by Colonel Dragutin Dimitrijević called the Black Hand, or sometimes the Union of Death. The Serbian government—King Peter and his prime minister, Nikola Pašić—was well aware that Dimitrijević trained terrorists. It also knew he was not amenable to control because the Russian military attaché provided him direct subsidies. In late spring 1914, the Black Hand learned that Archduke Franz Ferdinand, heir to the throne of Austria-Hungary, planned to attend military field exercises scheduled for late June in Bosnia and Herzegovina and then pay a ceremonial visit to Sarajevo, their capital. Here was an opportunity to strike at the hated foe close to home. Dimitrijević began plans for an assassination. When Pašić learned of the plot, he realized that war might well be the result and feared the preparations of the Black Hand might be too far advanced for him to stop. His nerve breaking, he had the Serbian minister in Vienna warn the Austro-Hungarian foreign office that the archduke might face danger—he could not be more specific without admitting the Serbian government's involvement. Of course, the Austrians ignored it. Franz Ferdinand and his wife, Sophie, oversaw the maneuvers and then traveled to Sarajevo, where they received a fine welcome. The Black Hand assassins were monumentally incompetent but the Austro-Hungarian security arrangements even more so. Riding in their open car, the royal couple were shot dead. The date was 28 June 1914: no one alive ever forgot the Appointment at Sarajevo.[8]

Initial reaction in Paris was muted. *Le Temps*, the newspaper widely regarded as the government's spokesman, reported that Franz Ferdinand was not a popular figure in Austria-Hungary and asserted, wrongly, "Neither the Serbian government nor the Serbian people are to any degree responsible." The Socialist party's *L'Humanité* came close to the truth in blaming the assassination on Austria-Hungary's annexation of Bosnia and Herzegovina. The right-wing monarchists of *L'Action française* speculated about conspiracy theories, favoring one involving the chauffeur whose wrong turn gave the assassins their opportunity. Raymond Recouly, foreign affairs analyst for *Le Figaro*, warned on 1 July that "the crime of Sarajevo" might have "incalculable consequences," but two days later predicted the crisis would pass. On 6 July, the mass-market daily *Le Matin* reassured, "All fears of Austro-Serb complications appear to have been eliminated." The Balkans were far away, the names too hard to spell or pronounce. And something else: the assassination of the archduke evoked a world where birth and privilege still determined standing. As Alfred Capus, Calmette's successor as editor at *Le Figaro*, wrote, "We French bourgeois are proud of our Revolution and incapable of indulging the prejudices of nobility."[9]

Distractions were abundant—and necessary, as Paris was sweltering this summer, the afternoon temperature often close to 90 degrees Fahrenheit. The best, because unifying, was a boxing match on 16 July 1914 in London between France's Georges Carpentier and America's Edward "Gunboat" Smith. Carpentier was the heavyweight champion of Europe, Smith the "White Hope Champion," a title created to denigrate Jack Johnson, the African American who won the U.S. heavyweight championship in 1908. In the sixth round, the British referee disqualified Smith for a "foul," and Carpentier returned to Paris for a hero's welcome as "White Heavyweight Champion of the World." Less good, because divisive, were legislative debates over domestic politics. The wealthy fixated on the progress of the income tax, with conservatives warning that its implementation would mean "social revolution." In fact, the version under consideration would affect only households with an income of more than 5,000 francs ($21,600 in 2011), meaning less than one in twenty, and the progressivity stopped at 2 percent.[10]

Potentially more important, but harder to explain and impossible to predict, was the proposed change in election procedure for the Chamber of Deputies from single-member districts (*scrutin d'arrondissement*) to department-wide proportional lists (*scrutin de liste, répartition proportionnelle*): both left and right favored the change, the center opposed it. A reminder of the stakes came in the announcement of parochial school closures, the latest instance in the contest between the Catholic Church and the anticlerical French Republic. Two new books ripped at this unhealed sore, the correspondence of a great anticlerical champion, *Lettres de Jules Ferry, 1846–1893*, and a novel by devout Catholic Paul Bourget, *Le Démon de midi* (The demon stirs). Leader of the moderate Republicans in the 1880s, Ferry established a new conception of national unity based on state schools providing free, mandatory, and secular primary education. For Bourget and his series of psychological novels that began in 1889 with *Le Disciple*, that education without religion led inevitably to the rationalization of sin and crime.[11]

Among the prudent and foresighted, the most important observation of the summer was calm on the Bourse, the Paris stock market: the long-term *(rente perpétuelle)* 3 percent state bonds held steady at 83.15 francs ($359.00 in 2011). Such financial confidence was critical because the treasury planned to cover 805 million francs of defense spending ($3.5 billion in 2011) from three-year service through new bonds at 3.5 percent to go on sale 7 July. The result was an extraordinary endorsement of government policy. Investors began lining up at 5 a.m., four hours before the Bourse opened, and then oversubscribed the 805-million-franc goal by more than 4,000 percent, committing 38 billion francs ($164 billion in 2011) to the new offering.[12]

To be clear, this result was an affirmation of Poincaré's policy, despite the legislative elections with their indeterminate result. In the Senate, a debate on military preparedness evoked charges and countercharges of failure to provide adequate equipment to the army and navy—in the past. Clemenceau exclaimed for effect, "There are hours when each must assume his responsibilities," but in adding, "The nation has always given its billions without counting when asked for the national defense and is ready to do so again," he referred to the 38 billion francs a week earlier. On Bastille Day, an imposing military review at Longchamps on the western edge of Paris thrilled a huge crowd with its image of strength and readiness. When the congress of the Socialist party voted two days later its support for a motion by Jaurès to impose a general strike in time of war, calumny rained down upon them. *Le Temps* warned that whatever *French* Socialists might do, *German* Socialists would certainly not join a general strike. Jaurès might well claim, "There is no contradiction between making the maximum effort to assure peace and if war breaks out in spite of us, making the maximum effort to assure the independence and integrity of the nation," but Jules Guesde, his competitor for leadership within the party, answered that the motion was "against national, republican, and socialist duty."[13]

In the midst of the controversy about the general strike proposal, Poincaré and Viviani began a state visit to Russia that had been planned for more than six months. They left Dunkirk on 16 July aboard the battleship *France*, which with its attending destroyers crossed the North Sea and the Baltic Sea and arrived at Kronstadt four days later. In *Le Figaro*, Recouly defined the significance of the trip: "The grandeur and prestige of France depends directly on its military power and the solidity of its diplomatic accords, above all its alliance with Russia." *Le Temps* added that because the Triple Entente was "ready for war, the three nations could work for peace." The government of Tsar Nicholas II ensured newspapers in St. Petersburg answered that the ties binding France and Russia were so tight that "any wound inflicted on one is felt by the other, that any triumph by one is a triumph by the other, that their hearts beat the same, that their powerful hands are forever joined for the peace of Europe and the prosperity of the world." The welcome was in the extravagant Romanov tradition: banquets and toasts in St. Petersburg, a review of forty thousand troops at the Krasnoïe-Selo retreat. The French leaders reciprocated with a formal banquet aboard the *France*.[14]

No formal record has survived of the Franco-Russian discussions, which took place before any intimation of crisis enveloped Europe. Poincaré and Nicholas must have considered the actions Austria-Hungary might potentially take against Serbia and whether Germany might become involved, as in 1908 and 1913. Russia had backed down twice and could hardly do so again without abandoning its Balkan policy. Poincaré surely promised French support for a firm Russian stand because if France refused to back Russia in such a crisis, the alliance had no meaning. Did Nicholas understand the pledge as encouragement to adopt intransigence over the Serbian question? Or did Poincaré also urge restraint—because, after all, he understood that the French had no desire for war? Actions mean more than words: the proof of how little Poincaré and Viviani anticipated an immediate crisis is that, after leaving Russia on 25 July, they maintained their plans to stop at Sweden and Denmark on the way back, their return to France set for 31 July 1914.[15]

Competing for attention with the presidential trip—and winning—was justice as theater, the trial of Henriette Caillaux, which opened on 20 July. Every major Paris newspaper covered it on the front page, and many added a verbatim account. Pride of place went to *Le Figaro*, the aggrieved party with a score to settle. Jean-Louis Forain, noted impressionist painter and lithographer, agreed to draw courtroom caricatures as illustrations for its reporting. *Le Figaro* anticipated revenge. *L'Action française* predicted acquittal, wagering against "republican justice" in the "trial of the Queen," but eager to despise "a pair of bandits," Henriette "the Bloody" (*la Sanglante*) and Joseph "the Crafty Devil" (*le Malin*). The monarchists meant "republican" to be disparaging in reference to the judicial process, but "repugnant" might have been justified. The disgrace of Victor Fabre meant his replacement as Paris attorney general by Jules Herbeaux, who had close ties to the Radical party and declared that he would prosecute the case personally. He scheduled the trial to coincide with the term of Louis Albanel as presiding judge of the felony court (*cour d'assises*), well aware that Albanel was a personal friend of Joseph Caillaux. The process of selecting the jury pool led to suspicion of tampering; having the police investigate all seventy-two potential jurors was its very definition. No wonder that *Le Matin* published a commentary by Guillaume Loubat, the attorney general for Lyon, under the title, "The Public thinks badly of the Felony Court."[16]

Without question, Joseph and Henriette Caillaux demanded special treatment. On 16 March when the police arrested her at the offices of *Le Figaro*, she hissed, "Do not touch me! I am a lady [*une dame*]," and she rode in her own car to the precinct station. Despite the favoritism she received in her cell at Saint Lazare, he complained that she was locked away "among common-law prisoners." With contempt, Maurice Pujo offered this distinction in *L'Action française*: "The term 'lady' refers to a higher degree of civilization, a delicacy and bearing arising from education and manners, curbing passions, having resources of dignity, silence, and sacrifice. But to Madame Caillaux, to be 'a lady' is simply to be a millionaire and to frequent other people rich and powerful, to arrive in her own automobile wearing a fashionable dress and carrying a fur muff in which there rests the revolver of a criminal."[17]

For her trial, Henriette Caillaux wore black—dress, hat, and gloves. She was haughty, declaring to the court, "I am of the bourgeoisie. In 1911, I married Monsieur Caillaux, the prime minister." The first phase of a felony trial in France is the interrogation of the defendant by the presiding judge. Rather than asking sharp questions, which by right she could refuse to answer, Albanel indulgently permitted her to speak for almost three hours and present her version of the case before the jury. She emphasized the brutal tenor of Calmette's editorial campaign, the snide comments she had to endure not only among her own social circles but from shopkeepers serving her, and the threat to her "situation," the possibility that her affair with Joseph Caillaux while he was married to Berthe Gueydan might become public knowledge. Now that her private life was revealed, "I must blush in front of my daughter." To claim that she acted on impulse and only after having been driven to distraction, she had to confront the issue of premeditation. On the afternoon of 16 March, she had both bought the Browning and left behind a note for her husband that concluded, "I will commit the act. If this letter reaches you, I will have carried out, or tried to carry out, justice." The pistol, she insisted, was merely for protection, and about the note, "I did not know what I was writing." At *Le Figaro*, she had to wait for Calmette to return from a meeting and had grown agitated. When he invited her into his office, she pulled the Browning from her muff, and "the gun went off all by itself." When Albanel prompted, "That's all you have to say?" she added, "It was fate. I regret infinitely the unhappiness I have caused." For *L'Humanité*, this performance was "simple and affecting"; for *L'Action française*, it was "childish and cynical egoism."[18]

On the following day, 21 July, Herbeaux began presenting the case for the prosecution. Novelist Bourget had been with Calmette just before the shooting and insisted that "his sense of delicacy" forbade publishing the 1909 letters. Calmette's chief lieutenant, Louis Latzarus, testified that Calmette did not have the letters and had made no effort to obtain them, but that he did have in his coat pocket "documents of extraordinary importance from a political point of view and from which all good Frenchmen would conclude the infamy and treason of Caillaux." He was referring to copies of the Quai d'Orsay

Greens and, in doing so, committed a serious tactical error. For coming next to the witness bar was Joseph Caillaux himself. Caillaux
began by describing the unhappiness of his first marriage to Berthe
Gueydan and how she had used the "Ton Jo" and the 1909 love letters to compel lucrative terms in their divorce. When Calmette published the "Ton Jo," he concluded that she had broken her promise to
destroy them and would take further actions to harm him and the
woman for whom he had abandoned her. When he shared his fears
with Henriette, she became hysterical. Here was the explanation for
the emotional distress that led her to shoot Calmette. Almost without a pause, Caillaux then began a defense of himself, figuratively
placing himself beside his wife in the defendant's box. The jury was
to understand that convicting her meant convicting him. He had,
he declared, dedicated his life to the service of France: the levy on
income was "the democratic tax of all great modern states"; his role
in the Rochette case "avoided financial difficulties"; the Treaty of Fez
successfully ended "the most arduous adventure France had known."
At that moment, he took advantage of Latzarus's mistake in referring
even obscurely to the Greens. Certain that the Quai d'Orsay would
have to deny their existence, he challenged, "Furnish your proofs if
you dare, for these are frauds!" After asserting his own patriotism, he
attacked Calmette's, alleging that *Le Figaro* accepted subsidies from
Germany and Austria-Hungary in return for slanting its reporting.[19]

Although Clemenceau immediately used his newspaper *L'Homme
libre* to charge Caillaux with treason, the day had gone badly for the
prosecution. *Le Figaro* dared ask whether Herbeaux was blunder-
ing on purpose because he also refused to coordinate with Charles
Chenu, attorney for the civil suit (*partie civile*) brought by Calmette's
family, which under French procedure was argued simultaneously
and before the same jury as the criminal case. Given the progress of
the trial, Henriette Caillaux's attorney, Fernand Labori, among the
most famous in France because he had defended Alfred Dreyfus at
the second court martial, found few reasons to intervene.[20]

The momentum for the defense continued on the third day when
Herbeaux's first act was to read aloud a formal statement from the
foreign ministry: "The government declares that the Greens are

pretended copies of telegrams that do not exist and have never existed. They can in no way be invoked to reflect upon the honor or the patriotism of Monsieur Caillaux." After Herbeaux offered not a word of commentary, Chenu sarcastically hailed "this certificate of national loyalty." From that moment on, he assumed responsibility for presenting the case against the Caillauxs, Joseph as well as Henriette. The first witness of the day was Georges Prestat, president of *Le Figaro*'s governing board, who formally denied the charges of German and Austro-Hungarian subsidies and defined the difference between Calmette and Joseph Caillaux in this epigram: "The lion attacks the living; the jackal attacks the corpse." When Chenu added, "No enterprise is more shameful than coming before a public audience to profane the tomb one's wife has opened!" the courtroom galleries erupted in spontaneous applause. Here was the first check for the defense and perhaps a glimpse of popular sentiment. Further witnesses that day, the gun dealer, some members of the Caillaux social circle, and various journalists, merely filled in the background of 16 March and proffered conflicting opinions about Henriette Caillaux's state of mind. For the first time, the trial was boring. Perhaps Chenu had restored equilibrium.[21]

That sense was fleeting because, on 23 July, Berthe Gueydan stood at the witness bar dressed, like Henriette Caillaux, entirely in black except for startling white gloves. The trial was about to spin wildly out of control. Gueydan described her unhappy marriage to Joseph Caillaux: how she discovered letters he had written to his mistress, Henriette Rainouard, and how, when he asked for a divorce, she used them and the "Ton Jo" to her advantage. The originals were gone, but she had photographs. When Labori intervened to declare that they should have been destroyed, Gueydan replied that she had explicitly refused and for her safety had kept the copies in a bank deposit box. She had them now in her purse and withdrew them. She suggested that Labori decide which if any should be made public. As much as he wanted nothing to do with these letters, he knew that he would have to enter them into evidence or leave the suspicion that they contained incriminating material. Blindsided, he told her, "Never yet in my career, Madame, has anyone done me such an honor."[22]

Dismayed by Labori's performance, Joseph Caillaux demanded an immediate opportunity to comment on his first wife's testimony. As Albanel permitted his return to the witness bar, Caillaux took over control of his wife's defense, which was, in truth, his own. His voice filled with scorn, he recounted how he had made a mistake in 1906 by marrying Gueydan, who was not of his "stock." Yet when he demanded a divorce four years later, he provided her a handsome settlement: "Rather than force a woman who has borne my name to live in penury, I made sacrifices equivalent to nearly half my fortune. I do not understand what protestations such a woman can raise!" Despite the presiding judge's demand for silence, catcalls and whistles filled the courtroom. Further damage for the defense came from the only other witness on this day, Barthou, who had been close to Calmette, was closer to Poincaré, and had read aloud the Fabre memorandum before the Chamber of Deputies. He had the stature of being the prime minister who enacted three-year service, and he now told the court that he "questioned the fidelity of Monsieur Caillaux's memory." The newspapers had a field day raking through the confrontations: like *Le Figaro, Le Matin* gave over almost the entire issue to the trial, while *L'Action française* headlined, "Monsieur Caillaux, you are a disgrace!"[23]

Well after the presses were running, reports arrived that would have substantially altered the layout of every front page. Late in the afternoon of 23 July, Austria-Hungary presented Serbia with an ultimatum—unconditional capitulation within forty-eight hours to ten demands. The most important was acceptance of representatives from Austria-Hungary in the investigation and trial of anyone involved in the death of Franz Ferdinand. Beyond the scope of the requirements lay the document's tone of arrogance, treating Serbia as unworthy of traditional diplomatic considerations. In the twenty-five days since the shots at Sarajevo, Austria-Hungary had plotted its response. On 5 July, a delegation had been dispatched to Berlin seeking support from Germany for Austro-Hungarian plans to punish Serbia. Kaiser Wilhelm II and Chancellor Theobald von Bethmann-Hollweg agreed but urged rapid action while shock at the assassination was fresh. They thereby issued a "Blank Check," promising German backing for whatever Austria-Hungary might do. Certainly, most of

Germany's leaders thought Austria-Hungary could mount a puni-
tive attack on Serbia without precipitating a broader war, but others
welcomed the possibility of a general conflict they believed could be
fought on favorable terms. In Vienna, opinion was now united that
the moment had come to end the Serbian problem and that Russia
would declare war as a result. Two corollaries followed inexorably:
harvest the fields before mobilization stripped them of farm workers
and complicate concerted action by France and Russia by delaying
the ultimatum to Serbia until French leaders had departed St. Petersburg and were at sea. And so Austria-Hungary had done.

In court on 24 July, no one mentioned that international relations
had taken a sudden and dangerous turn. The tension there was high
enough, beginning with a dispute over how many of the letters handed
over by Gueydan should be read aloud and leading quickly into a second
face-off between Caillaux and Barthou. Enraged at having been called
a liar, however discreetly, Caillaux paraded his political triumph over
Barthou in forcing the acceptance of an income tax to pay for the
three-year law. Barthou was in the audience and interrupted by calling out, "I am here! You have spoken of how I was broken into pieces.
Look well, the pieces are still good!" Later, the playwright Henri Bernstein, celebrated for his 1908 *Israël*, based on the Dreyfus affair, eu-
logized Calmette as the most dedicated of journalists who would have
undertaken his campaign against Caillaux only to save France from
such a man. The day was a disaster for the defense, but accounts of
the trial, which had been on the front page of Paris newspapers, now
went inside. Their place was taken by analyses of the Austro-Hungarian
ultimatum: for *Le Temps*, it was "unprecedented in its overbearing
tone and outrageous demands"; for *Le Figaro*, here was "incontestably
the gravest crisis in memory." Jean Jaurès in *L'Humanité* gave a sur-
prising endorsement of Poincaré and Viviani: "Our leaders can have
suspected nothing of this blow, or they would have hastened their
return." On the Bourse, the government 3 percent bonds fell below 80
francs for the first time since 1879.[24]

The forty-eight-hour deadline expired at 6 p.m. on 25 July 1914.
Before then, critical decisions had to be made. Austria-Hungary
assured Russia that it planned no annexation of Serbian territory.

Rejecting this pledge out of hand, Russia believed the ultimatum a prelude to Austria-Hungary's occupation of the Balkans and ordered preparatory steps for military mobilization. Acutely aware of its complicity in the assassination and its incapacity to face an Austro-Hungarian invasion, Serbia accepted the demands of the ultimatum with the exception of a joint investigation. Austria-Hungary declared the response insufficient and broke diplomatic relations. Germany urged Austria-Hungary to act rapidly in hope of "localizing" any war. Great Britain reacted tentatively, considering the Balkans beyond its interest, hoping for mediation, and not yet willing to promise siding with France and Russia in a general war. France reaffirmed support for its alliance partner Russia—but, having only sporadic radio contact with Poincaré and Viviani who were steaming for home at top speed after canceling their visits to Sweden and Denmark, their proxy, Jean-Baptiste Bienvenu-Martin, the minister of justice, was reluctant to act decisively. The Paris Bourse assumed the worst, "losing its head" in selling that was "absolutely disastrous," "a spectacle of panic."[25]

Headlines and editorials were dire. Jacques Bainville, the monarchist historian who had made his reputation by predicting the worst and frequently being right, pointed at the collision of two alliance systems. Jaurès called on "Socialists of all nations to use their solidarity against the dreadful catastrophe menacing the world" because "the idea of limiting the conflict appears more and more chimerical." *Le Temps*, which usually reflected official thinking, focused not on the Balkans but on Berlin: "Does Germany want war? Because if so, the entire political and diplomatic edifice constructed during the last three decades is in play." Coverage of the Caillaux trial now began on page 3 even in *Le Figaro*. The European crisis easily trumped a court session dominated by physicians and surgeons discussing the decision to stabilize Calmette before operating on his wounds. Four bullets had struck him, in the left thigh, in the center of the chest near the heart, in the lower left chest, and in the lower left abdomen. When Labori questioned their judgment, quoting from a medical textbook, Dr. Bernard Cunéo, who had performed the operation, replied bitterly, "attempting to present the illusion to Calmette's

children that their father could have been saved, in reality only as-
sassinates him again."[26]

After a one-day recess, the trial continued on 27 July with the case
for the defense. As revenge for the reading aloud of his love letters
to Henriette, Joseph Caillaux read aloud Calmette's will, emphasizing
that the bulk of his estate was money left him by a wealthy mistress.
Caillaux meant thereby to portray Calmette as a gigolo. When Chenu
protested that by law a will was a private document and demanded
to know how the defense had obtained it, Caillaux answered, "In the
same manner by which Monsieur Calmette obtained his copy of the
'Ton Jo.'" He then attacked the character of everyone who had spoken in Calmette's behalf. In the case of the dramatist Bernstein, he
decried, "When one has not fulfilled one's duty to the nation, one
is ill-equipped to give certificates of morality to others." And so the
threat of war finally came to the Caillaux trial. Alerted of the slur by a
friend's telephone call, Bernstein returned to the courtroom, pushed
his way to the front, and called out, "Caillaux! Are you there? Because
I do not insult adversaries in their absence! We are present at an in-
conceivable affair, a man climbing atop the coffin of his wife's victim
to speak to you more loudly!" As before with Barthou, no one even
attempted to stop him. Bernstein admitted that when drafted in 1894
he had deserted and taken refuge in Belgium. Then, after returning
under an amnesty, he enlisted in a combat unit: "I am an artillery
man. I leave on the fourth day of mobilization, and the mobilization
may be tomorrow. I do not know what day Caillaux leaves for the
front, but I warn him that during a war, he cannot have himself replaced by his wife. He will have to fire himself!" In the audience, men
leapt to their feet cheering in acclamation. Albanel had to suspend
the session. Outside the courtroom, the threat of war was hanging
heavy as well. Reports that Austria-Hungary had ordered mobilization overrode Great Britain's reluctance to act. Now, in hope of
peace, Britain proposed a conference and offered diplomatic support
to Russia but, in fear of war, implemented its agreement with France
to share naval responsibilities. Germany encouraged Austria-Hungary
to act rapidly, and anti-Russian demonstrations swept through its
streets. Based on radio messages from Poincaré and Viviani (still two

days from reaching France), Bienvenu-Martin had the minister of war, Adolphe Messimy, take preparatory military measures.[27]

Final arguments in the Caillaux trial began on 28 July, shadowed by the news that Austria-Hungary had declared war on Serbia. For the civil suit by Calmette's family, Chenu argued that Joseph Caillaux led his wife to believe Calmette would publish intimate letters destroying her reputation; that he hoped she would kill Calmette and so prevent revelation of what he truly feared, the Fabre memorandum; and that he now justified this "censorship by the bullet" through vilification of Calmette and his associates. For the prosecution, Herbeaux insisted that Henriette Caillaux bore the responsibility for killing with premeditation, but because she had done so under grievous emotional duress, the jury should temper justice with mercy. For the defense, Labori emphasized Henriette Caillaux's fears about the letters, fears Calmette himself had encouraged by publishing the "Ton Jo"; he dismissed the importance of the Fabre memorandum to Joseph Caillaux and, for an inspired conclusion, asked the jury to "save our wrath for our enemies beyond the borders. Let us stand always united and determined against the perils that advance upon us." The jury deliberated for less than an hour before returning a verdict of innocent.

Of course, *Le Figaro* headlined "The Verdict of Shame," because its editors were the declared enemies of Joseph Caillaux. Of course, *L'Action française* headlined "A Permit to Murder," because its movement was the declared enemy of the Republic. But even for them, the Caillaux trial was already the past in the present of national emergency. War loomed as all but inevitable. Maurice Barrès, who led the League of Patriots (Ligue des patriotes), evoked his best-selling novels of national energy as he thrilled: "At this moment, we are no longer factions, we are only France. We are a single great army, grave and resolute, massed shoulder to shoulder." Bainville urged sangfroid during these "agonizing hours." Remarkably for the anticlerical Republic, *Le Temps* entitled its lead editorial "Sursam Corda" (Lift up your hearts), the opening dialogue to the Eucharistic Prayer. Its language was blunt: "The time for fanciful dreams is over. While desiring peace, a proud people must be ready for war. The three-year service law, proposed by Briand, realized by Barthou, and firmly applied by Viviani, allows us to confront the worst eventualities with confidence."[28]

Those worst eventualities were coming. Russia announced its mobilization against Austria-Hungary. Germany sternly warned Russia to desist and bid for Great Britain's neutrality by promising not to annex any territory from France or Belgium. Unlike in 1908 or 1913, this time Russia did not back down before German demands, and Great Britain rejected what amounted to extortion. France's policy became stronger and more coherent when Poincaré and Viviani finally returned on 29 July: they renewed assurances of support for Russia and, to ensure that Germany would be seen as the aggressor, moved French troops back ten kilometers (about six miles) from the border. Russia's decision on 30 July to adopt general mobilization provoked the final crisis. Because Germany based its war strategy on the Schlieffen Plan, every day that Russia mobilized was one day less that it had to defeat France. On 31 July, Germany proclaimed "a state of threatening danger of war," issued a final warning to Russia, rejected Great Britain's request to respect Belgian neutrality, and sent an ultimatum to France—demanding its intentions if war began between Germany and Russia and, if France were to remain neutral, occupation by Germany of its border fortifications as guarantee.

In Paris, thousands had greeted the arrival of their president and prime minister with cheers for the Triple Entente: "Vive la France! Vive la Russie! Vive l'Angleterre!" Some even cried, "To Berlin!" When other thousands paraded against war, police broke up the demonstrations and made hundreds of arrests. Now was not a good time to be known as a friend of Germany—or as the beneficiary of questionable justice. Joseph and Henriette Caillaux packed urgently and left Paris. Jaurès believed he could still halt war by rallying the working classes of France and Germany against their governments. On 31 July he dared say to Louis Malvy, minister of the interior, "the France of the Revolution has been drawn by Russian Cossacks against the Germany of the Reformation." For such sentiments, a nationalist fanatic shot him that evening.[29]

The morning newspapers on 1 August announced the death of peace and the death of Jaurès. *Le Figaro's* Raymond Recouly, who almost alone in late June had recognized the danger, now wrote of "Imminent war. . . . In the terrible struggle to come, France gambles its destiny, to exist or not. All dissensions must cease, all quarrels end. From now on, the salvation of our country is all that matters." *Le Temps* challenged, "For nations as for individuals, moral character is affirmed through ordeal." Jaurès was called a martyr for peace and praised for his idealism by everyone—especially by his opponents, anxious about the possible disruptive effect of his assassination. *L'Action française* called it "more than a crime, a grave transgression against the nation," *Le Matin*, "an act of madness and folly," *Le Figaro*, "a contemptible murder." They need not have worried. Jaurès's lieutenants—Edouard Vaillant, Marcel Sembat, and Pierre Renaudel—rapidly made clear that the Socialist party would support any declaration of war. No one better conveyed the importance of their promise than the Catholic conservative de Mun, who wrote in *L'Echo de Paris*, "We must render homage to those whom I have combated the most, to the Socialists, smitten by the pacifist ideal, who despite the horrible, odious, and absurd assassination of their leader, provide the highest example of obedience to the national voice."[30]

The afternoon of 1 August brought the curt French reply to the German ultimatum: "France will be guided by her own interests." Simultaneously, the government announced general mobilization. Germany likewise decreed general mobilization and that evening declared war on Russia, the first declaration of war by one great power against another great power since 1870. On 2 August, Germany invaded Luxembourg and demanded passage for its armies through Belgium, which refused. On 3 August, Germany invaded Belgium and declared war on France. On 4 August, France and Great Britain declared war on Germany.

The spirit of sacred national union in France became manifest. Before an overflow crowd at the Salle Wagram near the Arc de Triomphe, Vaillant, now leader of the Socialist party, promised, "We shall fulfill all our responsibilities to the nation and to the Republic!" Charles Maurras, acerbic founder of the monarchist movement

Action française and co-editor of its newspaper, granted absolution to the Republic he despised: "National defense restores unity to French hearts and minds. The government will leave open the two hundred parochial schools it planned to close. The antimilitarist protesters will not be charged and will make good soldiers." No one yet imagined the slaughter to come. War could still seem noble, as in these words from Le Figaro's Capus: "No French man or woman will ever forget the last two days, unique in their intensity. Each of us is a representative, complete and absolute, of the French race, with all its inherent instincts, all its past, all its hopes. One sentiment vitalizes and exalts us, that of fighting not only for our soil but for civilization itself. We have all seen with a blinding clarity that barbarism marches at the head of the fearsome Germanic horde."[31] Poincaré called the Senate and the Chamber of Deputies into special session for 4 August. Under the constitution, the president of the Republic could address the legislature only through a written statement. The one Poincaré submitted was brief, calling for a reply to the German declaration of war. Bienvenu-Martin read it aloud before the Senate. The senators voted unanimously to declare war on Germany and then shouted, "Vive la France!" The Chamber of Deputies began with its president, Paul Deschanel, delivering a moving eulogy of Jaurès. Before he had finished, the deputies to a man were on their feet. They remained standing as Viviani read Poincaré's statement and then added his own words, "We are without reproach, and we shall be without fear!" He was cheered to the echo. When the deputies had taken their own unanimous vote to declare war on Germany, de Mun got up from his desk on the far right and walked across the front of the Chamber to the far left, where he embraced Vaillant. Until this moment, they had never spoken. Before, one was a conservative Catholic and the other a Socialist. Now, they were only Frenchmen.[32]

CHAPTER 2

Georges—The Defiant

Georges Clemenceau was unrepentant. "Yes, they told me to shut up, but damn it all! To hell with the Chamber, to hell with the majority if they failed to understand. . . . Nothing in the world could have stopped me." Two days earlier, on 20 July 1909, the words he could not resist uttering took him from premier to political oblivion. Before the Chamber of Deputies, this man called the "Tiger" roared out a personal denunciation of Théophile Delcassé, the much esteemed diplomat and architect of France's alliance system. Clemenceau then stood impassively at the tribune as a hue and cry of "Resign!" ascended. The formal declaration of "No Confidence," voted 212–176, was hardly necessary. When Clemenceau became prime minister, he was already sixty-five years old and a politician since 1870. He had waited a long time to exercise power, and he governed France for thirty-three months, the second-longest-lasting cabinet of the Third Republic. His age, but more the circumstances of his defeat, made any second chance unlikely. He was at his worst that day, angry, vindictive, self-destructive, literally out of control, as he invited his fate—and then savored the taste.[1]

The issue at hand was the state of France's navy. Between 1905 and 1907, the cruiser *Sully* went aground and sank in the Gulf of Tonkin, two submarines were lost while on maneuvers in the Mediterranean Sea, and the battleship *Iéna* exploded in the Toulon harbor at the cost of 117 lives. Ten years earlier, the French navy ranked second in the world, behind only the fleet of Great Britain. Now, it trailed far behind both the British and German navies and was hard pressed to remain ahead of Italy's. Accidents were one matter, incompetence and mismanagement something much different. Suspicion within the Chamber of Deputies first arose when Camille Pelletan served as minister of the navy from June 1902 until January 1905. The deputies authorized an investigation, but Clemenceau and Gaston Thomson, both closely linked to Pelletan in the Radical party, spiked the findings. Then, when Clemenceau became prime minister, he named Thomson to head the navy. The *Iéna* disaster led to a second inquiry, this time under Delcassé, who asked naval officers to write him directly about their experiences. His report, issued in conjunction with one from the Senate, blamed the explosion and subsequent gunnery incidents on the navy's "Powder B," which was subject to spontaneous combustion from chemical decomposition when stored for too long or in humid conditions. When Delcassé claimed before the Chamber on 18 October 1908 that the navy was incapable of reforming itself, Thomson chose to resign rather than force the cabinet to enter a losing debate. Clemenceau's reaction was scornful, replacing him with a civil servant and political nonentity, Alfred Picard, from the division of bridges and highways (*Ponts et chaussées*). Delcassé's response was to intervene months later, on 25 March 1909, to criticize Picard's plans as faulty and insufficient and to demand yet another investigation—the deputies agreed and made Delcassé its head. This new investigation's final report in June cited ministerial indecision, bureaucratic delay, insufficiently tested equipment, extravagant profits for major suppliers, and above all, failure to complete ships as rapidly as Britain or Germany.[2]

Angry debates dominated the mid-July sessions of the Chamber, and on 20 July 1909, Delcassé made Clemenceau the target by charging that four years earlier he had covered up mistakes and corruption under Pelletan. Clemenceau had an abundance of reasons to detest Delcassé, and he could not resist the temptation. Both men were republicans, but Delcassé had been allied to Léon Gambetta and the "Opportunists" (meaning "conservatives"), whom Clemenceau's Radicals had spent decades opposing. Both men had been lovers of opera star Rose Caron (Rose Lucile

Meunier), but Delcassé had supplanted Clemenceau in her affection. Delcassé had refused Clemenceau a favor: Charles Le Peletier, Count d'Aunay ruined his diplomatic career by supplying Clemenceau with confidential details about the negotiations of the Franco-Russian alliance in 1893, and Delcassé refused to reinstate him despite Clemenceau's entreaties. Delcassé sought the disgrace of Pelletan, who if not Clemenceau's boon friend was certainly a companion of many political battles. And so Clemenceau took the tribune:

> Delcassé has singled me out personally and said, "You knew the facts. Why have you done nothing?" What do I answer? I say, you were the minister of foreign affairs, and you carried out a policy which involved us in the greatest humiliation we have undergone. You brought us to the gates of war, but you had not made any military preparations. You know, all the world knows, all Europe knows that when the ministers of war and the navy were asked, they replied we were not ready. . . . I have not humiliated France, but I saw that Delcassé has humiliated her.

The reference was to the Tangier Affair of 1905, when France initially yielded to German threats over the expansion of French influence in Morocco. Yet the crisis subsequently led to greater support for France from Great Britain by demonstrating the increasing danger of German ambitions. Many of the deputies knew the details of Clemenceau's personal vendetta; many more could not excuse his twisting history to cover his own failings. Perhaps he believed he had the votes to sustain him anyway—Count Albert de Mun, the courtly leader of the Catholic conservatives, contended that the cabinet fell because Clemenceau assumed he had "fifty swinging Mamelukes to beat back any challenge." Instead, Clemenceau had surrendered to "the extraordinary wantonness that ever prevented him from being a statesman."[3]

This accusation always pursued Clemenceau. Auguste Scheurer-Kestner, his ally during the Dreyfus affair and a man he (wrongly) considered a friend, complained of "this irresponsibility the enormity of which can be measured only after having been around him a long time." Raymond Poincaré, often his political antagonist, said to novelist Roger

Martin du Gard of Clemenceau's writing, "He puts all his ponderous qualities into his style, all his fickleness into his life." If so, he came by it naturally. His father, Benjamin Clemenceau, local worthy, landlord, and rural physician in the backward Vendée region on the Bay of Biscay, was an improbable republican when France still had monarchs. In 1830, at the age of twenty, he walked—literally walked for thirty days—from the Vendée to Paris for the chance to study medicine, arriving just in time to participate in the revolution that overthrew France's last Bourbon king, Charles X. After another monarch, the Orléanist Louis Philippe, and another revolution in 1848, a new Bonaparte, Napoleon III, sat on the throne and regarded Benjamin Clemenceau so much an enemy that his police arrested him in January 1858. They threatened his exile to Algeria before releasing him a month later. Georges, born 28 September 1841, second child and first son, commented, "The normal state of my father is indignation." The principal influence he had upon his son was to inculcate a ferocious republicanism and an inflexible hatred of religion. When his father was arrested in 1858, Georges was so infuriated at the Second Empire regime and its clerical allies that, after breaking a statue of the Virgin, he retrieved the head and mounted it upon an inkwell, which he kept on his desk for the rest of his life. At home, he learned to ride, to fence, and to shoot; at school in nearby Nantes, he dutifully studied Greek, Latin, English, mathematics, and science—collectively, the cultural accoutrements of a privileged young man. Still in Nantes, he took up medicine, like his father, but to the accompaniment of complaints that he baited teachers who openly supported Bonapartism or religion. After a second reprimand, he decided that Paris would suit him better. His father promised financial support, went with him (by train, this time), and introduced him to the prominent republican politician Etienne Arago.[4]

With this send-off, Clemenceau spent more time on politics than medicine, using his father's money to found a weekly sheet, *Le Travail*, and in February 1862 won his own arrest after putting up posters that called for a demonstration to commemorate the fourteenth anniversary of the 1848 revolution. He spent seventy-seven days in Mazas Prison, sharing incarceration with Scheurer-Kestner. Once he was released, he set out to accomplish two goals. First, he bore down on his studies and defended his degree in May 1865, portraying himself as a Positivist and materialist "hostile to the transcendent, the miraculous, and the mystical." Second, he sought the hand of Scheurer-Kestner's sister-in-law, Hortense Kestner. Her family, including Auguste, rejected his suit—as did she, marrying in preference the solidly dependable republican stalwart Charles Floquet. Disappointed, in debt for *Le Travail*, and under scrutiny by the police, he returned to the family home at Aubraie near the Vendée coast. He expected a warmer welcome than he received.[5]

They were never noble, the Clemenceaus, but they lived "nobly." They were lawyers during the sixteenth, seventeenth, and eighteenth centuries, then physicians thereafter. Around 1700, one of the lawyers purchased "Colombier," a moated medieval manor with nearly two hundred acres of surrounding farmland. Benjamin Clemenceau was indeed a republican, but he was also the "Master of Colombier" who referred to the sharecroppers working its fields as "his peasants." He had a stern sense of order—his order. He married Emma Gautreau, daughter of a locally prominent family, and then adamantly refused to baptize their six children. When any of them behaved as he did, he coldly imposed penalties as an overbearing paterfamilias. Whatever he might have expected from his eldest son in Paris, the outcome was unsatisfactory. And so four months after coming home, Georges set sail for America, arriving in New York at the end of September 1865. He planned to translate John Stuart Mill's study of Auguste Comte into French, having adopted both men as intellectual guides. He wanted to see "American democracy" in action, having admired it from afar. Most of all, he wanted to be anywhere but France. To support himself, he had arranged with the important Paris newspaper *Le Temps* to contribute "Letters from America," for 150 francs an article ($800 in 2011), enough for a frugal living. He met Horace Greeley, editor of the *New York Tribune*; Edwin Stanton, secretary of war during the Civil War; and Ulysses S. Grant, who was soon to run for president. His articles described Reconstruction, the Fifteenth Amendment, and the impeachment of President Andrew Johnson. He completed his translation, which was published in 1867 as *Auguste Comte et le positivisme.* He gave medical consultations at a small office near Washington Square. He considered a career as a physician in Savannah or California. He dreamed of buying farmland in the Middle West. And he ran out of money. When his father refused any subsidy, he took a job teaching French and equitation at the school for girls of Miss Catherine Aiken in Stamford, Connecticut.[6]

On horseback and in the classroom, Clemenceau fell smitten with a seventeen-year-old girl, Mary Elizabeth Plummer, the orphan daughter of a New Hampshire dentist and the ward of her maternal uncle, Horace Taylor, a wealthy Manhattan stockbroker. Although intellectually naive and without a dowry, she was nine years younger and undeniably lovely. In June 1868, he proposed marriage, but Mary refused. Clemenceau then took the next ship to France and set about repairing his position. To pay off debts and provide for future expenses, he borrowed 25,000 francs ($133,250 in 2011), his elder sister, Emma, and her husband pledging one of their properties as collateral. From New York, he learned that Mary had reconsidered, and he sailed back to claim her. In the purely civil ceremony he insisted upon, they were married on 23 June 1869 at her uncle's home. Three days later they left for France, and in June 1870 she gave birth to their first child, Madeleine. A second daughter, Thérèse, and a son, Michel, would follow in 1872 and 1873. By then, Clemenceau was in Paris for good, leaving Mary behind in Aubraie. Did he ever love her or was she simply his rebound from Hortense Kestner? Certainly, Mary disappointed him. Difficult pregnancies stole her beauty. Her spoken French was halting. She cared nothing for the politics and culture that were his obsession. Her few surviving letters display "a great banality." She never won over any of the Clemenceau family, and her children preferred their absent father. Clemenceau felt no compunction about taking mistresses. When he discovered that she had taken a lover, he would react with fury.[7]

In mid-July 1870, France went to war with Prussia, and Clemenceau assisted with medical care in Paris. When the Second Empire collapsed at the beginning of September, republicans formed a "Government of National Defense." Some of them were Clemenceau's friends from the early 1860s, and he quickly assumed a position of leadership as mayor of the Montmartre district. From the outset he claimed for himself the Jacobin tradition: "We are children of the Revolution. Let us take inspiration from the example of our fathers in 1792, and like them, we shall conquer." He was wrong. The Prussians forced French leaders to request an armistice and then accept a humiliating peace treaty requiring the cession of Alsace and most of Lorraine and partial occupation pending payment of an indemnity. The National Assembly elected to constitute a new regime had a monarchist majority and was meeting at Versailles. Because this body was explicitly offensive to Paris and its republican sensibilities, the irrational reaction of many in the city was to rebel against the rest of a France that had elected such men. Thus originated the "Paris Commune": the idea of creating a modern-day, and republican, city-state in the midst of France. The triggering moment came on 18 March 1871, when the Assembly, headed by Adolphe Thiers, once prime minister under King Louis Philippe, sent soldiers to seize the cannon purchased by the citizens of Paris and emplaced on the Butte Montmartre to defend the city against the Prussian siege. Surrounded by a mob of Parisians, the soldiers fraternized with the demonstrators, who then put to death the two generals in command. Although both mayor of Montmartre and a deputy in the National Assembly, Clemenceau found himself helpless to alter a single moment of the violence that would stain the next months. He failed to halt the mob on 18 March. He failed to prevent the rush to civil war between Paris and the Assembly. He was deposed as mayor on 22 March and resigned as a deputy five days later. He could only watch as Thiers relentlessly broke down the city's defenses and Paris became an abattoir. During the "Bloody Week" of late May, soldiers massacred Communards, while Communards took revenge by killing hostages, including nuns and the archbishop of Paris.[8]

For half a decade afterward, Clemenceau lived meanly as he represented Montmartre on the Paris municipal council and operated a neighborhood medical dispensary. He paid occasional visits to Aubraie, twice impregnating the wife to whom he was less and less attracted. As the monarchist majority in the National Assembly bickered—until 1875—over which of the three varieties of French monarchy to endorse, support grew for a stopgap constitution. What became the Third Republic vested power in a bicameral legislature with a figurehead "President of the Republic," who might one day be exchanged for a constitutional monarch. Universal manhood suffrage, pioneered by the Revolution in 1792 and revived in 1848, would elect the lower house, the Chamber of Deputies. Local officeholders would elect the upper house, the Senate. Sitting together, the two houses would choose the president of the Republic. When the first elections for the Chamber took place in February 1876, Clemenceau stood as a candidate for the eighteenth district of Paris, Montmartre, and won. The Chamber of Deputies sat in the Palais Bourbon, in Paris just across the Seine River from the Place de la Concorde. Clemenceau took his seat on the far left, among the republicans who proudly called themselves "Radical."

Radicals defined themselves by recalling the First Republic, formed in 1792 after the overthrow of the monarchy. They called for eliminating the president and the Senate, neither of which were directly elected, in favor of a unicameral legislature; for establishing the freedoms of speech, press, and assembly; for removing clerical influence from government and education; for requiring mandatory military service of all young men; and for replacing the various property taxes with an income tax. Among republicans, Radicals were a minority, the greater number preferring to rejoice in the constitution they now had. Many of them could support in theory the Radical demands but would be willing to consider implementing them only when the time was "opportune"—thus the name, Opportunists. Their leaders—Léon Gambetta, Jules Ferry, Charles de Freycinet, Eugène Spuller, and Jules Méline—were "moderates," determined that this "Third" Republic not suffer the shipwreck of the "First" and "Second" Republics by failing to accommodate conservative social elements.

For Clemenceau, moderation in the defense of republican principles was no virtue. He denounced the Opportunists as "partisans more or less avowed to the politics of systematic adjournment and compromise . . . whose doctrine is the art of finding expedients more or less ingenious." Because no one else among the Radicals had his mordant invective or iron conviction, he quickly emerged as their leader. For his vehement anticlericalism, he was called the "Priest-

Eater" (*le Mangeur des prêtres*), for his savage attacks, the "Tiger" (*le Tigre*). He dared combine the Radicals with the antirepublican monarchists to attack and defeat Opportunist republican cabinets—and so within the Chamber came the reputation "Destroyer of Ministries" (*Tombeur de ministères*). Broader political influence required a newspaper, which Clemenceau launched on 13 January 1880, a four-page sheet with a circulation of approximately ten thousand copies called *La Justice*. To raise the founding capital of 1.5 million francs ($8 million in 2011), Clemenceau gave important hostages to fortune. His father contributed a substantial sum, probably half, with the understanding that his eldest son would thereby forfeit the bulk of his inheritance. The rest came from various friends and allies, the greatest amount from Cornelius Herz, an engineer and businessman from America, the origin of his fortune open to question. Approached to be a shareholder, Scheurer-Kestner declined because his political sympathies lay with the Opportunists and because he detested Camille Pelletan, the Radical whom Clemenceau proposed to be editor in chief. The other principal columnists would be Stéphane Pichon for foreign affairs and Charles Longuet, a son-in-law of Karl Marx, for social issues. Clemenceau took the title "Political Director," meaning that he dictated the paper's position on every issue. Léon Daudet, whose father, Alphonse, wrote popular novels and practiced the monarchist politics Léon would later adopt, was then among Clemenceau's friends and described him as "mocking, incisive, amusing, illogical, boasting, ferocious, capricious, scornful, disdainful, and goading."[9]

Beyond these attitudes of a frondeur, what were Clemenceau's politics? He chose the name for his newspaper instinctively. Like the Jacobins of the First Republic, his program was two words, justice and nation. For Clemenceau, "justice" was founded on liberty and equality, "nation" on popular sovereignty and nationalism. Such broad principles defy easy definition, but what he meant can be distilled from his intervention in the Chamber of Deputies. When Jules Ferry pushed forward France's conquest of Indo-China in 1885, Clemenceau attacked the very essence of imperialism: "There is no right of nations called 'superior' to impose their will on nations called 'inferior.' . . . Do not cloak violence in the name of civilization.

. . . Do not speak of right or of duty! The conquest you advocate is purely and simply to appropriate a man, to torture him, to extract all the strength that is within him for the profit of a pretended civilization. It is not right; it is the negation of right. To speak in this fashion of civilization is to join hypocrisy to violence." After soldiers fired on striking textile workers and their families at Fourmies on May Day 1891, Clemenceau embraced the laboring class, which he called "a new and redoubtable force of which political leaders have yet to take account." Because of its inherent collectivism, he was profoundly suspicious of socialist theory, but he recognized the necessity for reform and gestured to the right of the Chamber at Albert de Mun, who was converted to social Catholicism by his experience as a cavalry officer suppressing the Paris Commune: "so much did their desperation affect their enemy that he who shot them has become their defender." Yet Clemenceau had not the slightest sympathy for the religious faith that burned so brightly in de Mun. He countered Msgr. Charles Freppel by referring to "this great struggle between the church and the Republic which began long ago when the spirit of liberty arose in the world to counter the spirit of Catholicism." And in 1892 when de Mun, following the injunction of Pope Leo XIII, renounced royalism and "rallied" to the Third Republic, Clemenceau warned, "You say a hand is held out to yours? If you grasp it, you will be held so firmly that you cannot escape. You can, you will, be captives of the church, for it will never be in your power."[10]

Adolphe Thiers famously declared that France adopted a republic because "it was the form of government that divides us least." In an election rally on 12 August 1881 at the Cirque Fernando, Clemenceau provided a grander rationale: "If we have founded the Republic in our country, if we seek to institute a regime of liberty, we do so because we recognize that a system of repression has served nothing but to destroy the regimes adopting it." He went much further before the Chamber on 29 January 1891, when the prominent Opportunist Joseph Reinach analyzed the history of the French Revolution, placing the republican seal of approval on the moderation and seal of rejection on the extreme. For Clemenceau, this performance demarcated the line between Radicalism and Opportunism—and more important, why he was a Radical: "Reinach has just stood at the tribune to take up the great task of dissecting, in his fashion, the Revolution. He dissects in good conscience, and his work done, tells us seriously, 'I accept this, and I reject that.' Gentlemen, whether we like it or not, whether it pleases us or distresses us, the French Revolution is of one piece [*un bloc*]. Do you truly believe that its heritage can be diminished or augmented by the Chamber of Deputies?" History, Clemenceau argued, is not some game with the pieces to be colored by ideological fancy. Even the remaining partisans of king or emperor embraced the liberal reforms of the French Revolution, but a fair reading of history requires acknowledging that, without the Terror, the Revolution would have been defeated and all the changes—however perceived and divided up—reversed. More fully than anyone else, Clemenceau comprehended this essential truth.[11]

Dangerous it is to be right, and far more so because Clemenceau was Manichean in his judgments—ever segregating the good from the bad, the friend from the foe, the useful from the ineffectual, based on an idiosyncratic code. Scion of a family bourgeois for centuries, he was wellborn, well-bred, well educated, well dressed. He had money, and he had a certain social station. Radical politicians and their voters were from what Gambetta once termed the "new social strata" (*nouvelles couches sociales*): lower middle class, industrial workers, and peasants. Clemenceau was their "Master of Colombier." Having tired of his younger wife, he consoled himself with a series of mistresses, most often minor actresses he met through his frequent attendance at the theater. Two were so famous that affairs with them brought him a malicious celebrity: Léonide Leblanc, a great star of the stage who was called "Mademoiselle Maximum" for her luxurious tastes, and Rose Caron, a thrilling operatic soprano whose beauty was captured by Edgar Degas in an 1892 portrait. He counted dozens of social acquaintances. He attended the salons of Pauline Ménard-Dorian, Marie-Anne de Loynes, and Léontine de Caillavet. He frequented writers, like novelist Daudet, diarist Edmond de Goncourt, and poet Stéphane Mallarmé, and artists, like realist Jean-François Raffaelli and impressionist Edgar Manet, who both painted his portrait, and sculptor Auguste Rodin, who cast his bust. From Great Britain he added Admiral Frederick Augustus Maxse and from Denmark the critic Georg Brandes. Not one of them was from the new social strata; a number were noble. He counted as well a cast of political acolytes, most of whom he joined to *La Justice* as subordinates. His friends were few—and significantly younger, the better for him to dominate the relationship. For most of his adult life, Clemenceau's closest friend was Gustave Geffroy, fourteen years his junior, of Breton heritage with an interest in art and literature. Next came his brother Albert, born twenty years after him, who became a prominent barrister in Paris ready to defend any cause Georges espoused. The Greeks, whom Clemenceau admired from his childhood studies onward, warned that those whom the gods would destroy, they first make proud. Clemenceau was haughty, and he was vulnerable.[12]

The first fissure in his world came from within. In early 1891, Clemenceau's elder daughter, Madeleine, informed him that Mary, now forty years old, had taken for a lover the university student tutoring Thérèse and Michel. Using his political influence, he had police detectives arrest and take her before the Paris prefect of police, Henry Lozé, who threatened imprisonment for adultery if she did not consent to an immediate divorce and deportation from France. The ship carrying her to New York was slower than the one bearing the divorce decree, which was served upon her arrival. Although the entire Clemenceau family turned against Mary, they did not turn for Georges. Father Benjamin's reaction was renewed disappointment with his eldest son, whom he now excluded entirely from his will. At his death in 1897, Colombier passed to the second son, Paul, who displayed an infuriating schadenfreude. After making a fortune as an engineer with the Compagnie française de Dynamite, Paul married the elder daughter of Moritz Szeps, editor of the influential Viennese newspaper *Neue Weiner Tageblatt*, and she conducted the most Germanophile salon in Paris. Georges's mother and his two younger sisters, Adrienne and Sophie, sided with Paul. Only his elder sister, Emma, and his brother Albert, both long his allies, defended him.[13]

Unfortunately, more to defend was coming, as Clemenceau's world fissured from without. In the late 1880s, he made two serious political mistakes. First, he championed the ambitious General Georges Boulanger, who in a military hierarchy rife with Catholic monarchists was overtly "republican" and refused to attend mass. As minister of war (on Clemenceau's recommendation), Boulanger won national celebrity by posing as the man to lead a war of revenge against Germany— for which France was not yet ready. Both Opportunists and Radicals recognized him as a menace and returned him to regular duty. They were taken entirely by surprise when he conspired with monarchists to overthrow the Third Republic by exploiting the nationalism he had stimulated as "General Revenge" (*Général Revanche*). The plot collapsed when republicans threatened to charge him with plotting against the state, but no one forgot who gave Boulanger his start. Second, in the midst of "Boulangism," the president of the Republic, Jules Grévy, embroiled himself in the police investigation of his son-in-law for the sale of political favors. Because Grévy was one of their own, Opportunists tried to cover up Grévy's obstruction of justice. Because Grévy was an Opportunist, Clemenceau made certain that the allegation and then the facts became public, forcing Grévy's resignation. He had made himself a target.

The aiming at Clemenceau began with the Panama Canal scandal. Ferdinand de Lesseps had constructed the Suez Canal, which opened in 1869 and made his investors rich. In the 1880s, he proposed a new canal, this time through Panama, and thousands became shareholders in his company. Engineering difficulties combined with malaria and yellow fever to raise costs uncontrollably, and in 1888, the Panama Canal Company declared bankruptcy. Three years later came revelations that French legislators and journalists had accepted bribes to cover up these problems, and the name most prominently associated with the various charges of corruption was Cornelius Herz, who had provided so much capital to Clemenceau for founding *La Justice* and who in 1886 had been named a grand officer in the Legion of Honor. Clemenceau would admit much later, "Herz was, I have to say it, an accomplished scoundrel [*fripouille finie*]. Unhappily, that was not written on the end of his nose." In the midst of this crisis, he needed far more than a wry quip. From the far right in the Chamber of Deputies on 20 December 1892, Paul Déroulède, the Boulangist who founded the nationalist League of Patriots (Ligue des patriotes), demanded to know how a man like Herz, a foreigner, had accumulated

so much influence in France that he held the rank of *Grand Officier.*
The answer, he insisted, was "a Frenchman, a powerful Frenchman,
influential, audacious, who could introduce him to ministers, to journalists. . . . This obliging, this devoted, this tireless intermediary, so
active and so dangerous, all of you know him, his name is on all of
your lips, but not one of you dares to speak it because you fear his
sword, his pistol, and his tongue. So I shall brave all three and say
aloud: it is Monsieur Clemenceau!" This challenge struck a lightning
bolt across the Chamber. From the far left, Clemenceau immediately
responded. He denied ever using his influence as a deputy or the influence of *La Justice* to assist Herz in any fashion. Reaching the essence
of Déroulède's denunciation, that he had acted against the interests
of France, Clemenceau exploded: "That I have betrayed my nation,
betrayed my homeland, that in service to some foreign interest I have
sought to do damage to my country, sought to cause disturbance in
my homeland—that is the charge you have made against me. . . . To it,
only one response is possible: Monsieur Déroulède, *you have lied!*"[14]

Honor required that such an accusation and such a response lead to
a duel, the risk of life. Although dueling was formally against the law,
the authorities frequently kept their eyes wide shut. From childhood,
Clemenceau had practiced marksmanship and swordsmanship. Because he was left-handed, he was a confusing opponent with an épée;
he was a crack shot with a rifle, but dueling pistols had smooth bores
and were notoriously inaccurate. In November 1871, during testimony about the origins of the Commune, Major Constant Poussargues
described Clemenceau's role using insulting language. When Clemenceau challenged him, he chose pistols. After Poussargues fired and
missed, Clemenceau wounded him in the thigh, declaring that he was
unwilling to kill a French officer. In December 1888, he quarreled with
a right-wing deputy, Alphonse Maurel. They faced off with swords,
and Clemenceau was lightly wounded in the right shoulder. Now, he
arranged to meet Déroulède with pistols at the Saint-Ouen racetrack
on the northern edge of Paris. Because the insults were so grievous,
they agreed to exchange six shots, three apiece, at twenty-five paces.
As more than 250 people gathered to watch, gendarmes maintained
order but apparently were commanded not to interfere with the duel.

Each shot was high drama: a man facing his opponent who leveled a pistol at him from approximately sixty feet away—without flinching. To great amazement, each shot missed. Afterward, Clemenceau stared at his pistol and exclaimed in disgust, "Splendid!" He sought a second duel a month later in January 1893, but Déroulède was unwilling to tempt fate twice.[15]

In the 1885 elections for the Chamber of Deputies, Clemenceau's star had shone so brightly among Radical voters that he won two seats half a nation apart: for Montmartre and for Draguignan, in the Var, almost on the Mediterranean Sea and some sixty miles from the Italian border. He chose to represent the Var, thinking to leave behind the rougher urban politics of Paris for a reliable and semirural district. But the rapid spread of primary education and the increased circulation of newspapers meant that voters anywhere could read the details of every accusation hurled against him. Even the most outrageous accusation had believers, the allegation that his friendship with Admiral Maxse proved him an agent for Great Britain. So much so that in the 1893 election campaign, he had to address them openly in a remarkable apologia: The political world was filled, he cautioned, with

> shameful emotions, vengeful appetites, interests in jeopardy, crushed hopes, thwarted ambitions. . . . For more than thirty years, I have been a republican warrior. . . . I have fought ideas, not individuals. . . . Of corruption, there is no proof, not the beginning of proof, not a trace! I settled the debts of my youth through a loan which remains outstanding today. I married my wife without a dowry. I have lived in the same apartment for the last six years, the bill for the furniture and the carpet paid off little by little with a balance left. Where are the millions I am accused of receiving?

Assailed by rumor, attacked from all sides, Clemenceau still led in the initial round of voting, but he lost the runoff on 2 September 1893. With justification, he believed his political career finished.[16]

What next? After a grim trip to Aubraie marked by his father's lacerating critique of his prospects, Clemenceau returned to Paris and took up journalism full-time. During the next ten years, he wrote 1,445

articles—one every two or three days—for various daily newspapers, most often *Le Journal, L'Echo de Paris, L'Aurore, Le Français, La
Dépêche de Toulouse*, and his own *La Justice*. Many of these columns
he republished in collections, *La Mêlée sociale* (The social struggle;
1895), *Le Grand Pan* (The great Pan; 1896), and *L'Affaire Dreyfus* (The
Dreyfus affair; in seven volumes, 1899–1903). For a fourth time, his
words led to a duel: in July 1894 against the debonair Paul Deschanel,
who before the Chamber of Deputies accused *La Justice* of defending
anarchism. After Clemenceau's next column replied, "Monsieur Deschanel is a coward. Monsieur Paul Deschanel has lied," they fought
with swords southwest of Paris at Boulogne-sur-Seine. A large crowd
gathered once again, seeing Clemenceau end matters rapidly by
slashing Deschanel above the right eye. Were his duels the kind of celebrity that won him a coveted invitation to the March 1895 banquet
celebrating gossipmonger Edmond de Goncourt? After a brief hob-
nobbing with literary gents, Clemenceau experimented by writing a
novel, *Les Plus forts* (The strongest; 1897) and a one-act play, *Le Voile
du bonheur* (The veil of happiness; first presented 4 November 1901)
before recognizing that his world was realistic, not imaginary. A fair
estimate for the income all this writing generated is thirty thousand
francs a year ($160,000 in 2011), enough to live a life of relative ease
in bourgeois fashion, enough to pay off his debts, and most satisfy-
ing, more than enough to spite his father. By comparison, the salary
of a deputy was nine thousand francs ($48,000 in 2011), and that of a
schoolteacher, one thousand francs ($5,330 in 2011).[17]

Yet the personal and political blows he suffered had their effect.
Clemenceau turned inward, mistrusting the loyalty of men he had regarded as friends or allies. In 1896, he moved from the hubbub of Paris
to a spacious apartment on the Rue Franklin in Passy, a quiet and
fashionable western suburb. He had a rose garden in the courtyard
and enough room for two servants—his valet, Albert, and cook, Marie, both of them careful of his moods and likes. The utter regularity
he adopted betrayed how much he now withdrew from life. Waking
long before dawn, he heated the onion soup he had every breakfast,
and then he sat at the semicircular desk in his study wearing a robe,
felt slippers, and a checked tweed cap. He wrote with a quill pen and

dried the ink with powder, the old-fashioned way. When he ran out of ideas, he retrieved his small pistol and shot at the rats running down the drain pipes, always pleased to wake up the Jesuits who were his neighbors. Lunch was exactly at 12:30, after which he usually walked his dogs in the nearby Bois de Boulogne. The afternoons he spent at one or another newspaper office, but he returned home for dinner at 7:30. If he went out afterward to the theater or some social function, he was back early. The Manichean quality he had always manifested— ever characterizing, by his definition, the good and the evil—goaded him to view the world as a cruel amphitheater within which humankind engaged in perpetual gladiatorial games. He was ever more contemptuous, ever more contumacious. Three decades later, when he wrote of the historical figure he most admired, he defined himself as well as the Athenian orator Demosthenes: "Call that man happy—for it is the lot of all to suffer—who has suffered for a noble cause, and grieve for him who, having sought nothing outside of himself, has known only the cinders of life, of egoism vainly consumed."[18]

Clemenceau took on all and sundry in his articles until he found his issue in the Dreyfus affair. Initially, he sided with the military high command, even considering them too lenient. Following the court-martial in December 1894 that convicted Captain Alfred Dreyfus of selling secrets to the Germans and sentenced him to life imprisonment on Devil's Island off French Guiana, Clemenceau wrote, "If, in the scale of punishments, the penalty of death is the ultimate sanction, I believe it should be reserved for the greatest crime, which is surely treason." His mind was unchanged as late as October 1897, when he left *La Justice* to become editor in chief of *L'Aurore*. Soon afterward, however, he came to know Mathieu Dreyfus, who was devoting every resource to prove his brother innocent, and Lt. Colonel Georges Picquart, the counterintelligence officer who believed that the evidence pointed to Major Ferdinand Walsin-Esterhazy as the real traitor. They convinced Clemenceau by using the word dearest to him, "justice," but perhaps more so by presenting the defenders of Dreyfus as oppressed, unpopular, and ill-used. An eternal duelist, he thrilled at challenge, at combat. When his turn came to recruit for the Dreyfusard cause, he would repeat his mantra, "We shall be alone. We shall have all the world against us. But we shall win!" And they did. The decisive moment came in January 1898, when France's most celebrated novelist, Emile Zola, wrote an open letter to the president of the Republic charging that high military and political officials had conspired to convict an innocent man, Dreyfus, and to acquit a guilty one, Walsin-Esterhazy. Clemenceau ran the letter as the front page of *L'Aurore* under a banner headline, "I Accuse . . ." (*J'accuse . . .*). The evidence Zola laid out began to turn public opinion for Dreyfus, but much hard slogging was left to go.[19]

A month later, on 26 February 1898, Clemenceau fought his fifth duel, against Edouard Drumont, the vituperative editor of the anti-Semitic daily scripture *La Libre parole*: pistols, and as with Déroulède, no wounds. Another year later, on 16 February 1899, Félix Faure—the president of the Republic Zola had addressed, an Opportunist, and a determined opponent of reopening the Dreyfus case—died from a stroke during a rendezvous with his mistress after a large luncheon. Clemenceau's comment the following day in *L'Aurore* was derisive: "President Faure has just died. France is not one man the less." During the next seven months, Déroulède attempted a ludicrous coup d'état at Faure's funeral; France's Court of Final Appeal (*Cour de Cassation*) ordered a new trial for Dreyfus; and this second court-martial resulted in the absurd verdict "guilty with extenuating circumstances." On 19 September 1899, Faure's successor as president of the Republic, Emile Loubet, granted a pardon. Clemenceau protested that by accepting it, Dreyfus was acknowledging guilt, preferring instead that he die on Devil's Island as a martyr for justice. Even Mathieu Dreyfus sided briefly with the "man of iron and steel" before he urged his brother to embrace this salvation while continuing to seek a formal declaration of innocence. That vindication came finally on 12 July 1906.[20]

Clemenceau rode the Dreyfus affair to political rehabilitation. Flush with victory and restored finances, he withdrew from *L'Aurore* to found a weekly journal, *Le Bloc*, taking the name from his famous reference to the French Revolution in 1891 and to the painting of a massive luminous rock given him by his new friend Claude Monet, a Dreyfusard. Writing almost every word, Clemenceau kept *Le Bloc* going for sixty issues, just long enough to win election to the Senate. Given his new stature, local officeholders in the Var wanted to make amends for his defeat in 1893 and offered their support. A cardinal element of Radicalism had always been a unicameral legislature elected by universal manhood suffrage, but the guarantee of a seat in the Senate for a nine-year term and its nine-thousand-franc salary trumped principle. Clemenceau was elected on 4 April 1902 and soon enough his claws were extended: "Yes! We have guillotined the king; long live the State-King! Yes, we have dethroned the pope; long live the State-Pope! . . . The State has a long history of murder and blood. All the crimes of this world, the massacres, the wars, the derelictions of justice, the stake, the wheel, the tortures—all have been justified by the interest of the State, by reason of State." He served notice that the Tiger who had savaged Opportunist ministers from the Chamber would now savage Radical ministers from the Senate. For the Dreyfus affair brought power and influence to the men of the political left who had been prominent in the Dreyfusard cause. The 1902 legislative elections gave a majority in the Chamber of Deputies to them as the Bloc des Gauches. Their leader, Emile Combes, made a fetish of punishing the real or purported sins of the army and the Catholic Church. The army was to be purged of officers conspicuous in their religious devotion; the schools run by the church were to be closed; the 1801 Concordat linking church and state was to be abrogated. Clemenceau approved separating church and state but rejected any state monopoly of education. He had no sympathy for pious military officers but called penalizing them unjust. He instinctively recognized Combes as an enemy, just as Combes recognized the same of him. Combes ordered police surveillance of Clemenceau, who watched a detective hide behind a laundry wagon near his apartment in Passy and then cried "peek-a-boo!" in his direction. As he told the story at *L'Aurore*, "That afternoon at the Senate, Combes came toward me with his hand extended. I put my hands in my pockets."[21]

Forever an outsider, forever singular, Clemenceau raged against institutions demanding unquestioned obedience—once the church, now an all-powerful state. Had the lesson of Alfred Dreyfus been forgotten so soon—or learned so imperfectly? The 1901 Associations Law facilitated the formation of organized political parties, and when the Radicals took the required steps, Clemenceau refused to join. His "radicalism" was as ever a "radical individualism," defined on his terms. Among journalists, he recruited two new apostles: from *Le Temps*, the brilliant foreign affairs editor André Tardieu, and from *L'Aurore*, another Manichean like himself, Georges Mandel. He was preparing for combat and took measure of the other contenders. Among the moderates, the best was Raymond Poincaré, whose pragmatism, prudence, and diligence were his antithesis. Somewhere between them—no one ever knew exactly—was Aristide Briand, supple conciliator, believing in nothing, sympathetic to all. Three decades later when they were all dead, Wladimir d'Ormesson, editorialist for *Le Figaro*, compared them: "Briand tells you, 'Yes, but . . . ,' Poincaré, 'No, because . . . ,' Clemenceau, 'No.'" The great comer in the Radical party was Joseph Caillaux, wealthy, arrogant, unprincipled, and considered corrupt: the traits they shared made them detest each other all the more. Of Jean Jaurès, a Dreyfusard who had unified the disparate elements of French socialism into a single reformist party, Clemenceau said, "Do you know how to recognize an article by Jaurès? All the verbs are in the future tense."[22]

March 1906 brought Clemenceau's chance. Radical stalwart Jean Sarrien sought to form a cabinet in the midst of disturbances over the separation of church and state and asked him, among others, to his house for consultation. Passing the drinks tray, Sarrien asked what each would have, to which Clemenceau replied, "the Interior." He was sixty-four years old and in charge of domestic order, but he had no intention of stopping there. Seven months later, Clemenceau had so vigorously restored order that he took over as premier from the utterly overshadowed Sarrien, who was afterward called "the Tiger's meal." His most perceptive biographer, Jean-Baptiste Duroselle, described the attitude Clemenceau would take now that he had power: "For him, it was pride and will. His faith in the Republic, in liberty, in France was joined to a potent scorn for most other men, by an inflexible harshness which, with age, led him to a preference for order, for authority that must be obeyed." Clemenceau spoke vaguely of social reforms, but he spent money on modernizing France's national bureau of criminal investigation, the Sûreté générale. Its head, Célestin Hennion, called these new forces his "Tiger Brigades." When electrical workers went on strike in March 1907, Clemenceau called out troops, restored power, and when Jaurès demanded by what right he acted, replied, "In the name of society's right to live, in the name of the government's right to assure that life." Ten months earlier before the Chamber, in June 1906, he had derided Jaurès: "He speaks from the mountainside, absorbed in his sumptuous mirage while I, down on the plain, till a barren soil. . . . You claim to create the future but we will make that future." When an overproduction of wine in 1907 caused a collapse in prices and led vintners to foment violence, Clemenceau had them arrested. In July1908, he called in cavalry units to break strikes at Vigneux and Villeneuve-Saint-Georges. When the largest union, the General Confederation of Labor (Confédération générale du travail), threatened to call a general strike, he had all of its leaders jailed. He called himself France's "top cop [*premier flic*]." Jaurès now said he was an "evil man."[23]

Clemenceau broke with Jaurès over foreign policy as well. The Socialists had convinced themselves that an international brotherhood of workingmen could—surely would—preserve Europe from any future war. Clemenceau denied that brotherhood of any sort existed, and he detested Germany for seizing Alsace and Lorraine from France in 1871. In the best Jacobin fashion, he was a patriot and a nationalist. He opposed imperial ventures not only on principle but because they distracted French concentration from the blue line of the Vosges River that was the border with Germany. When Clemenceau discovered that Caillaux favored German economic hegemony as long as France could share in the spoils, he became the deadly antagonist of this "demagogue-plutocrat." In 1905 Germany had threatened France over Morocco. In September 1908, tempers flared over the "Casablanca Affair," involving three German deserters from the French Foreign Legion. Imperiously confronting Clemenceau, Prince Huero von Radolin, Germany's ambassador to Paris since 1901, demanded that France adopt the German position or he would have to return to Berlin for consultations—a threat to break diplomatic relations. Radolin should have known that Clemenceau reacted badly to threats, especially when he believed they had little substance. Retrieving a train schedule, Clemenceau replied, "Excellency, the train for Cologne leaves at nine. It is now seven. If you do not want to miss it, you must hurry." Shortly afterward, Germany agreed to arbitration. Yet near the end of 1908 in what came to be called the First Balkan Crisis, German leaders threatened France's ally Russia with war for objecting to Austria-Hungary's annexation of Bosnia and Herzegovina.[24]

During his thirty-three months as premier, Clemenceau came to rely on Briand, the minister of religion, to promote peace within the cabinet. The true proof of Briand's skills came in his quietly negotiating an entente with French Catholics after the 1905 separation of church and state. Clemenceau ostentatiously ignored the details and replied to Pelletan's mocking question, "Is the road to Canossa beautiful?" (a reference to Holy Roman Emperor Henry IV's humiliating submission to Pope Gregory VII in 1077), with "I don't know; Briand takes us there in a closed carriage." Yet when Clemenceau provoked his own downfall in July 1909, Briand was the obvious successor as premier. He would continue Clemenceau's policies with less insolence. Clemenceau could step back: "I can amuse myself with the idiocies of others instead of committing them myself." He could potter at the house he bought in 1908 near Bernouville, not far from Monet's in Giverny, eventually having a garden with fifty white lilies, fifty climbing roses, ninety geraniums, and three hundred stock roses. He could visit his favorite spa in Carlsbad with his Danish friend Brandes. He could travel to South America on a lecture tour in 1910. He could submit to an operation removing his prostate in 1912 by the celebrated surgeon Dr. Antonin Sébastien Gosset—and recover not in a state hospital but at a nursing home staffed by the Little Sisters of the Poor, where Sister Théoneste cared for him as if to establish that he had been wrong about the church all his life. The joke went round that when tigers grow old, they are made into bedside rugs.[25]

Not yet: in January 1912 Clemenceau roused himself to take on Caillaux, whose negotiations with Germany the previous fall during yet another crisis over Morocco strongly implied French weakness. A burst of nationalism followed, bringing to power Poincaré, who combined his painstaking caution with an obdurate hatred for all things German since the loss of his native Lorraine in 1871. As premier, Poincaré brought a new vigor to foreign policy, and cabaret singers celebrated with a pun on his name: France had its fists clenched (*ses poings carrés*). When January 1913 brought the election for president of the Republic, Poincaré declared his candidacy, sensing that he could transform the office into a locus of power. For classically Radical reasons and because Poincaré, as a moderate, was certain to rely on votes from the political right to win, Clemenceau objected loudly. When Poincaré won nonetheless, relations between them, never warm, grew testy. But because they both sensed a new war with Germany looming, Clemenceau supported Poincaré's most important legislative goal, which was to lengthen the term of service for conscripts from two years to three (it had been reduced in the wake of the Dreyfus affair) and thereby increase the size of the French army. On 22 February 1913, Clemenceau told Maurice Paléologue, who was close to Poincaré and would soon become France's ambassador to St. Petersburg: "The foreign situation appears more worrisome each day. We can save the peace only with a strong army. So, we must immediately revert to three-year service. No matter the expense, the same sacrifice for all, even if the country does not understand." For Poincaré, Clemenceau, "despite his grave faults of pride, jealousy, rancor, and hatred, . . . is endowed to the highest degree with national fortitude; he is a patriot like the Jacobins of 1793." On 23 May, Clemenceau promised that, "if a crisis dangerous to national interest opened," Poincaré could count on him to form a cabinet.[26]

Just beforehand, Clemenceau began another newspaper, *L'Homme libre*, with his friend Geffroy and disciple Mandel, the first issue appearing on 6 May 1913. Clemenceau intended to give daily proof that the Tiger still had his claws and his teeth. Fifteen months later, the war he had apprehended engulfed almost all of Europe. Germany issued a declaration of war against Russia on 1 August 1914, then against France on 3 August, and Belgium on 4 August. Great Britain and France replied by declaring war on Germany. In France, the cabinet was enlarged to encompass all parties—but despite Poincaré's entreaties, Clemenceau refused to join this *Union Sacrée* (Sacred Union). He was unwilling to serve with men he detested, disliked, and mistrusted —Delcassé, Alexandre Millerand, and Louis Malvy, respectively. He did trouble to upbraid Malvy for failing to arrest the revolutionaries and pacifists listed in the interior ministry's *Carnet B* (Notebook B). Regarding the assassination of Jaurès on 31 July by a nationalist fanatic, Clemenceau would say, years later, "I can never think without a shiver of the first, the very first, cause of victory: the murder of Jaurès." For now, on 26 August 1914, he wrote in *L'Homme libre,* "We demand a government of steel, indestructible, unyielding," yet he reacted with fury when Malvy censored the newspaper after Clemenceau reported serious inadequacies in the military infirmaries. On 8 October following a week-long suspension, *L'Homme libre* reappeared as *L'Homme enchaîné*—the "Free Man" becoming the "Chained Man." The legislature had adjourned when the fighting began but reconvened in January 1915, with Clemenceau sitting on the Senate's army committee and its foreign affairs committee, where he made himself expert in the conduct of the war. From October 1915 onward, he visited the trench lines that ran across northern France from Switzerland west to the North Sea finding evidence beyond question that the Sacred Union was not winning the war. Ignoring every danger, he won the trust and admiration of the soldiers—the *poilus,* the "dirty hairy ones" who had stopped the Germans, were holding the Germans, but who were dying in extraordinary numbers—more than half a million by the end of 1915.[27]

The battles of Verdun and the Somme, names for the 1916 hecatombs, multiplied the suffering and death. March 1917 brought revolution in Russia, April, the utter failure of new French offensives followed by the mutiny of some frontline units. Behind the lines, pessimism grew and gained a name, *défaitisme* (defeatism), and a program, peace at almost any price. Two newspapers—the moderate *Le Journal,* partly owned by Senator Charles Humbert, and the extreme-left *Le Bonnet rouge*—were suspected of accepting German subsidies. Various men and women appeared to be acting as German agents, either of influence or of espionage. More than a few had connections to Caillaux, who had connections to Malvy, minister of the interior since May 1914 and suspiciously unwilling to act. With Mandel ferreting out the evidence, Clemenceau opened his own investigation and in a sensational speech before the Senate on 22 July 1917 assailed the spread of pacifism, defeatism, and treason. He singled out Malvy for tolerating it: "You have betrayed the interests of France." During the next months, a parliamentary commission ordered Malvy to stand trial before the Senate as *Haute Cour* (high court), and the *Sûreté générale* arrested a senator (Humbert), a deputy (Louis Turmel), various journalists and editors (Miguel Almereyda, Paul Bolo-Pasha, Pierre Lenoir, and Emile Joseph Duval), and an adventuress (Margaret Gertrud Zelle, known as Mata Hari) for treason or complicity in treason. And during the next months, the military situation grew dangerously worse. Italy, which joined the side of France, Great Britain, and Russia in 1915, suffered a catastrophic rout at Caporetto. The United States, which declared war on Germany in April 1917, had not yet sent a single soldier to Europe. Russia was near collapse. Poincaré recognized that the critical moment had arrived. France had to choose between seeking a negotiated peace and fighting on to the death, between Caillaux and Clemenceau. In his diary he wrote that Clemenceau "wants to go to the limit [*jusqu'au bout*] with the war and with the judicial cases. . . . He is without doubt the right man. He has qualities which, given the troubles we have, outweigh his failings. Above all, he is a patriot."[28]

Poincaré's description of his meeting with Clemenceau on 14 November 1917 is justly celebrated: "The Tiger enters. He is fatter. His deafness is worse. His intelligence is intact. But his health? His will? More and more I sense the peril of the endeavor. But this devil of a man has behind him the support of patriots." And so they agreed that Clemenceau should form the cabinet he had promised for the moment of France's greatest need. On the following day, *L'Homme libre* published the last editorial Clemenceau would ever write, which began, "The hour has come to govern, because that is the first condition of a republican regime." He meant a revived Committee of Public Safety as in 1793–94, with himself as a new Maximilien Robespierre. Other than his longtime friend Pichon as minister of foreign affairs, he chose second-stringers to fill out the cabinet positions: he meant to run things—everything—himself, assisted by Mandel and by General Jean Jules Henri Mordacq, whose toughness impressed him during a visit to the trenches. On 20 November, he addressed the Chamber of Deputies calling for energy and victory, for the cause of France was the cause of Justice, of civilized nations against the barbarian.

"One day," he thrilled in closing, "from Paris to the most humble village, acclamations will welcome our conquering standards, soaked in blood, torn from shells, the magnificent specter of our great dead. This day, the grandest of our race, we have the power to accomplish." The vote of confidence was 428 to 65, with Malvy and Caillaux among the 25 who abstained. Afterward, Clemenceau told *New York Times* correspondent Wythe Williams, "I intend to do two things. One, I will destroy the German Empire. Two, I will destroy Caillaux." Poincaré agreed that Caillaux should face trial for cultivating connections to treason. On 14 January 1918, Clemenceau ordered Caillaux's arrest, to serve as a warning against anyone who would doubt victory.[29]

History rarely offers a clearer verdict: on 11 November 1918, a total of 356 days after Clemenceau took power, France and its allies won the war. Nine months earlier, in February, the outcome had been much less certain. Clemenceau had stiffened spines, but France and Great Britain were running out of soldiers, even as Germany, with Russia knocked out of the war, could concentrate its might against the Western Front. The Americans were coming—were they coming in time? On 8 March 1918, the eve of a new German offensive, Clemenceau gave his greatest speech, telling the Chamber of Deputies: "I wage war! . . . In domestic affairs, I wage war! In foreign affairs, I wage war! Always, everywhere, I wage war! Russia has betrayed us, and I continue to wage war! . . . Before Paris, I wage war! Behind Paris, I wage war! If we retreat to the Pyrenees, I shall continue to wage war, and I wage war until the last quarter hour, because the last quarter hour will be ours!" Watching from the gallery was Winston Churchill, who copied down every word as if he divined that someday he would need to deliver exactly the same speech, and he wrote later that Clemenceau "ranged from one side of the tribune to another, without a note or book or reference or scrap of paper, . . . he looked like a wild animal pacing to and fro behind bars, growling and glaring." The German attack struck on 21 March, driving at the junction of French and British forces near Amiens. Great fear spread among civilian and military leaders. To restore confidence and to establish greater coordination, Clemenceau proposed a single commander for all French and British forces on the Western Front, proposing General Ferdinand Foch—despite his having a Jesuit as a brother.

The British accepted, both armies defied greater German numbers, and they held Amiens. A second wave came in late May at Chemin des Dames, near Soissons, where victory would put the Germans at the northwest approach to Paris. Their initial success inspired panic, but in the midst of the tumult, Clemenceau remained confident. By early June, Foch rallied reserves and stabilized the line. To any criticism came Clemenceau's withering reply: "If, to win the approval of some who judge hastily, I must abandon the leaders who have so well served the nation, that is a treachery [*lâcheté*] of which I am incapable." When the Germans mounted a third assault, this time in July near Reims, Foch launched a counterattack at Château-Thierry using 350 tanks, 13 French divisions, and for the first time, 3 American divisions, which pushed the Germans backward and represented the turning point of the war. The destruction of the German Empire then came on apace.[30]

And the destruction of Caillaux? When Clemenceau became premier, he proclaimed, "There have been crimes, crimes against France, which call for prompt punishment. . . . All the guilty before courts-martial. The soldier in the courtroom united with the soldier in battle. No more pacifist campaigns, no more German intrigues. Neither treason nor semitreason. The war! Nothing but the war! Our armies will not be caught between fire from two sides. Justice will be done. The nation will know that it has been defended." Regarding the soldier in battle: between November 1917 and November 1918, Clemenceau devoted ninety days, in three-day intervals, to visiting the soldiers in their trenches, frequently coming within two hundred yards of German lines. The most famous moment came on 6 July 1918, when he sought out the troops of General Henri Gouraud at Les Monts in the Champagne hills who were awaiting what would be the final German offensive. They knew well, as he certainly did, that most of them were marked for sacrifice. They had nothing to present him but a bouquet of chalk-white wildflowers. Overcome, he pledged that he would keep this gift forever: desiccated and brittle, a few remain as a treasure of the Musée Clemenceau, the rest lie with him in his casket. Regarding pacifist campaigns and German intrigues: the deputy, Turmel, and one of the editors, Almereyda, died in prison; the other journalists, editors, and the adventuress were shot; Humbert alone was cleared. In August 1918, the senators, sitting as the High Court, convicted Malvy of having "failed in, violated, and betrayed the duties of his office" and sentenced him to five years' exile. Eighteen months later in February 1920, they found Caillaux guilty of illicit correspondence "furnishing the enemy with information deleterious to the political or military situation," with the penalty of three years in prison and loss of political rights for ten years. The nation knew that it had been defended.[31]

By the fall of 1918, Austria-Hungary was near collapse and Germany, not France, sought a negotiated peace. On 17 September, in the Senate, Clemenceau replied with ice, "Insanely, Germany believed that victory would amnesty everything in hosannas of fire and blood: our countryside devastated, our towns, our villages ruined by mines and fire, by methodical pillaging, by refined cruelty. Their victory did not come, and the most terrible account of a people to a people is now to be opened. It will be paid. . . . Germany wanted a military decision. Let it be as Germany wanted!" Six weeks later, Germany was beaten, and on 11 November as the Armistice took effect, Clemenceau was acclaimed as *Père-la-Victoire* (Father Victory) by huge crowds as he arrived at the Palais Bourbon late in the afternoon to address the Chamber of Deputies. His eyes overflowed, but his voice was strong: "At this formidable hour, grand and magnificent, my duty is accomplished. In the name of the French people, in the name of the French Republic, I salute Alsace and Lorraine recovered. Honor be to our great dead who have given us this victory. Because of them, France, yesterday the soldier of God, today the soldier of Humanity, will always be the soldier of the Ideal." Yet that evening, when his daughter Madeleine saw him darkly morose and begged, "Papa, tell me that you're happy," he replied, "I can't tell you that because I am not. It will not have done any good."[32]

What is victory at the cost of more than 1.3 million men dead, more than 1.1 million left with permanent disabilities, that is, 6 percent of France's population and a quarter of the men aged between twenty and twenty-seven? What is victory when France's north, which accounted for 60 percent of coal production, 66 percent of textile production, and 55 percent of metallurgical production, lay in total ruin? Clemenceau was convinced that Germany would recover and seek to reverse the verdict of 1918. He refused to believe that idealistic schemes could alter human nature. Of the American president Woodrow Wilson's Fourteen Points speech in January 1918, Clemenceau remarked, "God himself only had ten, and we see how well they have worked."[33] At the Paris Peace Conference held from January to June 1919, he sought French security through a buffer state to be created by detaching from Germany the so-called Rhineland, between the Rhine River and France. President Wilson and British prime minister David Lloyd George adamantly refused. They proposed instead that the Rhineland be permanently demilitarized and occupied for up to fifteen years, and more important, they proposed a treaty of guarantee, renewing the wartime alliance of the three democracies. Given France's exhaustion and economic dependency because of wartime borrowing from its allies, Clemenceau had to give way. Foch and Poincaré could not contain their vehement objections. Poincaré wrote in his journal that Clemenceau was "heedless, excessive, vain, bickering, jesting, shockingly reckless, deaf intellectually as well as physically, incapable of reasoning, of reflecting, of following a discussion." He sent long memoranda to Clemenceau, who later recalled, "Every time I saw his dainty little handwriting, it threw me into a fury." Clemenceau told Wilson, in English, "You must give me help from these two fools."[34]

The Bolshevik Revolution in Russia and the collapse of Austria-Hungary into ethnic minorities squabbling for territory severely complicated the negotiations. Any predictions about the future of Europe had to be based more on conjecture than on reality. In this exercise of imagination, the French delegation, led by Tardieu, did at least as well as any other. In the midst of it, on 19 February, Clemenceau, who scorned personal security, was shot as he left his apartment in Passy. Although hit three times, he staggered back inside, where an examination revealed that the only serious wound was to his shoulder blade. Sister Théoneste returned to nurse him, and eight days later he was back at work. The would-be assassin was a young anarchist, Eugène Cottin, using a Browning automatic. Clemenceau joked that Cottin needed further instruction at a pistol range and, when Cottin was condemned to death for the attack, insisted that Poincaré commute the sentence to life imprisonment. The treaty that emerged from the peace conference was signed with much ceremony in the Hall of Mirrors at Versailles on 28 June 1919. When the Chamber of Deputies debated its ratification, the principal issue under discussion was whether France could trust the promises made by Wilson in the name of the United States. Clemenceau did not hesitate to remind the deputies that, while France had held the Germans at the Marne and at Verdun, "we could never have won the war without our allies beside us. That is the truth. . . . Nothing obliged the Americans to come to our assistance. They came." Against the complaint that the treaty condemned France "to the politics of vigilance," he rejoined, "I, myself, see life as a perpetual struggle, in peace as in war. . . . All existence is but a struggle."[35]

Because the United States failed to ratify the treaty and Great Britain supported softening the strictures against Germany, a refrain arose that Clemenceau had "won the war but lost the peace." He had always disdained the very idea that the Republic should have a president, but with Poincaré's term expiring, he believed the office might make a capstone for his career. For once, however, Clemenceau failed to reckon with rancor. Every enemy he had ever made—Catholics on the right, Socialists on the left, moderates in the center, and dozens of others with a score to settle—rejoiced at this moment to take revenge. On 16 January 1920, they voted instead for Paul Deschanel, who still had the scar from his duel in 1894. Clemenceau had always denigrated the election for president of the Republic with the jest *"Je vote pour le plus bête"* (I vote for the biggest fool): the irony must have been appealing. He immediately resigned as premier and withdrew permanently from public life. To escape from France, he traveled first to Egypt and the Sudan, where British authorities received him with magnificence, and then to India. At the peace conference Ganga Singh, the maharajah of Bikaner, had invited him on a hunting expedition, and Clemenceau now accepted. He shot two tigers on 14 January 1921, another irony he must have appreciated, given the target and given the date. Almost exactly a year earlier, his enemies had figuratively shot the Tiger in the vote for president of the Republic.[36]

To Major General Edward Louis Spears, who served as liaison between the British War Office and the French Ministry of War, Clemenceau remarked: "I had a wife, she abandoned me; I had children, they turned against me; I had friends, they betrayed me. I have only my claws, and I use them." The truth was more complicated. Regarding his wife: In 1900, eight years after her divorce and deportation, Mary Clemenceau quietly returned to France. She lived in Paris until her death in September 1922, frequently seeing her children but never her former husband. Regarding his children: His only son, Michel, trained as an agricultural engineer in Zurich after a dismal record at several French schools. For a time he made his career in Hungary, where he married and had two children, before returning to France in 1905. He involved himself in various schemes to win military supply contracts and to manufacture automobiles and aircraft, all of them irregular and leading to charges of fraud. For a time, Clemenceau cut all ties, but he renewed them when Michel fought bravely in the war, killing at least one German officer in hand-to-hand combat while suffering a serious wound in the thigh. His elder daughter, Madeleine, married a wealthy attorney twenty years her senior who shot himself when he discovered her adultery with an associate and left a will entrusting guardianship of their child to his friend Poincaré—infuriating Clemenceau. His younger daughter, Thérèse, married a handsome and often inebriated idler who deserted her after seven years. Because she was without support, Clemenceau permitted Thérèse and her two daughters to live with him for a time in Passy—if all three slept in the same room. Regarding his friends: The men closest to Clemenceau, with the single exception of Tardieu, were always fiercely loyal. His associates, not a few of whom turned on him, were never his friends.[37]

After Clemenceau returned from his travels, he sold the house at Bernouville, which he had hardly visited during the war. He wanted a refuge in the Vendée, but he had refused to set foot in Colombier since his brother Paul became chatelain. The estate of Major Amédée Luce de Trémont, Catholic and royalist but a profound admirer, lay to the west of Aubraie, right on the Bay of Biscay. Just above high tide there was a cottage, really little more than a shack (*bicoque*), called Bélébat. Trémont offered it to Clemenceau for free but settled on a rent of 150 francs a year ($211.00 in 2011), to be donated to the local poor. For the rest of his life, Clemenceau spent about a third of each year entranced by this seaside solitude. He called it "my horizontal château." His claim to have "taken possession of *my sky, my sea, and my sand*" testified how bitterly he regarded the loss of his birthright. He walked for hours along the coast because he felt too old to fish. Against all odds in the sandy soil, he grew irises, roses, hydrangeas, peonies, hollyhocks, chrysanthemums, lilies, and anemones. He liked going to the local market and chatting with the stall keepers. Although the roof leaked and mildew was a constant threat, he brought some of his treasures from Passy. In the living room he hung Monet's water-color of the old Spanish gate in the Kaaba of Oran; in the bedroom, a tiger skin; and in the study where he wrote early in the morning, the stuffed head of the animals he shot on safari, "for company." His doctors—Antoine Florand, for his asthma, rheumatism, and diabetes; Charles Coutela, for his cataracts—and his dentist, Arthur Hugen-schmidt (the illegitimate son of Napoleon III and Virginia Oldoini, Countess of Castiglione), all came to him. He received visitors: his children, his brother Albert, Monet, Mandel, Mordacq, Pichon, and in September 1925, the writer René Benjamin, who explained his es-teem concisely, "I don't have to wear a German helmet, and I owe that to you." Clemenceau bounced back and forth to Paris along primitive roads in a little Citroën automobile. André Citroën insisted on giving it to him; Clemenceau insisted on giving the factory workers who had assembled it ten thousand francs ($14,080 in 2011).[38]

Occasionally, Clemenceau could be lured out. In June 1921, Ox-ford University presented him with an honorary doctorate. That October, a statue of him by Louis Sicard was unveiled at Sainte-Hermine, where he asked the melancholy question, "What does it serve to say, 'Our fathers were great men,' if from their tombs they judge us diminished?" The following year in May, the Lycée de Nantes was renamed for him, and he asked the boys: "How do you see me? Perhaps like one of those old owls, beating their wings against the wind, nailed by our peasants to the doors of their barns for the crime, according to the fable writers, of seeing clearly in the night." He was profoundly apprehensive about the weakness of France and its isolation under the leadership of Poincaré and Briand. No one had ever forgotten his stinging line from two decades earlier: "Poincaré is a man who knows everything and understands nothing, while Briand knows nothing but understands everything." At the banquet celebrating the school on 27 May 1922, he warned, "Better to die with honor than to live in shame. We have no need to live in glory, but we want to live in honor." From here, he was ready for one final sortie, an appeal to the Americans on their home ground. The *New York World* offered to cover his expenses in return for his writing six articles for its regional newspapers. He arrived by ship in New York on 18 November 1922. He was welcomed by the undersecretary of state, Robert W. Bliss, who had served as a councilor to the American embassy in Paris during the war and whose wife had nursed the French wounded; by Myron T. Herrick, the current ambassador, who returned for the occasion; by Wilson's close advisors Colonel Edward M. House and Bernard Baruch; and by France's ambassador to Washington, Jules Jusserand. Clemenceau looked in vain for the house he had rented in 1857. He placed flowers on the grave of Theodore Roosevelt, who had supported France without stint during the war and whose defiance of fate Clemenceau recognized as his own.[39]

From 21 November until 12 December, he gave a series of speeches in New York, Boston, Chicago, St. Louis, Indianapolis, Dayton, Baltimore, Philadelphia, and Washington. He reminded his audiences:

> You mixed your blood with ours, . . . you do not have the right to leave us this way without trying to help. . . . You swore before the world that you would issue your guarantee. You proclaimed it in the treaty. I ask you, why did you go to war? Was it to help others preserve democracy? . . . There can be no doubt that Germany is preparing a new war. Nothing can stop that except an alliance of the three democratic powers: America, Great Britain, and France.

President Warren Harding received him at the White House but had no intention of adopting policies more accommodating to France. Clemenceau found him courteous but uncultured—as did many Americans. He met with Wilson, partially paralyzed from the stroke that felled him in October 1919 but still keen of mind. He had discussions with Colonel House; General John Joseph Pershing, commander of the American Expeditionary Force; and Charles Evans Hughes, the current secretary of state. He visited Mount Vernon and laid a wreath at the Tomb of the Unknown Soldier. He spoke before the Banquet of Good Will sponsored by the American Committee for Devastated France. His ship home departed on 13 December and arrived a week later. The French press pretended that the trip had changed minds in the United States. Clemenceau was well aware that he had not.[40]

What makes a valedictory for a Tiger? In May 1923 Clemenceau had a visit from Marguerite Bonzon Baldensperger, the wife of a distinguished expert in comparative literature at the Sorbonne. She was herself an editor at the publisher Librairie Plon and proposed that he contribute a book to its series *Nobles Vies—Grandes Oeuvres* (Noble lives, great works). During further meetings, they agreed upon Demosthenes, the Athenian orator from the fourth century BC, as his subject. And during these meetings, Clemenceau perceived in Baldensperger a profound sadness. Eventually, she told him that the eldest of her four children, a daughter, had died some fifteen months earlier and that she had found no means to console her anguish. Greatly moved, he bent toward her: "Place your hand in mine. I shall help you to live, and you will help me to die. That is our pact. Let us embrace." During the next six and a half years, he would write her 668 letters. His affection for her was the purest act of love in his long life.[41]

Under her inspiration, Clemenceau wrote three books. Librairie Plon made a fortune from their sales; Clemenceau gave almost all of his royalties away. First, in 1926, came the promised study, terse and discerning, of Demosthenes, who warned that the conquest of the Greek city-states by Philip of Macedon and his son Alexander would mean the destruction of their liberty, culture, and ideals. Here was "a drama of the sword against the idealism of the human conscience." And although Demosthenes was not heeded in time, "There is no irreparable defeat except for a cause that is abandoned. . . . There is a superior lesson in tragic lives, wherein everyone can find a subject of meditation fitted to his capacity." Writing in the midst of the troubled 1920s, Clemenceau saw Germany as a twentieth-century

Philip, "a conqueror who, under a thin varnish of Hellenic culture, poorly concealed a blind thirst of conquest." In 1928 he added a second book to the *Nobles Vies* series, *Claude Monet: Les Nymphéas* (Claude Monet: 'The Water Lilies'). During the war, Monet began creating large panel paintings of the water lilies in the branch of the Epte River flowing through his garden at Giverny. On the day following the Armistice, he offered them to the nation as his observance of victory, and Clemenceau ordered the Orangerie renovated to house them. When Monet's work flagged as his sight failed from cataracts, Clemenceau urged a surgical intervention by his own ophthalmologist. Reluctantly, Monet consented to an operation on his right eye, and afterward his vision suffered from a yellowish tinge. He did eventually complete twenty-two panels but died in December 1926 before they could be installed. Clemenceau's slight and extolling essay was written in expiation for having harried his friend. In between these brief biographies, he completed the long philosophical meditation, *Au soir de la pensée* (*In the Evening of My Thought*), he had worked on haphazardly since 1921. Beginning with the hypothesis that the universe is entirely materialistic, he argued for a sense of morality based on the effort to achieve justice and liberty. He was, in fact, defending his entire life. Much of the argument was obscure, but he was fumbling toward ideas that resemble existentialism.[42]

Clemenceau's final book required no inspiration but instead erupted from within him. On 17 April 1929, he received an advance copy of *Le Mémorial de Foch* (*Foch: My Conversations with the Marshal*), memoirs based on interviews with Raymond Recouly, the longtime foreign policy analyst for *Le Figaro*. Foch had died less than a month earlier on 20 March, and at his funeral, Clemenceau said sorrowfully, "They are all going away and leaving me." The grief turned to outrage as he turned the pages: Foch blamed Clemenceau for negotiating a treaty that failed to render Germany incapable of ever posing a threat to France again, of negotiating a treaty that "was not peace but a truce for twenty years." Asking the universe—because he would never ask a deity—for six months' time, he gathered his most fervent apostles, led by Mordacq and Mandel, to write a reply. Clemenceau got seven months, and they completed a book of nearly four hundred pages. Librairie Plon published *Grandeurs et misères d'une victoire* (*Grandeur and Misery of Victory*) posthumously. Anyone reading it then or since can testify that the Tiger's claws remained sharp—and lethal.[43]

Clemenceau suffered a small stroke in early July 1926, then another at the end of September 1929. He was now eighty-eight years old, diabetic, and uremic. His heart and lungs were failing. He had survived a prostatectomy in 1912 and three bullet wounds in 1919. For more than a decade he had worn thin grey leather gloves to hide the eczema that made it painful for him even to touch a sheet of paper barehanded. Death was closing in: his sister Sophie in 1923, his friends Geffroy and Monet in 1926, his physician Florand, his sister Adrienne, and his brother Albert in 1927, his sister Emma in 1928. He felt bitterly the betrayal of Tardieu, who accepted a portfolio in the cabinet that Poincaré had formed in 1926; breaking with him forever, Clemenceau sent this telegram: "Invincible repugnance for raggedy old slippers" (*vieilles pantoufles éculées*). On 21 November 1929, he collapsed at his desk and the following day sank into a coma. He died just before 2 a.m. on 24 November. Albert, his valet, claimed he briefly regained consciousness about a half hour before and asked to be buried upright, facing Germany.[44]

In strict accordance with the will Clemenceau signed on 28 March 1929, his children and apostles transported his body to the Vendée, to Colombier, to be buried beside his father. In the casket with him, they laid the iron-headed walking stick he had used all his life, the little edition of Pierre de Beaumarchais's *Le Mariage de Figaro* that his mother gave him as a child, his goat-skin travel case, and a portion of the flowers the soldiers had presented him at Les Monts. The burial was private and without ceremony. He had accepted the offer from Louis Sicard, sculptor of the statue at Sainte-Hermine, to place a stele of the Greek goddess Athena at the grave site. The only epitaph he needed he wrote in the opening pages of *Grandeurs et misères*: "I am what I am. Qualities and failings. . . .There is strength in expecting nothing except from oneself."[45]

CHAPTER 3

The Thibaults

During the first eight decades or so following the chaos and innovation of the 1789 Revolution, the French bourgeoisie fashioned
a world of order and stability. From *Liberté*, they generated "classical liberalism," laissez-faire economics, and individual freedoms of
speech, press, assembly, and religion. From *Egalité*, they replaced
privilege based on birth with equality before the law and a guarantee of due process. From *Fraternité*, they transformed a kingdom of
subjects into a nation-state of citizens whose allegiance proceeded
from popular sovereignty and nationalism. They bent the authority
of the Catholic Church before the confidence of science and the material progress of the Industrial Revolution. They diminished rebellion and revolution through the spread of primary education and the
rise in living standards. Then, beginning in the middle 1880s, established certainties became less certain. Because sufficiency stultified,
risk enticed. Because the reasonable bored, the mystical beckoned.
The economy stalled against new competition. The working class
embraced the vision of socialism. The bourgeoisie lost confidence.
Claims for the unconscious and the *élan vital* sapped rationality.
Celebrated conversions revived the Catholic Church. Distant hints
of danger became a rising chorus. Stability foundered before energy.
However much a mystic, Léon Bloy caught the mood: "I await the
Cossacks and the Holy Ghost."[1]

So the world the nineteenth century had made was dying before the Great War administered a killing blow. The brilliant fictional portrayal of this society sagging toward collapse was Roger Martin du Gard's *Jean Barois*, the surprise best seller of 1913. As his symbol, the protagonist adopts Michelangelo's "Captive Slave," the figure only half emerged from the marble, "struggling to free his aching limbs and rebellious shoulders from their stony thrall." When Martin du Gard had begun the manuscript three years earlier, he chose the title *S'affranchir* (To Free Oneself), and abandoned it reluctantly as the book went to press. For Jean Barois is a seeker, after truth, after meaning. He casts off the tepid Catholic faith of his youth, leaves behind his simple pious wife, takes as friends freethinkers with advanced political views, and becomes a leading leftist intellectual as editor of *Le Semeur* (*The Sower*), a journal dedicated to propagating these opinions. But over time, the new growth does not live up to the seed he plants, a new irrationalism eclipses his scientific relativism, and his health collapses. Already discouraged, he is stupefied when his daughter reveals her decision to become a nun: "the vows I shall take will pay a little of the family debt, they will make some compensation for—for what your books have done." Returning to his wife and the home of his childhood, he desperately seeks some certainty, makes his confession, and dies grasping at a crucifix. Barois is drawn back into his past, his freedom an illusion.[2]

The success of *Jean Barois* vindicated Martin du Gard's insistence on making his career as a writer. Born 23 March 1881, he was a scion of the established and wealthy bourgeoisie, the essence of "right-thinking" (*bien pensant*): prudent investments, discreet behavior, observant religion. To prepare for admission to the Sorbonne, he attended a Catholic academy, the Ecole Fénelon, where he fell under the influence of abbé Marcel Hébert, who preached a symbolic interpretation of Christianity soon to be called "Modernism." This effort to reconcile Catholic dogma with modern discoveries in physics, chemistry, and biology failed utterly. For believers in modern science, it was pretentious nonsense. For Pope Pius X, it was heresy, condemned in the 1907 encyclical *Lamentabili sane exitu*. Martin du Gard himself briefly embraced Modernism when he underwent a crisis of faith as an adolescent, but then he abandoned religion altogether. He also failed to distinguish himself as a student at either the Ecole Fénelon or the Sorbonne. Literature alone attracted him, and he asked his father for permission to pursue a career in writing. Although disappointed at how his son had thus far perceived his responsibilities, this prosperous attorney offered a shrewd compromise: his blessing, but only if Martin du Gard prepared a backup. Almost on a whim, he decided to become an archivist and enrolled at the famous Ecole des Chartes, renowned since its establishment in 1821 for training in paleography. He spent six years there, interrupted during 1902 and 1903 by his required military service, which he fulfilled with a logistical support unit in Rouen. For the first time, he applied himself seriously, graduating in 1905 near the top of his class. He wrote his thesis on the Benedictine Abbey of Jumièges, founded in 654 by the Merovingian Saint Philibert. Here was a hint that his convictions about religion remained unsettled. The rigorous discipline of scholarship formed his mind: "I acquired a kind of scientific conscience, the taste for truth, an obsession for documentation, and the habit of precision."[3]

Martin du Gard had covered the bet on literature and adopted new perspectives, but a topic eluded him. After some tentative outlines, he settled on what he knew best, a young writer trying to write. His character André Mazerelles has ambitions beyond his talents and comes to bitter failure through implacable fate. He gave this first novel the title *Devenir!* (To Become!) and was himself so ambitious for the literary world to recognize his talent that he paid the publisher Paul Ollendorff a handsome subsidy to release it in 1909. When the literary world ignored *Devenir!* he appreciated the irony. Possessed with the confidence arising from a privileged upbringing, he was convinced that his genius would eventually tell. After all, he could afford a certain amount of failure: he was a rentier with investments and prospects of inheritance. But only a certain amount, for three years earlier he had taken a wife, Hélène (née Foucault), and now they had a daughter, Christiane. Following more casting about, he took up the issue that for long had resonated in his mind, the conflict between religion and science for the soul of modern civilization. And so he wrote *Jean Barois*.

The novel opens in the small town of Buis-la-Dame, about fifty miles north of Paris in the Oise. The mother of Jean Barois has died of tuberculosis, and he has inherited a disposition to the disease. His father, a physician with a practice in Paris, orders a program of food, fresh air, and rest, while warning, "All existence is a struggle; life is simply winning through." The local priest, abbé Joziers, counsels, "The suffering of every creature is willed by God. . . . He made it a condition, indeed the prime condition, of life." As devout as obedient, young Jean prays as he strengthens. A few years pass, he is healthy and wins admission to the Sorbonne, where he studies both medicine and natural science. Although what he is learning shakes his faith, he finds a temporary refuge in Modernism, but only temporary—like Martin du Gard himself. A critical moment comes when his father, ill and failing fast, returns both to Buis-la-Dame and to the religious belief he had long discarded. On his deathbed, he first adjures Jean to marry Cécile Pasquelin, his childhood sweetheart and daughter of his godmother, then explains his conversion, "that unknown quantity—it's a terrible thing to face." No longer devout but still obedient, Jean marries Cécile. He accepts a position teaching science at a Catholic school, Wenceslas College, but, to expiate his father's weakness, adopts an ever more strident materialist philosophy before his students. When Cécile, whose simple faith seems a rebuke, begins a novena in hope of becoming pregnant, he ridicules her. The rector of the college admonishes him and Cécile weeps hysterically, but Jean coldly replies that suppressing his views would mean "abandoning all my human dignity, all decency of mind." He resigns his post and agrees to a separation from Cécile. Months later, he learns that she has given birth to their daughter. In a poignant scene, once more in Buis-la-Dame, he holds the baby she has named Marie and remembers "how naively he had dreamt of giving and receiving perfect happiness."[4]

More years pass and Barois, now in his middle thirties, is living alone in Paris. He has gathered in his apartment a group of high-minded friends who are determined, like him, to parade their idealism before the world. They decide to found a journal, *The Sower*, and to take as their motto "Something we know not is stirring in the world today." The words are from Félicité de Lammenais, the French priest whose support for political and religious freedom in the 1820s and 1830s led to his censure by the Vatican. Although *The Sower* starts with only thirty-eight subscriptions, it gains prominence through an early and passionate stand in the Dreyfus affair. By disputing the evidence used to convict Captain Alfred Dreyfus of treason, by questioning the resistance of the army and the government to an open examination, Barois and his friends make themselves targets of a public opinion fiercely convinced otherwise. When public opinion begins to shift, when the number of "Dreyfusards" begins to match the number of "anti-Dreyfusards," they ride the wave of change. The culmination of the Dreyfus affair means not only the pardon and eventual exoneration of Alfred Dreyfus but the political victory of the Radicals and Socialists who take up his cause—significantly later than *The Sower*. For the men closest to Barois, this triumph has the ugly feeling of a Roman circus. Marc-Elie Luce is suspicious: "*We* were a handful of 'Dreyfusistes'; they are an army of Dreyfusards." When the Radicals prove to be as "political" and as prone to corruption as their predecessors, as likely to act not for the interest of ideals but for "the interest of state," François Cresteil d'Allize reacts with disgust: "We lanced the abscess, we counted on a cure—and now gangrene's set in."[5]

Not long after, Cresteil kills himself. He had given up his commission in the cavalry and estranged himself from his aristocratic family to take a stand for "truth." But "duty, virtue, goodness—they're all just make-believe, . . . fine-sounding names to cover up selfish instincts. . . . all roads lead to the same place, the same dark hole." Barois himself nearly dies in a carriage accident and, when he regains consciousness, recalls that just before the impact he began to recite, "Hail, Mary, full of grace." Fearing the example of his father, he writes a testament to his belief in science and to his rejection of religion, because "I know nothing more harrowing than to see an old man, whose whole life has been devoted to the furtherance of some noble idea, go back in his declining years on the principles that inspired his life's work and play traitor to his past." Yet something has broken within him: he cannot regain his health, and he no longer has the same spirit of combat. To his surprise, Marie, whom he has seen only a single time, appears at his door. She wishes to spend her eighteenth year with her father, to fulfill a provision in his separation agreement with Cécile that he had long ago dismissed as ridiculous. In her face, he has a "vision of Cécile as a girl, of the unrecoverable past," and he agrees. Only after she spends the year reading everything he has ever written, only then she tells him of her decision to take the veil. To his protests, she replies, "But don't you see, Father, that if my faith could be shaken by arguments it wouldn't be faith?"[6]

At *The Sower* the most dogmatic of his colleagues, L. Breil-Zoeger, preaches a militant atheism that might once have attracted Barois. Now, he asks, "What's the obscure force that urges me toward right conduct if not a deep-seated religious feeling which has survived my loss of faith?" Yet the revived mysticism of nation and Catholicism that he discovers in the new generation entering their twenties and thirties frightens him as much. He meets two of them in his office and hears them denounce "that sterile navel-gazing contemplation; . . . the France that has been through the Agadir crisis and lives under German threat has no use for it!" They tell him, "What's indispensable to us, if we are to keep our will to action vital and alert, is a moral discipline behind it." Barois comprehends the power of these convictions and would rather stand with these young men than with Breil-Zoeger, but he recognizes full well that they regard him as the enemy. He decides to resign as editor, telling Luce, "I'm not sure of having sowed the good seed." When he explains himself, Luce says only, "I can do nothing to help you—now." He finds his direction when he and Cécile meet for the first time in almost twenty years, at the ceremony in which their daughter formally joins her convent in Belgium after a year's novitiate. Marie tells him, "Father, in every line you wrote, I realize that you are seeking God." She embraces them as she begs, "Please stay together now."[7]

Barois joins Cécile in Buis-la-Dame. As the tuberculosis he held at bay now savages his lungs, he is desperate and afraid. He turns to the new young priest, abbé Lévys, and sobs, "So now I know my quest is ended, . . . and I shall joyfully obey; yes, all now is clear, crystal-clear. At last everything has a meaning." When Luce visits, Barois tells him, "Only see for yourself how calmly I can face death, now I know I shall live again beside Him. . . . You and I were sowers of doubt, my friend. May God forgive us." Later when Lévys walks him to the railroad station, Luce complains that Barois has returned "to those consoling fairy-tales." Lévys responds, "Were you capable of consoling him? No. Whereas I brought him peace." A few days later, a dying Barois receives extreme unction and dies, like his father, grasping a crucifix. As Lévys and Cécile go through his papers, they discover the testament he drew up after the carriage accident. From the opening sentences they recognize the voice of the materialist editor and intellectual. Lévys watches as Cécile casts the pages into the fire.[8]

Does life hold meaning in a world without God? Can the principles of science contend with the morals of religion for ultimate truth? Is human civilization a mere collection of vanities? At the age of thirty-two, Martin du Gard was writing about issues that were critical to the modern age. One of France's most important publishers, Editions Barnard Grasset, shied from them, choosing to accept instead Marcel Proust's *Du côté de chez Swann* (*Swann's Way*). Another, Librairie Gallimard, eagerly grabbed *Jean Barois* upon the recommendation of its rising star, the novelist André Gide, who wrote, "a remarkable manuscript, publish without hesitation." In 1913 at least, Martin du Gard far outsold Proust. Less than a year later, he had the unenviable privilege of confronting these fundamental questions personally on the battlefield as France went to war. Mobilized on 2 August 1914, he served as a sergeant in the army's logistical branch, overseeing some twenty supply trucks attached to the First Cavalry Corps in northern France. Hélène volunteered as a nurse at the military hospital in Vichy and was joined there by his parents, who looked after Christiane, now six years old. From the outset, Martin du Gard was appalled: "I see daily the savagery of all. . . . It is not civilization against barbarism, it is the same vileness, the same cruelty, instincts reawakened, two barbarisms grappling." The optimism of the "Catholic" newspapers like *La Croix* and *L'Echo de Paris* disgusted him. After six months of fighting, French casualties were approaching a million men killed, wounded, or missing. Among them was his good friend, his oldest friend from the Ecole Fénelon, Gustave Valmont, killed on 6 September at Courgivaux as the battle of the Marne began.[9]

Like every soldier near the fighting, death preoccupied Martin du Gard. On several occasions, artillery shells impacted so close that he was surprised to find himself alive. To one friend he confessed that his greatest regret at dying young would be the books he could not write, "especially the next, which already possesses and haunts me." In August 1915, Hélène's brother, Henry Foucault, suffered a severe head wound from shrapnel at Arras. Transported to Bordeaux, he was almost given up for dead because he had lost so much brain tissue, but after two months of care, he regained, one by one, the use of his limbs and his mental capacity. Soon afterward, Martin du Gard read the latest novel from Paul Bourget, *Le Sens de la mort* (*The Night Cometh*), and reacted strongly against its didactic plot—which opposed the suicide of an atheist surgeon, Dr. Ortègne, who fears the suffering of cancer, to the heroic death from wounds of a simple Catholic soldier, Le Gallic, who bears his agony without complaint. When Marcel Hébert, his preceptor at the Ecole Fénelon—and to whom he had dedicated *Jean Barois*—died on 12 February 1916, Martin du Gard was granted leave to attend the funeral in Paris. Among the many former students present was André Fernet, magistrate, novelist, playwright, and now pilot in France's aviation corps. They shared a cab and a sense of loss at Hébert's death, but nothing else, not even a friendship any longer. Martin du Gard called the war abhorrent; Fernet called it the altar of sacrifice. Two months later, Fernet wrote him:

> That this war is an atrocious thing, that these daily massacres are abominable, that is understood, and you will not do me the injury of believing that I admire them. . . . But I could not live with the secret shame of not having done everything that I can. If I could not be a pilot, I would be an infantryman. Whatever happens, I am ready with the sacrifice of my life . . . because it is necessary. If everyone tried to hide away, it would be the end of our country, the end of all that we have been, are, and will be.

Martin du Gard offered a placating reply, "You risk your life to make observation flights, and that is enough to impose silence on me." Six weeks later, on 1 June, Fernet was killed when his plane crashed behind German lines near Morhange in Lorraine.[10]

The sixteen months between February 1916 and May 1917 were hecatombs for the French army: 337,000 casualties at Verdun, 204,000 at the Somme, 187,000 at the Aisne—a total of 728,000. After the last, the so-called Nivelle Offensive, many frontline soldiers revolted, declaring that they would defend their positions but not undertake any further attacks. Martin du Gard was in the rear of the fighting at the Somme River and witnessed "a massacre *without precedent. . . .* What horror, what depths of horror!" By the end of 1916, he was predicting defeat. He wrote a friend, "I have the absolute conviction that the war is in vain, that its outcome will be disastrous for us, and that nothing can be done to alter this destiny." His unit spent the winter near Compiègne, close to the German lines, where he learned the plight of French men and women in the regions under occupation by the Germans, "the true material misery, the incessant harassment, the agony of always being menaced, hounded, pressured." He was close to breaking down, decrying *"the bankruptcy of morality*, of religious bombast, of grand words devoid of sense and reality, Universal Justice, Human Dignity, Law, Civilization." After the May mutinies, he exclaimed: "You will see, you will see. I am certain that *no further offensive is possible* along the French front. Not a single leader will risk it." Hélène did collapse, her nerves frayed from work and worry. She and Christiane took refuge at her parents' country retreat, Le Tertre, northwest of Paris at Bellême in the Orne.[11]

France as well seemed close to collapse in the fall of 1917, some ready to adopt Joseph Caillaux's "defeatism" and seek whatever peace Germany would be willing to grant. The appointment of Georges Clemenceau as prime minister represented a last-ditch effort to fight on. Through his policy of "all-out war" (*guerre à outrance*), the French stiffened their spines and clad themselves with new determination. Convinced that Germany could be beaten, and would be beaten, Clemenceau rallied the army to hold. He ensured greater coordination among French, British, and (soon enough) American troops through a single overall commander for the Western Front, and he charged defeatists and German sympathizers with treason.

Sick at heart from the loss of close friends and from the savagery surrounding him, Martin du Gard doubted Clemenceau's success, especially deploring the "scalp dance" around Caillaux. Even when this new girding brought France to the brink of victory in the fall of 1918, he bridled: "the collapse of Germany does not make me cry with joy, but the collapse of militarism, yes, because the best means of striking down our own is to eliminate any pretext for it by destroying its adversary. And that should be the true 'war aim'!" From antimilitarism he would move to pacifism. Like so many of his generation and status, he had founded his life on order and coherence even while admitting the power of the irrational. War was the reign of absurd chaos, the claims of brutality and folly overwhelming the individual and a civilization revealed to be surprisingly fragile.[12]

Demobilized in March 1919, Martin du Gard moved with his wife and daughter to an apartment in the Latin Quarter of Paris, on the Rue du Cherche-Midi not far from the square at Saint Germain des Près. Almost forty years old, he had expectations to meet, and he planned to do so through the project he had conceived during the war, a roman-fleuve, the extended chronicle of family in which he could explore every idea that fascinated his imagination. After spending more than a year in preparation, he wrote friends that his work on *Les Thibault* (*The Thibaults*) was under way: "my book will cover forty years, divided into thirteen periods, each of which will constitute a book; with more than twenty-five characters, you can imagine the intersecting plots of all these jumbled lives." And: "I am not sure where I am going, but I am going there joyously." Three months later, in late summer 1920, he worried that he had completed only eighty pages and blamed the delay on worries about Hélène's health. She had never truly recovered from her breakdown in 1917 and was now suffering from serious depression. When he learned of one friend's approaching marriage, he warned, "the wedding is only the point of departure, and you cannot rest a single second because the conjugal future is inherently unstable. I have had so many ideas about it that seemed good to me: I bought and paid for them, one after another." Yet when he complained, "I work badly, too much family," he added, "but my wife and my daughter fill my lungs with good air."[13]

In fact, by anyone else's standards, Martin du Gard worked exceedingly well. By mid-1921, he was promising his publisher, Gaston Gallimard, the initial part of *Les Thibault* by October and added in jest—or maybe not—that he wanted it to appear quickly, "before the new war that is coming." He did better, finishing the next part by January 1922. Gallimard published the first on 15 April as *Le Cahier gris* (The grey notebook) and the second on 15 May as *Le Pénitencier* (The penitentiary). Exactly two years had passed since he wrote the first page. Tirelessly, he prepared by compiling the evidence necessary for a detailed and realistic portrayal—a legacy of his training at the Ecole des Chartes. As the novel opens, one of his principal characters attends a Catholic school, and Martin du Gard could rely upon his memories of the Ecole Fénelon for those details. Another character is a medical student, and for him, Martin du Gard researched carefully the intricate relationships of medical students to each other and to their mentors. He drafted each scene "always four, five, eight times" before he considered it sufficiently polished. In June 1922, Romain Rolland, who had won the 1915 Nobel Prize for Literature for a ten-volume roman-fleuve, *Jean-Christophe* (1903–12), wrote him that these first two segments of *Les Thibault* were "true, alive, original, brave, sound—I liked them a great deal." Martin du Gard was more than willing to believe the praise: "I confess to my closest friends the presumption that the current readers of these first volumes will be only a small fraction of the readers I hope to have later when *Les Thibault* is complete."[14]

The third part, published in two volumes as *La Belle Saison* (The summer months) came out in October 1923, at least half a year behind schedule, the causes for delay many. Martin du Gard began spending more and more time in the solitude of Le Tertre. He found postwar Paris wearisome, consumed by the questions and politics of reparations. He feared the future, and his prediction was uncanny: "a new war with Germany, this time with France fatally alone, our rapid defeat, and our subjection to a pan-Germanism blended with Bolshevism which will be far worse than our shameful, rickety, nationalist Republic." He blamed Raymond Poincaré, president of the Republic from 1913 to 1920, for France's involvement in the Great

War and now deplored his policies as prime minister since January 1922, especially the occupation of Germany's Ruhr Valley in 1923 to compel its payment of reparations. Personal motivations counted more heavily. The health of his parents was failing fast, his mother suffering from uterine bleeding, his father from heart disease and arteriosclerosis. Hélène's wartime depression became recurrent, and he complained that she was "always under the weather, tired without reason, nervous to excess." Their marriage had become a desert after she learned of his attraction to men. Without, his ingrained discretion prevented any public disclosure, and her devout Catholicism precluded divorce or even a separation. Within the marriage, they fought for influence over Christiane, with Martin du Gard more often the winner.[15]

While writing *La Belle Saison*, he admitted that this third part was "hard to get started" and worried that *Les Thibault* was too large and unwieldy to complete: "The more I go, the more I sense that my project is insanely reckless." Much worse was to come. His father died from a massive stroke in early April 1924. Already weakened by a painful uterine ablation three months earlier, his mother plunged into despair. She had advanced cancer, but her family and physicians kept the diagnosis secret. Yet she must have suspected because her treatment now included radiation. Over the next nine months, she died slowly and in great pain. Hélène rarely left her side, sleeping in the same room. Martin du Gard watched the agony, transfixed by dread. "It is ghastly. She is spared nothing, the most hideous and degrading physical miseries. She has morphine day and night." "Purulent ulcers, we live in horror." Until finally, on 13 January 1925, "Mama has ceased to suffer. However expected, the blow is severe." Almost immediately, Hélène herself broke down, worn out by nursing her mother-in-law for so long. She was only in her early forties, but the traumas of the last ten years had done their damage. As Martin du Gard would write one friend, "I believe that the war, in overturning everything, all the accepted notions, has created a generalized state of mental disequilibrium." For more than a year he had made almost no progress on the fourth part of *Les Thibault*: "You ask me, 'And the work?' It is impossible for me to concentrate."

With his parents buried but his wife taken to her bed, he confessed, "My life has been harshly shaken and bruised, my literary efforts at a standstill." And in a metaphor he had hard earned, "For a year I have been surrounded by the shades of death and have escaped blind and gasping for breath." By May he was apologizing to Gallimard for what was certain to be a long delay before he could complete the next installment.[16]

During the summer of 1925, Martin du Gard made a fateful decision. Le Tertre would eventually be Hélène's after the death of her parents, but he would arrange with them to take over the property immediately in return for a cash settlement. She adored the old Norman estate, and if he used his own inheritance to restore and modernize it completely, they could live there year-round. Acting "as if the future belonged to [him]," he planned to "set down roots, to restore the house, to construct an addition, to move in forty cases of books—all that for *Les Thibault*, to establish the setting for the twenty-five years I grant myself for the project—the *enormous* project—which each week becomes more important to me." He vastly underestimated the complications. The necessary renovations proved more extensive than he had supposed. Inventories, divisions of property, and the moving of household furnishings devoured his time. The architects were "donkeys with diplomas." He personally directed the teams of workers. After some eighteen months, he came to acerbic conclusions:

> Before having taken on the job of construction chief, I had thought with some confusion about my easy life, about my work as an "intellectual." But in watching them on the job, I realized that I had the right to hold my head high, that beside me, not one of them had the right to speak of making an effort, taking pains. And me, I earn almost nothing from what I do. These laborers work like soldiers, singing, watching the clock, rolling a cigarette, stealing time in order to do no more than the construction chief, myself, can require of them. Then, they deride my "fine château," treating me like some idle bourgeois who knows nothing of construction or of the exhausting proletarian life. Yes, I live off my investments, and yes, I inherited

money, but though I have no working-class consciousness, I am conscious of being a worker whom they have no right to ridicule.[17]

The long delay for *Les Thibault* lasted until 1928, but by then Martin du Gard had made up the lost time. He gave Librairie Gallimard an enormous manuscript, which it published as part 4, *La Consultation* (The consultation) and part 5, *La Sorellina* (The little sister). Certainly, the renovation of Le Tertre had been a trial, but the estate was now his "refuge," his "good life in the provinces," where during the winter fastness he could stare out at his forest covered in snow. He called his study "a true factory, a Thibauderie," where he locked himself away for ten hours a day beginning in the early morning. This dedication was not a grasping after royalties: in his best year (1924) writing brought him only 19,100 francs ($22,256 in 2011). Not to win honors: he reluctantly accepted the Légion d'honneur in July 1926, put it in a drawer never to be worn, and called Edouard Herriot, the prime minister who awarded it, "a profoundly sincere and possibly dangerous utopian." Not to please Hélène: she made her own life at Le Tertre. Not to enchant Christiane: after her eighteenth birthday in 1926, she escaped the parental struggle over her by studying in Great Britain. Of her flight, Martin du Gard jested, "England is a country more remote from us and more barbarous than Afghanistan" and bragged that the new world of experiences would make her "more than a little girl from the old French bourgeoisie." Both he and Hélène missed her desperately.[18]

The reason for Martin du Gard's treasures of patience, application, and perseverance lay in his profound conviction that destiny compelled him to write a roman-fleuve for the ages: "More than ever, I believe that *Les Thibault* will be my great work; I shall need twenty years more to see it through as I must." He was sensitive and emotional. When the writing went well (understand that he prepared draft after draft until he had sedulously eliminated any imperfections), he was buoyant, even joyful. When not, he was "distraught, frightened at what I do but not discouraged; I think of *Les Thibault* as a bullet that must, no matter what, pass through the grooves of the gun barrel." He set himself the highest standards: "The daunting quality of what I attempt is always having to push further, the problem of taking my characters to a precise psychological point in life and *then go beyond*! Not just to *continue* but to *advance*, to gain ground on the unknowable, to mine the depths. Am I up to it?" He worried that he might not be, sensing that the incessant concentration and the infinite troubles that were the very basis of his daily regimen were aging him. And if so, would he have the strength to finish?[19]

The question loomed ever larger as Martin du Gard pressed forward into part 6, in which the patriarch of the Thibault family dies after months of physical and spiritual suffering. The physical pain derives from kidney failure, the spiritual from fear that his public devotion has concealed private hypocrisy. For the manifestations of disease and misery, Martin du Gard drew on the vivid memory of his mother's deterioration before an inexorable cancer. For the priestly care of souls, he had the examples of his parents on their deathbeds, but neither of them was a hypocrite in a crisis of faith. Because he had never formed a close relationship with any ecclesiastic other than the long-dead Hébert, he turned to the devout novelist and playwright Henri Ghéon, who provided him with "exactly" the information he needed. Writing the manuscript of what was published in 1929 as *La Mort du père* (The death of the father) was a dark journey through family distress and individual agony—all the more so because he prepared six drafts before he was satisfied. He recognized that it did not make for cheerful reading, "but death and suffering exist, they are not my inventions, and too many people know nothing about them." But his true subject here—as throughout *Les Thibault*—was the necessity for choice in a world where the rules have lost meaning: "I sense the terrible fragility of moral customs, moral appearances, this thin moral mask, and I deny with despair that morality can be founded on anything other than religion. Anyone who claims to do so is uttering hollow phrases."[20]

That fragile moral mask appears early in this grand roman-fleuve. Antoine and Jacques Thibault are scions of economic privilege, born into France's upper middle class. Their father, Oscar Thibault, has made a fortune in business and regards this success as a tribute to his own shrewd capacity and as the blessing of God upon his righteousness. He is ostentatiously Catholic, proud of his position as a lay personage in the church and always consulting his confessor, abbé Vécard, before taking any important decision. The time is June 1904—Antoine is twenty-three and a medical student, Jacques is fourteen, attending a Catholic school. As the novel opens, Jacques has run away from home—but worse, he has absconded with Daniel de Fontanin, not merely studying at a lycée, one of the elite state secondary schools, but a Protestant. Oscar Thibault calls him "that wretched little heretic." Abbé Binot, the rector at Jacques's school, has found a grey notebook that the boys used to exchange letters, and the tone of fervid emotion raises suspicions about their relationship. After presenting this evidence, Binot adds primly, "Yes, we know only too well what lies beneath the sanctimonious airs of Protestants." Antoine thinks Jacques will return on his own, and unafraid of sullying his hands or endangering his soul through consort with Protestants, he dares go to the Fontanin home, where he meets Daniel's mother, Thérèse, and younger sister, Jenny. The households are mirror images: Oscar Thibault's wife, Lucie, died giving birth to Jacques while Thérèse de Fontanin's husband, Jérôme, has largely abandoned her to pursue affairs with other women. Jacques and Daniel have taken a train to Marseille and plan to find passage to the French colony of Tunisia. For Jacques, rejecting his birthright and making a new life far away is the ultimate rebellion against his father's strictures. For Daniel, the escapade is an adventure, not much more than a caprice. Gendarmes pick them up on the road from Marseille to Toulon and bring them back to Paris. Thérèse de Fontanin embraces Daniel with joy and relief. Oscar Thibault barely acknowledges Jacques as he excoriates, "He's a young scoundrel, with a heart of stone. Was he worth all the anxiety we've gone through on his account?"[21]

In retribution for his sins, Jacques is confined at his father's monument to right-minded virtue, the Oscar Thibault Foundation at Crouy. Some fifty miles north of Paris, it is a reformatory for hooligan youth that relies upon stern discipline, manual labor, and daily mass to eliminate delinquent habits—and for additional persuasion, a diet of bread and water. Jacques is spared the worst of this regime, but his father's edict demands, "The young ruffian! We've got to break his will." Although forbidden to inquire after his brother's welfare, Antoine goes to Crouy after ten months and finds it "reeks of the prison-house." He offers to take charge of Jacques himself and enlists Vécard on his side by insinuating that the guards engage in sexual abuse. When his father objects and insists on the right to mete out discipline in his own fashion, the priest compares him to a Pharisee. The accusation stings Oscar Thibault: "His shoulders sagged and he dropped back into his chair. He was picturing himself on his deathbed, and a dread came over him that he might have to face his last hour empty-handed. He tried to reassure himself by recalling the high esteem in which the world held him." Then, he relents. The arrangement brings a chastened and more composed Jacques back, not to his father's house but to a separate apartment he shares with Antoine. He spends his days and nights preparing for the competitive examination that determined admission to the summit of universities and liberal arts in France, the Ecole normale supérieure. His only recalcitrance is a secret and sporadic correspondence with Daniel against his father's specific edict.[22]

Antoine continues his medical studies and makes hospital rounds with the attending physicians who are his mentors. Increasingly self-satisfied, he regards himself "as a fine figure of a man, built on exemplary lines. What particularly pleased him was the look of grim determination on his face." He shares this trait with his father and insists that "pride comes in very useful as a driving force." Aside from passing liaisons with young women well below his social station, he avoids social entanglements. But like Jacques, he is drawn to the Fontanins, who are easy, informal, pardoning—so different from the Thibaults. In Antoine's case, the draw is Thérèse, whose mature sexuality is a perfume he inhales deeply as he tells her, "Your Reformation was a revolution on the religious plane, for it opened the door to ideas of spiritual freedom." His mere presence in her house, a Protestant, a married woman estranged from her husband, would have scandalized Oscar Thibault. And if he could overhear their conversation, the praise of heresy would not be the worst of his worries. For Antoine was dismissing any requirement for ultimate truth: "I don't claim . . . that science explains everything, but it tells me what things are, and that's enough for me. I find the *how* of things sufficiently interesting for me to dispense with the vain quest of the *why*."[23]

Five years pass. Jacques has prepared so diligently that he obtains the third-highest score on the examination to enter the Ecole normale supérieure. Antoine has specialized as a pediatric physician and is increasingly recognized as the most talented of his generation. Seeing only the externals, Oscar Thibault proudly takes credit for the achievements of his sons and takes the legal steps necessary for them to inherit his full name, as in Antoine Oscar-Thibault, to distinguish themselves from Thibaults who have accomplished less. He knows nothing of how far they diverge from his ideals. Within Jacques, the old resentments still rage. Sometimes, he contemplates submitting to his father's conventional bourgeois patterns, "get his degree, become a cogwheel in the machine." More often, he imagines giving "full rein to the destructive forces that surged within him . . . against morality, the cut and dried life, the family, society." Within Antoine, the rebellion is insidious. Called to treat a young girl hit by a delivery van, he discovers that she is hemorrhaging severely and will die before she can be taken to a hospital. He has to carry out an emergency operation in the family's dining room and saves her life by suturing a ruptured femoral artery. Afterward, he is attracted to one of the neighbors who assists him. This Rachel Goepfert would excite his father's disapproval in every way. She is half-Jewish and has been a ballerina, a circus horse rider, and the mistress of a scoundrel, Hirsch, who has fled to the African Sudan to avoid arrest. She seduces Antoine immediately, telling him, "A night like that works you up!" Gazing at her the next morning, he feels "like a starved jungle creature whose raging hunger nothing, nothing could ever quiet."[24]

This section of *Les Thibault, La Belle Saison*, centers on carnal morality. Among the Fontanins, Jérôme's profligate affairs excite his son, Daniel, to emulation and his daughter, Jenny, to revulsion. Daniel has become a successful painter whose association with the prominent art dealer and publisher Ludwigson has brought him the sales and the flamboyant notability that assure sexual conquests. Jenny thinks her brother is sullied by "impurity" and worries that he "may end up losing . . . the sense of sin." Perhaps from his experiences at the reformatory but more because he sees himself as a rebel who holds himself to a higher standard, Jacques has a similar sense of abstention. During brief furtive moments, Jenny and Jacques confess to each other their fears and believe they share a profound, and utterly chaste, love. For Antoine and Rachel, confession provokes a crisis. Her sensuality enraptures him—"Rachel's nakedness in all its splendor"—her salacious comments arouse him—"My dream for when I am old is to . . . run a brothel. . . . I'd like to be sure of having young folk around me, fine young bodies." But further revelations unnerve him. By her first lover, she had a daughter who died as an infant. And Hirsch, though an arms smuggler, murderer, and sexual pervert, is the only man she will ever love. Trepidation twists his heart, and Antoine senses in himself "the antipathy of a domesticated animal for the prowling denizens of the wild that are a menace to the home." When Rachel announces that she must leave for the Congo to look after her investments there, Antoine is relieved.[25]

In the much-delayed next three parts of *Les Thibault—La Consultation*, *La Sorellina*, and *La Mort du père*—Martin du Gard has advanced the plot from 1910 to 1913. The focus shifts decisively to the meaning of disease and death, with Antoine the principal character. Jacques is absent until near the end of *La Sorellina*, having disappeared just as he is to enter the Ecole normale supérieure. During a heated confrontation with his father, Jacques declares his love for Jenny; his father forbids any relationship with a Protestant, especially a member of the Fontanin family; and Jacques threatens to kill himself. Because he has left no trace for three years, Oscar Thibault fears he has driven his son to suicide. This guilt burdens him all the more grievously because he recognizes the approach of his own death from kidney failure. Antoine oversees his father's treatment, but his practice is pediatrics. He has an excellent reputation, and his appointment hours are busy, filled with the children of the prominent—to his father's great satisfaction.

Would the so-Catholic Oscar Thibault comprehend the casuistry his elder son has to apply? A friend brings his frail stepdaughter for an examination. Antoine diagnoses advanced tuberculosis, a hopeless case. Because she has a few months of normal life left, he does not blight them by delivering a sentence of death. A German teacher at the Lycée Charlemagne recounts how he and his wife married in their early middle age, and because he never expected that they might have a child, he did not tell her of having syphilis when he was younger. They do have a child, a son who is mentally deficient. The father wants to know whether he is responsible. Antoine wonders what can be gained from assigning blame. Again, he chooses to mislead, assuring him that the boy's condition is not his fault. The infant daughter of two friends is in great pain from an ear infection that has penetrated to the brain. When they call in Antoine for a consultation, the attending physician explains that the child will certainly die within a few days and suggests ending her misery through an overdose of barbiturate. Antoine refuses and, to make certain that his colleague will not do so, administers the proper amount himself. Afterward, he wonders: "The laws of nature are the only laws that count; they, I admit, are ineluctable. But all those so-called moral laws, what are they really? A complex of habits, foisted upon us by the past."[26]

The casuistry extends to home. Antoine believes that the strategic use of morphine to relieve his father's pain prevents him from realizing the nearness of death. He is wrong: Oscar Thibault bravely insists to his longtime secretary, "there comes an hour when rest is all one yearns for. Death should have no terrors for a Christian." He is not too weak for bombast, giving Antoine one more lecture on bourgeois morality: "I have always been proud of belonging to that prosperous middle class which in all ages has been the mainstay of my country and my Church. But, my boy, that relative affluence imposes certain duties. . . . Ah, the Family! I ask you, are we not the pivot on which turn the middle-class democracies of today?" Yet in the opiate haze, he grows maudlin. He recollects his wife, Lucie, their courtship and early marriage, then her death twenty-three years ago giving birth to Jacques. And of Jacques, what torment he now feels for the way he treated his younger son. Has he always blamed him for Lucie's death? What retribution is he to face in the life to come for this sin? Aware that his father is failing rapidly, Antoine revives the efforts made earlier to discover his brother's fate. The search then had been in Great

Britain, but he turns to Switzerland after reading a long story, "La Sorellina," in the Geneva-based magazine *Calliope*. Although the plot is set in Italy, he recognizes immediately the resemblance to his brother's brief life. The author is Jack Baulthy, a pseudonym transparent to anyone looking for Jacques Thibault. Antoine travels to Switzerland and locates him in Lausanne, sharing a rooming house with sundry socialists and anarchists. At first Jacques is unwilling to return but finally bends before Antoine's insistence that he make a final peace with his father.[27]

The brothers arrive just in time as Oscar Thibault suffers extreme pain from kidney blockage. He calls for abbé Vécard to make a final confession, but the words of absolution do not comfort. With dread he considers his life: "Selfishness and vanity. A thirst for riches, for ordering others about. A display of generosity, to win honors, to play a specious part. . . . That 'life of an upright man'—he was heartily ashamed of it. He saw it now as it had really been. Too late. The day of reckoning has come." He is in true agony, spiritual as well as physical. Antoine draws morphine into a syringe, an amount well beyond the usual dose, an amount certain to provoke death. He injects it, persuaded that he grants mercy not only to his father but to everyone around the deathbed witnessing this anguish, this disintegration of a human being. Afterward, "the thought came to him, stark, clean-cut: 'And it was I who killed him.'" To one mourner he replies, "Your sympathy is wasted, Madame. I did not love my father." The last will and testament directs the funeral mass to be celebrated at the Oscar Thibault Foundation, that is, at the reformatory at Crouy. Sharing a compartment with Antoine as they return to Paris by train, Vécard offers this didactic summation: "Can you imagine what it's like . . . coming to the brink of eternity without faith in God, without discerning, on the further shore, an almighty, merciful Father stretching out His arms in welcome? Do you realize what it means, dying in utter darkness, without a single gleam of hope?" Antoine replies with fervor, "I, perhaps, have seen more unbelievers die than you have. . . . And quite sincerely, I wish for myself that, at that moment, I may be open to all the consolations faith can give. I dread a death without hope as much as a death-agony without morphine."[28]

Martin du Gard had taken *Les Thibault* to the same impasse as *Jean Barois*. Nearly ten years of writing, multiple volumes, and a plot woven like an intricate variegated tapestry from the lives of so many well-developed characters have led once again to the fundamental question as to whether life has any meaning without belief in God and the afterlife. As before, he offered no answer. *Les Thibault* stands as a remarkable portrait of a time, the Belle Epoque and its illusions before the Great War, a perceptive and ironic psychological sounding of bourgeois life in France, but nothing more profound. When some close friends expressed their disappointment, Martin du Gard defended his aloof, distant, objective, agnostic approach. He was most like his character Antoine, the rational materialist physician who follows his own rules while acknowledging the power of faith and recognizing that he himself might not be immune to the relief it could bring. The next seven years tested this detachment severely.[29]

In November 1929, Christiane announced her intention to marry Marcel de Coppet. This declaration came without warning and sent her parents reeling. Christiane was twenty-two, Coppet forty-eight. He had made a brilliant career in the colonial service and, initially as governor general of Chad, would be taking her to the far reaches of Africa. Their secret romance was a double betrayal because Martin du Gard had, for a quarter century, considered Coppet his best friend. Initially, he put up a good face, describing the "mutual passion before which we must give way" and insisting that "no one is more worthy of being loved than Coppet." Less than two weeks later, he could not contain his lamentation: "My feelings are infinitely complex, especially the grieving. I must keep silent. And go on. I shall do so, keep on living once they are married and departed. Until then, I have to remain calm, remain courageous, and wait as the days pass." And: "I watch my only child depart for two, three, four years perhaps, to the heart of Africa! Letters take eight weeks to reach Fort Lamy, so five months to ask a question and get an answer! Fears torment me—the risks of travel, the living conditions, the climate, with so few medical resources."[30]

By January, his tone was sharper, with a target: "Christiane hands her future to a man who can give her in return only a charged and

troubled past. I am too old for illusions. I wanted her to have a marriage, a family," and then, "You know Coppet has carried off my
daughter in the flower of her youth and taken her away to the center of Africa. I am shattered by it." He worried himself sick and was
confined to bed with what began as a cold and turned into serious
pulmonary congestion accompanied by phlebitis. Hélène's health
had been delicate for several years. Their frailties and their anguish
drew them together, made them "tighten the loose bonds" of their
own marriage—all the better to nourish a profound hatred: Martin
du Gard was never again more than correct to Coppet, and Hélène
devoutly wished him dead. But their hope that Christiane would
abandon him and return home vanished after she gave birth to their
first grandchild, Daniel, on 19 March 1933.[31]

Frailties were minor compared to the injuries Martin du Gard and
Hélène suffered on New Year's Day 1931. Driving that evening near
Le Tertre, they went into a skid on black ice, and their automobile
crashed into a shallow ravine. The holiday delayed their rescue, and
they lay in the wreckage for three hours. Hélène suffered a crushed
sternum, three cracked ribs, and deep cuts to her face, the skin below
her right eye torn away. Martin du Gard had a fractured tibia, serious
damage to his knee, and lacerations to his right hand. The cast on his
leg brought a recurrence of phlebitis. After treatment at the Dela-
genière Clinic in nearby Le Mans for ten weeks, they sought warmer
weather near the Mediterranean coast, at Sauveterre in the Gard, for
a long recuperation. Briefly, Martin du Gard could jest, "We're idiots
to settle in the cold fog of the north when such a pleasure comes
from living in perpetual sunshine. Marseille should be the capital
of France." When pain in Hélène's chest persisted, an X-ray examination revealed a small tumor, which she had removed in late July.
The pathology report revealing it benign ended Martin du Gard's
"terrible fear." During their ordeal, Christiane could offer only encouragement to her parents from distant Chad. Almost another year
would pass before she and Coppet returned to France for the first
time since their wedding. Their obvious happiness—"beaming with
joy"—provoked Hélène's resentment. The initial cold reserve she
adopted at their arrival transformed into withholding every tender

act once she learned of Christiane's pregnancy. Martin du Gard admitted that "Hélène was in a bad state" and speculated that restoring her equilibrium would "require killing four or five people, beginning with every member of Coppet's family."[32]

Such a slaughter would have been only a distraction from the painful reality of the Great Depression. Together, Martin du Gard and his wife had an impressive portfolio of blue-chip stocks, government bonds, and real estate. By late 1930, all of them were generating less income (dividends infrequent, interest payments reduced, renters hard to find), yet none could be sold except at a loss. Their accident and extended recovery occasioned new heavy expenses, and by the spring of 1932, Martin du Gard complained, "During the past year, my sources of revenue have dried up one by one, and we find that the organization of our life no longer matches the extent of our means." Now, "my material existence, which for fifty years I took for granted, has been abruptly compromised. . . . Properties not rented and impossible to sell, stocks and bonds whose revenues have fallen by two-thirds. Even my royalties reduced. And each month, I must find some 10,000 francs [$8,412 in 2011] to pay for servants, taxes, insurance, and the like." He regretted having spent so much renovating Le Tertre, where now for economy Hélène was making the beds and doing the housekeeping, and where they refused the slightest excursion to save on gasoline. They felt trapped: "Impossible to sell Le Tertre, but impossible to send away all the help and close it up because humidity would rot everything and make the property even more difficult to sell in the future." Just before Christiane and her husband arrived to visit, Martin du Gard had concluded that remaining at Le Tertre was financially disastrous, that whatever the risks of leaving it deserted, he and Hélène should find some inexpensive lodging in southern France and wait for better times. No wonder she was in such a foul mood and unable to share her daughter's joy.[33]

For Martin du Gard, "the salvation would be to dive into work," but the water was murky. To follow *La Mort du père*, set in 1913, he had originally planned to bring the Thibault brothers to the outbreak of the war in another long section with the title *L'Appareillage* (The setting off). He wanted to explore their lives in depth and at length. But as he wrote, first Christiane's marriage and then the injuries from the New Year's Day accident interrupted his work. During the long delays, he reconsidered the detached approach he had adopted toward his characters and their time. By the spring of 1932, he decided to jump directly to the outbreak of the Great War, in which they would meet death. If so, he could complete *Les Thibault* in one more long segment. Once he had organized the plot, he reassured his publisher, Gaston Gallimard, and less than a year later was boasting, "I am working hard. I am completely re-energized. I am digging away at the mobilization and the war. I want to capture the pathos of July 1914, to portray my characters as leaves in the storm." He and Hélène rented rooms—first in Cassis, then in Marseille, finally in Nice. He worked ten hours a day on the manuscript, which he would complete by the end of 1935. She cooked their meals. The troubles they had endured, the toll of her injuries and the surgery, made her cling to him. The dependency worried him—"she is not valiant"—the debilitation much more—"stamina declining, slowly, regularly." He rejoiced that she rallied to assist Christiane at the birth of a son, Daniel, in March 1933, and a daughter, Anne, in November 1935. Both cheered Coppet's transfer from Chad to Dakar, then Djibouti, and finally Mauretania, not merely a series of advancements but much improved climate and so much closer that "it is almost a Parisian suburb."[34]

Money was so tight that Martin du Gard set aside *Les Thibault* for five months in 1933 to prepare a screenplay of Emile Zola's *La Bête humaine* (*The Human Beast*), because he was offered 30,000 francs ($26,260 in 2011). For 1934, he planned to take out a mortgage on Le Tertre—not merely a submission to fate but an emblem of failure that would have been horrifying to the ideals of the French bourgeoisie. His pride forbade accepting the loan offered by a good friend, writing, "things go badly, but not to that point." The following year, the need to come up with 15,000 francs ($11,041 in 2011) to pay the taxes on Le Tertre forced him to sell paintings that had been in his family for more than half a century. He was frantic—"I lie awake in the middle of the night. I don't have the first penny!"—and accepted far less than the appraised value. Even then, he was

running up debts that he could pay only by writing a best seller—
and soon. No wonder that he completed this new section, *L'Eté 1914*
(*Summer 1914*), at an extraordinary pace: approximately 280,000
words in fourteen months.[35]

Martin du Gard's decision to thrust the Thibault brothers into
the maelstrom of the Great War proceeded from his fear that a new
and more terrible conflict loomed. In March 1932, he spent ten
days in Berlin, where he found Germans to be "friendly, direct, so-
ciable, well-organized, so much more like us than Anglo-Saxons . . .
or Swiss, or even Flemish Belgians." For him, the only followers of
Adolf Hitler were "imbeciles, obstinate workers, and the narrow-
minded to whom he promises paradise in exchange for misery."
Ten months later, Hitler was chancellor of Germany and was rapidly imposing a totalitarian regime. By the fall of 1933, Martin du
Gard was admiring the stern warnings about Nazi ambitions given
by Wladimir d'Ormesson, former diplomat turned foreign policy
analyst, in his columns for *Le Temps*. Five years earlier, d'Ormesson
had sounded the alarm in a widely disregarded book, *La Confiance
dans l'Allemagne?* (Confidence in Germany?). Now, after reading
Hitler's *Mein Kampf*, Martin du Gard found d'Ormesson prophetic.
February 1934 brought the revelation of government corruption in
the Stavisky affair, violent demonstrations by the extremes of the
political right and left, resignation in fear by the Edouard Daladier
cabinet—all profound and dislocating to the established order. For
Martin du Gard, "in these days since the riots, I sense a departure,
that something, call it 'a new French revolution,' has begun. Not a
revolution like 1830 or 1848 with the sudden victory of a faction and
the substitution of one regime for another. Instead, intermittent up-
heavals, hours of respite following hours of violence in a long rising
turmoil. . . . I am preparing myself, my heart full of anguish, to live
through this grand adventure."[36]

The next two and a half years brought the "adventure" into clearer
focus. Because he was inherently individualistic and mistrusted all
political groups, Martin du Gard was made least uncomfortable by
the organized disorder of the Radical party. Like them, he favored
a foreign policy of conciliation, of general disarmament, of collec-

tive security, of confidence in the League of Nations. But what was to be done now, facing a rearmed and provocative Germany? Could any French leader risk failing to prepare the nation for a war that appeared ever more likely? And if so, might the "psychosis of war" lead to revolution either before or after? Martin du Gard foresaw a war of appalling dimensions, rightly predicting "the conflict between Germanism and Slavism—sought by both sides." Any of Martin du Gard's remaining idealism vanished after the League of Nations failed to take strong action when Fascist Italy invaded Abyssinia in September 1935. Were the leaders of France and Great Britain afraid of Benito Mussolini, "this gangster, one of the baleful monsters Hell periodically vomits forth to the misery of humankind?" And if so, "Law and Civilization have been shown up as shameful imposters, with no one—or almost no one—willing to avow their unmasking. Let us find a deserted island and establish a splendid little colony."[37]

The privilege of having rumors of war and war itself was Europe's in 1936: March brought Hitler's remilitarization of the Rhineland and July the outbreak of fighting in Spain between Republicans and Nationalists. Between them in May came the victory of the Popular Front in France—a coalition of Radicals, Socialists, and Communists—followed in June by massive strikes ended only through extraordinary concessions, the forty-hour workweek, two-week paid vacations, and substantial wage increases. Nearly ruined by the Great Depression, Martin du Gard called himself "anti-capitalist," as did many intellectuals in democratic countries, and like them made casual denunciations: "I believe that capitalism is the cause of the troubles from which we suffer and that we cannot be saved from them by the delegates of capitalism." When authentic revolutionaries like the Communists, whom he already rejected for their collectivism, came near to power in the Popular Front, he retreated quickly. The true goal of communism was, he claimed, a Bolshevik-style revolution in France followed by a dictatorship of the proletariat. The day they revealed their true selves, "*general panic*" would sweep France. Worse for Martin du Gard, communism was not just the sworn enemy of fascism but ready to lead a war of extinction against it. Martin du Gard had come to an irrevocable personal conviction: "*Anything*

rather than war! Even fascism in Spain! . . . Even fascism in France!
. . . Nothing, *no hardship, no servitude,* can be compared to war, to
all that war can engender. . . . *Anything*; Hitler, rather than war! And
besides, war would straight away become civil war, with the triumph
perhaps of communism after years of blood, of destruction, of sor-
rows without name."[38]

The pages of *L'Eté 1914* give proof of this conviction in magnificent
and stirring drama. Jacques Thibault has returned to Switzerland following his father's death. He has refused his share of the estate and
lives humbly in Geneva, renting a single room on the income from
writing occasional articles for obscure newspapers and magazines.
His milieu is the collection of socialists and anarchists who congre-
gate at a cheap hotel. He sees them as two types, either Apostles,
"generous-minded mystics" hoping for a new internationalism of
peace and freedom, or Experts, professional revolutionaries ready
to use violence. Their acknowledged leader is Meynestrel, called
"The Pilot," an Expert who preaches insurrection because reform-
ers underestimate the resistance of the bourgeoisie, capitalism, and
the nation-state. Beside Meynestrel, and most of the others, Jacques
is a moderate, replying, "I'm positive that no true progress can be
achieved by sordid methods. It's sheer nonsense glorifying violence
and hatred as means to bring about the triumph of justice and fraternity." Because Jacques cannot escape his heritage as bourgeois and
French, another Expert retorts, "A dilettante, that's what you are!"
The date is 28 June 1914, but none of them have yet heard news of
the assassination in Sarajevo.[39]

Three weeks later, in mid-July, Jacques recognizes the threat of
war and has volunteered for the effort to encourage a general strike
of the European working class to prevent it. When he arrives in Paris,
he seeks out his brother, Antoine, who has spent the last months taking full advantage of a substantial inheritance. Now, he calls himself
"Antoine Oscar-Thibault," wears only the finest clothes, has lavished
money on remodeling his father's house, and has converted one floor
into a modern laboratory. His father's investments were gilt-edged
equities and bonds that generated modest but stable returns. Having
spent so much and requiring a greater income to support his new

pretensions, Antoine has shifted to Russian state obligations that pay higher interest but at greater risk. He has taken on an additional risk—an affair with a married woman, Anne de Battaincourt, who is older and of dubious reputation and whose daughter was once his patient. Frustrated to find Paris consumed with fascination for the Caillaux trial and oblivious to any danger of war, Jacques turns on Antoine: "How at home he seems in all this luxury! . . . He has Father's vanity, the aristocratic vanity of the bourgeois." "What made me a revolutionary," he exclaims, "is having been born here, in this house, the son of a bourgeois father. It's having had to witness as a child, day after day, all the injustice which keeps our privileged class on top." Antoine replies with condescension, "Every social system's doomed to reproduce the failings, the incurable defects of human nature. So what's the use of running the risks of a general upheaval?"[40]

The next scene is the only one in the more than seven hundred thousand words of *Les Thibault* that seems contrived. Martin du Gard has to bring the Fontanin family into *L'Été 1914* and does so by having Jenny burst into Antoine's house begging for him to care for her father, Jérôme, who has shot himself in a nearby hotel. Four years earlier, Jenny and Jacques were profoundly, and innocently, in love, but Jacques disappeared after his father vehemently rejected any relationship between his son and a Protestant. He has not seen or contacted her since, and she believes that he has utterly rejected her. Neither finds a word for the other, and Jacques vows a quick return to Geneva. Antoine displays his professional calm and competence, telephoning for a surgeon to meet him at the hotel. A telegram goes out to Daniel de Fontanin, Jenny's brother and Jacques's childhood friend, who is completing his required military training—extended an additional twelve months by the three-year service law of 1913—as a sergeant at Lunéville, near the border with Germany. At the hotel, Antoine and his associate immediately recognize that Jérôme is without hope. Estranged from his wife, Thérèse, he has recently arrived from Vienna, where he left behind a young mistress and accusations of fraudulent financial dealing. As he put the gun to his temple, he must have thought no escape remained. The papers, bills, and letters he leaves behind are painful for Thérèse to examine.

Jacques's return to Geneva is brief because he is unique among the Apostles and Experts in having access to a fortune, the inheritance he refused, which Antoine has honorably kept safe awaiting his possible change of mind. When he reveals his willingness to turn the money over to the "International Socialist Committee" for use in an antiwar campaign, he becomes, dilettante or not, Meynestrel's most valuable asset. Back in Paris on 23 July to retrieve the funds, he learns that Jérôme has died, that Thérèse will go to Vienna to clear her husband's name, that Daniel will sell his new paintings to pay his father's debts, and that Jenny—well, "How was she to quell that insensate yearning to be happy which her meeting with Jacques had revived?" Jacques tells her, "when once there has been between two people what there has been between you and me, when they've been drawn to each other as we were drawn, glimpsed such boundless hopes, such visions of the future, what difference can the lapse of four years, ten years make?" He also discovers a Paris suddenly and intensely concentrated on the threat of war. After Jérôme's funeral on 25 July, Daniel waits for the train to take him back to Lunéville, aware that the first battles of a war will engulf him. Antoine recalls that he is to report to a military medical unit at Compiègne the first day of mobilization. On 26 July, his mentor, Dr. Philip, who is old enough to remember the Franco-Prussian War of 1870, warns against hoping for the best, "at my age it's hard to count on reason vanquishing stupidity." Rumelles, a high official at the Quai d'Orsay and long Antoine's friend and patient, acknowledges that war is likely, "What would you have us do? . . . Let Russia down and stand entirely alone?"[41]

While awaiting the settlement date on the sale of the securities constituting his inheritance, Jacques anxiously haunts left-wing gatherings. To Jenny, who tags along dreamily, he explains his choice, "I realized that it was absurd to fancy justice would triumph easily or quickly, . . . my instinct of revolt . . . joined forces with other rebellious spirits like mine for the betterment of mankind." When he finds most French labor leaders succumbing to nationalist propaganda, he is bitterly disappointed and eventually demands to speak. "My friends, you ask, 'What is our duty?' Well, it's simple, and it's clear. We must have one aim only: peace. We must drop party differences and unite. Unite in saying 'No!' and fighting against war." His words thrill Jenny, but the workers walk out. Later, an old-time syndicalist printer sums up: "Nine out of ten of our famous revolutionary leaders—shall I tell you what I really think about them? They'll never be able to bring themselves to adopt 'unconstitutional' methods. That being so, well, the conclusion's inescapable."[42]

Antoine as well is suffering the collapse of the ideals in which he has believed. On 30 July, Russia ordered general mobilization, and on 31 July, Germany announced "a state of threatening danger of war," refused to guarantee Belgian neutrality, and sent an insolent ultimatum demanding French intentions. Antoine's "morale, till now intact, was badly shaken. . . . He was suddenly discovering the impotence of intellect; and . . . the futility of the virtues which had been the mainstay of his industrious career: common sense, moderation, wisdom and experience, the cult of justice." Even so, he still had a moral order to defend when Jacques—representing Martin du Gard's position—cries out: "Anything rather than the madness, the horrors of a war! . . . I won't take part in any war, whether they label it 'just' or 'unjust,' whatever its origins and motives." Antoine upbraids him, "the man who joins his regiment when he is called up for service is obeying the collective will of the nation—whatever his personal views may be." The Thibault brothers stand on opposite sides of the social contract. Jacques insists, "I deny that the state is justified in forcing a man, for any reason whatsoever, to go against his conscience." Antoine replies, "To refuse to do one's duty at such a moment is to sacrifice the public's interest to one's own."[43]

That night, a nationalist fanatic shoots dead Jean Jaurès, leader of the Socialist party and the most eloquent spokesman for preventing conflict between nations through a general strike of their workers. Confronted the following day by the German declaration of war against Russia, Jaurès's lieutenants quickly promise support for whatever decisions French leaders take—meaning the order for mobilization that goes out a few hours later with the injunction, "We rely on the loyalty of every Frenchman, knowing full well not one of us will fail the call of duty." Had he survived his wounds, Jaurès almost certainly would have done the same. Reading the posters declaring that 2 August was Day 1 of Mobilization, Jacques feels "a cold, disdainful rage. . . . For weeks he had lived in a fool's paradise, fondly trusting that justice, truth, and man's fraternity would triumph in the nick of time." He knows he must leave France quickly to avoid being arrested as a pacifist, a dissident, or even a traitor. He asks Jenny to flee with him, to make a life together in Geneva.[44]

On 2 August just before the border closes, Jacques does take the train to Geneva. He has the money from his inheritance but not Jenny. With both of them overwrought from the announcement of mobilization and thinking her mother still in Vienna, Jenny has Jacques sleep beside her—both fully clothed—at the Fontanin apartment. Thérèse arrives unexpectedly and is mortified by her daughter's conduct. The following morning, Jenny cringes as her mother says, "You've been led astray by an infatuation I'd never dreamed possible. . . . You should be ashamed of yourself!" Later at the train station, she tells Jacques that she cannot go with him, that she cannot abandon her mother with Daniel on the front line and Jérôme in his grave only a week. Maybe she will join him later. Jacques has been planning, in that quaint nineteenth-century expression, "to make her his own" after they reach Switzerland. Now, they have only a couple of hours before the train leaves: "She dared not refuse him this last joy. Her cheeks crimson, she looked away with a wan little smile."[45]

Jacques is free from every emotional commitment, free—in the existential sense—to pursue a defining act which, though likely futile, is magnificent in conception. Using a portion of his inheritance, he will print up many thousands of leaflets denouncing the war, load them into a small plane, and release them to the wind as he flies over the French and German lines in nearby Alsace. He thinks, "How it would grip the imagination of the world at large! 'The Peace Plane!' 'A message from the air!'" When brought to account, he will proclaim, "There is a higher law than yours, the law of conscience." But on 10 August, when the preparations are complete and he is waiting for the plane to take off, he recognizes bitterly, "I'm acting as I'm doing only out of despair. To escape from myself. I shan't stop the war. I shan't save anyone—except myself." Over the battlefield, both sides open fire on the unmarked plane, which crashes to the ground before he can toss out a single leaflet. Jacques is badly injured. French troops reach him first and assume he is a spy. He is being carried to the rear on a stretcher when a German attack makes him an unnecessary liability. A soldier shoots him dead, muttering, "Scum!"[46]

Librairie Gallimard published *L'Eté 1914* as a three-volume set in late 1936. Evoking the implacable menace of the Great War—not two decades over—resonated strongly in a France now beset by political polarization and economic collapse, faced with the threat of new conflict, and increasingly incapacitated by recriminations and fear. In a letter to Martin du Gard, Raymond Aron, soon to ascend the heights of the French intellectual world, confessed his own reaction: "Are we seeing today the preparation of the next war through a similar sequence of errors, irresponsibility, and weakness? I suspect strongly that the tragedy of history is repeating itself." During the next months, sales were excellent, and Martin du Gard began paying off his debts, a long process he thought. Then without warning, on 11 November he received astonishing news: he was the 1937 Nobel Prize Laureate for Literature. A couple of days later he wrote a longtime friend, "Damned happy, but crushed by the weight of this wildly disproportionate reward for my merits." He reassured his publisher: "This Nobel Prize . . . consecrates my books and me. But it should change nothing. I have no intention of getting fat or presumptuous." In his letter accepting the award, Martin du Gard speculated, "if the Swedish Academy has chosen the date of 11 November, the anniversary of the Armistice, to draw public attention to the author of *L'Eté 1914*, the reason is that these books of anguish, where I have tried to revive the anxious turmoil of the weeks preceding the mobilization, might, in some manner, serve the cause of peace by recalling to all the tragic lesson of the past."[47]

Private, self-effacing, and solitary, Martin du Gard never sought personal celebrity, and so few photographs of him were available that some newspapers published ones of his younger cousin Maurice, a journalist. At Stockholm in early December, he and Hélène were more the center of attention than at any other point in their lives. The experience was, he admitted, "a fairy story. Incredible. But I am not made to play the star, and I sense myself emptied of all instinct for sociability for a long time." Suddenly wealthy, they took the long way home, traveling through Copenhagen, Berlin, Dresden, Prague, and Vienna. What they saw raised their most profound apprehensions. Germany was "terrifying." Vienna "enchants us . . . not an ounce of vulgarity." But by their return in late March, Germany had seized Austria, while France and Great Britain did nothing but offer vain protests. "My tour of Europe has lasted four months, and I return with the most *sinister* impressions, which everything seems to justify. Repeated capitulations by the democracies, the unequal contest of the clay pot against the iron pot." They reopened Le Tertre as a refuge: "The world is insane, all is absurd. . . . Here is calm and overwhelming silence." There, he planned one final addition to *Les Thibault*, a coda based on the journal of Antoine Thibault, who is "gassed late in the war, knows that he has no chance of recovery, and records his thoughts in a tête-à-tête with death."[48]

That spring, he was confident of completing this *Epilogue* rapidly: "if the summer of 1938 is not a 'Summer 1914,' I hope to finish this last book by the end of the year." He even took on a pet, a little black French bulldog—"I lead him around to 'go pipi,' and that forces me to get out a little." But 1938 was, in fact, shaping up to be a year of crisis, and by mid-June, he worried, "I am on the eve of completing my *Thibault*, and something tells me that I must hasten, that unforeseen evils menace us and, if these ordeals befall us, the suffering for me would be increased by my having not finished my work when I could have done so with greater application." By late August and early September, with war tension high over Hitler's demand for Czechoslovakia's Sudetenland, his mood was black. "I take solace in work, but how long will the madmen and the criminals of this world permit me to bury my head in the sand. I am profoundly discouraged, and I would like to dissociate myself from *everything*, to turn my back on all." He wrote another friend, "In these days heavy with anguish, I feel as if I am reading the newspapers of July 1914." And to yet another, "Nothing has changed, and no one has learned anything in these twenty-four years. I should write a 'Summer 1938.'" The "miraculous announcement" on 28 September that France, Great Britain, Germany, and Italy would meet the following day at Munich to resolve the crisis gave him hope: "I believe the immediate danger averted." Afterward, some condemned the Munich Agreement as a "humiliation," the ultimate appeasement, because France and Great Britain avoided war by agreeing to Germany's seizure of the Sudetenland—when France had a mutual defense pact with Czechoslovakia. The accusation made him furious: "We had to choose either a negotiated *capitulation* or *general war*! A war that would have cost forty million lives, ruined a civilization, and which would have begun with the massacre and devastation of these Czech 'friends,' in whose name, for the sake of 'honor,' we 'should have' unleashed the conflict! . . . Nothing is worse than war. It is not inevitable, no matter what anyone says."[49]

At the end of the year, Martin du Gard's writing was far from done. The Munich crisis was wrenching for him. Hélène, who "for three years had accepted a mediocre life and the exile of rented rooms in Nice," who had been for him "every day the single, unobtrusive, quiet, understanding confidante" of his work, was left distraught when her sister died from tuberculosis and then her father from a cerebral hemorrhage during a single week in December. They longed to escape, and the opportunity came through a sudden windfall of American dollars: the Viking Press was preparing a two-volume English translation of *Les Thibault*, and the Literary Guild decided to adopt both as "Books of the Month." At the beginning of March 1939, they boarded the French ship *Barfleur* bound for Guadeloupe and then Martinique. During the voyage, they learned that Hitler, in violation of his promise at Munich, seized the remainder of Czechoslovakia and that Mussolini invaded Albania. Soon after their arrival, they heard of Hitler's demand for the Polish Corridor and Danzig. Despite being unable "to escape the anguish of Europe"—or perhaps impelled by it—Martin du Gard completed the last pages of the *Epilogue* in May and wrote Gallimard that "*it brings* Les Thibault *to a close.*" As he entrusted the manuscript to international mail, he declared, with relief, "this enterprise, which for nineteen years has been the framework of my life, has reached its conclusion, the Thibaults exist, independent of me, whole and complete—finished."[50]

Finished indeed: the *Epilogue* opens in May 1918, with Antoine recovering at a hospital near the Mediterranean, in Le Mousquier, after
exposure to mustard gas six months earlier. Persuaded by his physicians that he will eventually recover, he is keeping a detailed record of
his symptoms and treatment for future publication. He has avoided
Paris entirely since his mobilization nearly four years earlier in August
1914. Through Rumelles, his contact at the Quai d'Orsay, he learned
of Jacques's death in Alsace. From letters, he discovered that Jenny
became pregnant from her single tryst with Jacques and gave birth to
a son, Paul. Now, he has news that his father's longtime housekeeper
has died, and he decides the funeral is reason enough to go home. The
trip by train is exhausting and reminds him of how weak he remains.
At the Thibault house, which has been closed and empty since his departure, he has an overwhelming sense of loss: "He saw the past now
bathed in roseate light, the glamour of youth and health. Ah, what
would he not have given to retrieve the atmosphere of that bygone
family life, that lost serenity!" An accumulation of mail awaits him,
and he picks out a package, postmarked March 1915 from the General
Hospital, Konakri, French Guiana. Within, he finds a necklace of honey-
golden amber set with tiny rings of ambergris between the beads, the
necklace that Rachel Goepfert always wore—"And suddenly the past
had risen before his eyes, vivid as reality." That night, he dreams of his
father. Is he recalling a world long gone, or does a conscience uneasy
at his departure from his father's values assail his sleep?[51]

Thérèse de Fontanin and Jenny have converted the old Thibault
country retreat northwest of Paris at Maisons-Laffitte into a hospital for soldiers recovering from their wounds. Daniel is there with a
prosthetic leg. Antoine is not surprised to find Thérèse superbly capable of running things, because she managed to fend for herself and
her family with a husband like Jérôme. Jenny as well knows how to get
things done and has charge of the laundry. She is defiantly defensive of
Jacques's memory and entirely indulgent of her son. Antoine notices
that while "maternity and its obligations had filled out her hips and
bosom, thickened the lower portion of her neck, . . . the expression
of her eyes . . . still had that faraway look—of loneliness, serene courage, and melancholy." Other than play with Paul, Daniel does almost

nothing, and his sister says harshly that he "has never had any sense of his duties to society." She does not know that the shell fragment that tore off Daniel's leg also left him emasculated. The burden of nostalgia weighs heavily on Antoine as he remembers when "all of them were young, rejoicing in their youth and prospects for the future, without an inkling of what lay ahead—the cataclysm the statesmen of Europe were preparing for them behind the scenes."[52]

The following day, he goes to the office of his longtime mentor, Dr. Philip. They agree about the war and its impact, Philip saying, "Who knows if, in the years to come, historians won't write us down as a generation of fools and simpletons who gulled themselves with wishful thinking, with illusions about man and his capacity for civilization?" He examines Antoine, listens carefully to his lungs and heart, and try as he may, he cannot prevent himself from revealing the result. "Philip's look, his whole expression, seemed to be saying: 'Your case is hopeless—and there is no escape.'" For the first time, Antoine admits to himself, "Way down deep I too knew it: I knew there was no hope." And so Antoine returns to Le Mousquier prepared to die, but true to his organized nature, he first has preparations to make. In a series of letters to Jenny, he discloses his condition and declares his intention to make Paul his sole heir. Ever bourgeois, he suggests that Jenny marry him to give Paul legitimacy, but she adamantly rejects the idea as a betrayal of Jacques. After writing to French Guiana, he receives a note explaining that Rachel was brought to the hospital suffering from yellow fever. Before dying a few days later, she entrusted her nurse with the necklace and Antoine's address in Paris. Because no one claimed the body, she was buried in a pauper's grave. She left behind a black French bulldog called "Hirsch."[53]

Antoine now knows all he can ever hope to know about his life and its meaning. He begins a diary that he hopes Paul will find and read someday. Memories of his father haunt him. "He was a difficult man to love. I judged him with much harshness and, I suspect, did him less than justice. . . . His defects set everyone against him and his very real virtues won him no liking. . . . I believe he was aware of this and that the knowledge of his isolation made him suffer terribly." He questions his father's wish for his sons to adopt the name Oscar-Thibault:

"There was much more to it than the proprietary instinct. . . . It was something finer—a craving to leave some trace behind him, not to be utterly blotted out by death." Memories of his only true love haunt him even more. "Thought of Rachel. In these sultry nights the perfume of the necklace is overpowering. She, too, had a stupid end, in a hospital bed. Alone. But one's always alone, dying." He realizes, "The associations of this necklace may concern a paltry love-affair, but, when all is said and done, that paltry love-affair was about the best thing in my paltry life."[54]

As Antoine approaches his end, he casts aside the last baggage he has carried. On 8 July 1918, he records, "Thirty-seven today. My last birthday." He warns Paul, "Impossible to rid one's mind wholly of the futile desire to find a 'meaning' in life. Even I, reviewing my career, often catch myself wondering: What was the point of it? It had no 'point.' None whatsoever. . . . And nothing matters—except perhaps, to get through this short lease of life with the minimum of suffering." When the chaplain asks to hear his confession, he thinks, "Could bring myself to do it if I thought it would give anyone pleasure. But nobody that I can see would be the happier if I pretended to die a Christian death." He lives to see the Armistice, but a week later he is in great pain and fears he may slip into a coma. He wants to die on his own terms and has prepared a lethal dose of morphine: "High time—or my strength may fail. All's ready; I need only steel my will, reach for the syringe. Struggled all night. High time. Monday, November 18, 1918. 37 years, four months, 9 days. Simpler than one thinks. Goodbye, Paul."[55]

On 1 September 1939, Germany's invasion of Poland brought the new conflict Martin du Gard had long feared. France and Great Britain were again at war with Germany. Far away in Martinique, he and Hélène listened with dread to the radio. The next mail delivery demonstrated the suspension of peacetime expectations: all the letters had been opened and read. When Hitler did not attack Western Europe that fall after defeating Poland, they decided to return home. Finding a ship was difficult, but eventually they got to New York and boarded an Italian liner, the *Conte de Savoia*, which brought them to Genoa. From there, they took to the train to France, finally arriving at Le Tertre in mid-December. Christmas was anything but merry.[56]

CHAPTER 4

Shifting Ground

The Great War laid waste to France. Broad measures stagger: the dead, 1.3 million; the severely wounded, 1.1 million; the damage to the region of the Western Front, 88.7 billion francs ($151 billion in 2011); the debt incurred prosecuting the battle, 177 billion francs ($301 billion in 2011); the losses from Bolshevik renunciation of tsarist obligations, 26 billion francs ($44.32 billion in 2011). The details numb: more than one-quarter of men aged between twenty and twenty-seven died, 600,000 widows and 750,000 orphans mourned, births diminished 1.4 million.

To grasp the meaning of these statistics, imagine that the United States has just fought a war on its own soil for the last four and a half years and suffered losses comparable to France's between 1914 and 1918. The population of the United States today is approximately 775 percent more than that of France then (310 million to 40); the economy of the United States today is 1,200 percent greater than that of France then ($14.5 trillion to $1.2 trillion). Applying these multipliers, the United States would have suffered 10.1 million dead, 8.5 million severely wounded, damage of $1.1 trillion, debt of $3.6 trillion, losses from foreign investment $312 billion, 4.6 million widows,

5.8 million orphans, and a quarter of the men aged between twenty and twenty-seven dead. If this comparison is unconvincing, one blunt fact remains: the 1.3 million French who died in the Great War are more than the total number of Americans who have died in all the wars fought by the United States, from the American Revolution to Afghanistan and including the Civil War.[1]

Harder to calculate in cost are intangibles: the war and its aftermath completed the destruction of the world the nineteenth century had made. Traditions waned, innovation waxed. Prudence and restraint were the essence of the French bourgeoisie and thus of the Third Republic, but they were challenged now by growth and consumption. Economic mobilization for the war crushed small enterprises in favor of large industries. Inflation in the 1920s and depression in the 1930s eroded inherited wealth. The rentier—who by living on dividends and interest could devote his life to the arts, to writing, to politics, to service—faded in significance. The long departure of men to the front had left women in charge and afterward unwilling to give up a new emancipation economic, social, and sexual. Working-class militancy burgeoned, any deference to elites vanished after the communality of the trenches. New immigrants, encouraged to replace the dead, resisted assimilation. Artists deracinated Cartesian heritage to chase the dark specter of the irrational through Dada and Surrealism. Domestic politics polarized and intensified with dangerous new enemies for parliamentary democracy, the Communists on the far left and fascist imitators on the far right. International relationships were a shambles. Defeated enemy Germany remained recalcitrant. Ally Great Britain declined collective defense. Turncoat Russia portended communist subversion. Wartime savior America remained perplexed with economic might but political isolation. The time was out of joint: O cursed spite that wounded France was left to set it right.[2]

For French novelists confronting this broken world, the experience of the war raised questions of courage and fear, suffering and death, glory and shame. First among them was Henri Barbusse, a journalist who enlisted in 1914 at the age of forty-one. Assigned to an infantry unit, he faced combat for seventeen months until his injuries required his transfer to a clerical post. There, he wrote *Le Feu: Journal d'une escouade* (*Under Fire: The Story of a Squad*), which was published in December 1916, won the Prix Goncourt, and sold nearly a quarter million copies. His was the first realistic account of battle on the Western Front and was based, he claimed, on notes he took while in the trenches. Nothing about the brutality of war is omitted, and the dedication reads, "To the memory of the comrades who fell by my side at Crouÿ and on Hill 119 January, May, and September 1915." Through its sales and its tone, *Le Feu* may well have promoted the defeatism that spread in France during the first half of 1917. Barbusse himself began as a socialist, but his political trajectory was much further left. He moved to Russia in 1918, joined the Bolshevik party, and eventually became an apologist for Stalin.

Barbusse gave *Le Feu* the appearance of a journal kept while serving with the French Sixth Battalion north of Amiens. In his graphic scenes, heroism is meaningless when life is full of dread, food rank, water foul, trenches claustrophobic, and death stark. The men of Corporal Bertrand's squad are from different regions of France, worked at various jobs before the war, and range in age from their early twenties to mid-forties, but now they have in common "the simple nature of men who have reverted to the state primeval." Poterloo, a miner from the Pas de Calais, wears boots he took from a dead Bavarian machine gunner after emptying them of "some bones and bits of sock and bits of feet." They mock the propaganda distributed by the government and published in the newspapers as "brain stuffing" (*bourrage de crâne*); they avoid the chaplain who tells them that "God is with us" (*Dieu avec nous*) because the German priests say the same (*Gott mit uns*). They wonder if the German soldiers, the "Dirty Boche," are not, "at bottom, . . . men pretty much like us"—but the German officers, "they're not men, they're monsters. I tell you, they're a specially filthy sort o' vermin. One might say they're the microbes of war."[3]

The squad watches the Eighteenth Battalion marching to the rear after four days in the frontline trenches. The captain "walks with difficulty, by reason of his old wound at the Marne battle . . . and there are other pangs, too. He lowers his hooded head, and might be

attending a funeral. We can see that in his mind he is indeed following the dead, and his thoughts are with them." Poterloo was born in
the nearby town of Souchez, which has been in German hands since
early in the war. When the French finally retake it, he goes searching
for his home. He finds a corpse on the main street with a letter jut-
ting from the pocket: "My dear Henry, what a fine day it is for your
birthday": "the man is on his belly; his loins rent from hip to hip by a
deep furrow . . . on temples and neck a kind of green moss is growing." He does not find his house: "You know, it's too much, all that.
It's wiped out too much—all my life up to now. It makes me afraid—it
is so completely wiped out." Another in the squad, Lamuse, is fascinated by a young woman he sees wandering through the villages
behind the lines. When he finally speaks to her, she recoils, "Leave
me alone—you disgust me." Later, he finds her dead from an artillery
blast and cannot resist embracing the body, "as I should have hugged
her once on a time if she'd let me. I've been half an hour cleaning
myself from the touch of her."[4]

They reserve their greatest scorn for shirkers (*embusqués*), who
manage to avoid service—or if in uniform, avoid combat. Volpatte
spends two months at the rear recuperating from a wound and on
his return to the squad denounces "the dead-heads . . . they're all
alike and all rotters. . . . We're divided into two foreign countries. The
Front . . . where there are too many unhappy, and the Rear . . . where
there are too many happy." Bertrand adds, "There are some times
when duty and danger are exactly the same thing; when the country,
when justice and liberty are in danger, it isn't in taking shelter that
you defend them. On the contrary, war means danger of death and
sacrifice of life for everybody, no one is sacred." He is prophetic, for
when the orders come to attack and take Hill 119, more than half
the squad is killed, Bertrand among them. Although victorious, the
survivors are devoid of sensation: "When you hear or see the death of
one of those who fought by your side and lived exactly the same life,
you receive a direct blow in the flesh before even understanding. . . .
It is only later that one begins to mourn."[5]

Le Feu closes with the remainder of the squad adopting a pacifism
both armed and aggressive. The soldiers are worn to futility: "War

is frightful and unnatural weariness, water up to the belly, mud and dung and infamous filth. It is befouled faces and tattered flesh, it is the corpses that are no longer like corpses even, floating on the ravenous earth. . . . No more war! Enough of it! . . . Two armies fighting each other—that's like one great army committing suicide!" Yet they recognize that an end to the fighting can come only through defeating their malignant enemy: "Germany and militarism . . . they're the same thing. They wanted the war and they'd planned it beforehand. They *are* militarism. . . . War must be killed in the belly of Germany."[6]

The reverse of Barbusse on the war was Henri de Montherlant and his novel *Le Songe* (The dream), which appeared in 1922. Scion of a penurious aristocratic family, indulged by his mother and grandmother, profoundly influenced by the nationalism and cult of the self in the novels of Maurice Barrès, Montherlant was the very definition of egotism. Expulsion in 1912 at the age of seventeen from his Jesuit preparatory school for a homosexual affair with a fellow student merely intensified his conceit. He eagerly anticipated his mobilization in 1916 as a moment to prove his virtue—and he did so, serving in the infantry and suffering a serious wound. *Le Songe* celebrates Alban de Bricoule, a thinly disguised Montherlant, who sees war as a means to harden his body and his soul. Here, the horrors that overwhelm the characters in *Le Feu* are merely the backdrop before which Bricoule parades a taste for heroism and sacrifice. He idealizes his fellow soldiers as close comrades, ardent and strong, faithful to the end, the fraternity of war. Women do not belong in this world; their sentimentality and their sexual charm sap the virility necessary for combat, for conquest.[7]

Unlike Barrès, who well before 1914 chose collective nationalism over individual self, Montherlant's Bricoule is supremely solipsistic. Early in *Le Songe* he muses, "I count on myself alone. I take counsel with myself alone." He is convinced that "everything he desired would be his, that each of his goals would be achieved one after the other; and the calm with which he welcomed these victories would render him all the more worthy of gaining more. 'Nothing can stop me—except sickness, or death.'" And if the latter, "Certainly, a violent death would be sufficient for me. I could accept such a death."

He believes himself capable of friendship, capable of desire, but incapable of love, and that companionship with male contemporaries brings out the best in him. Cultivating asceticism, he spurns sensual gratification as vulgar and enervating. Sexual desire inflames him, but he refuses its allures. His relationships with women have been fleeting because each has eventually insisted on entering "that little circle of pleasure from which I desperately sought to pull them." One woman alone captivates him, Dominique Soubrier. With her, he has fashioned "a wondrous camaraderie." They talk of purity—not just of the Holy Virgin but of Greek maidens, for the Parthenon was the "temple of the young girl." Bricoule is so immersed in himself that he has not the slightest comprehension that Soubrier is fiercely in love with him.[8]

When he learns that a former classmate has been killed in battle, Bricoule volunteers for service without waiting to be mobilized. He will join the "holy manly order" of warriors, imagining that the Western Front is a re-creation of the Peloponnesian wars he has studied in school. Assigned to an infantry unit in the Vosges region, his first thought sets a tone of rigor: "if necessary, let me die in this place, because it would be dying in a manner I approve." When another soldier, Stanislas Prinet, warns, "It's hard here," he replies, "Would you prefer to be tested only by mediocre ordeals?" They become comrades in arms, braving the trials, but the primal conditions soon enough sully heroic conceptions. After killing a German soldier at close quarters, Bricoule senses "an ancient hatred well up in the most bestial recesses of his being simply because this unknown was born on one side of the frontier and he on the other." Crouching over the body "like a cat on a mouse," he astonishes himself with a primal growl. Later, when he finds Prinet dead, he has a moment of disorientation: "Everything is black, everything is empty, no support left on which to lean." Then, he rallies to his ideal: "He will lean on the divine."[9]

With Bricoule off to war, Soubrier volunteers as a nurse at a rehabilitation facility for officers. The horrific wounds and the random depredation of death erode her belief in any exalted values. When contingency reigns, only the moment matters. She decides that "the hour permits everything," for "what good is this immense disorder in the world if not to grant us the right to be exceptional ourselves? . . . The rules no longer exist, good is no longer good, bad no longer bad, customs, illusions, all the old established ways are overturned." When Bricoule has leave and comes to see her, she reveals her passion for him: "I love you, my friend, and neither you nor I can prevent my loving you." Until that moment, he could see her as another comrade, but now she is merely a woman tempting him with her flesh. She recognizes his decision from his eyes: "She has offered her heart and all it holds, its splendor, its marvel, its essence; she has given him all, freely, as one does in dreams. And he is rejecting it all." Bricoule returns to the trenches. Despite what he has experienced, willingness to risk death remains for him the essential definition of virtue.[10]

Of course, this romanticized attitude, a remnant of chivalry, made little sense in a modern industrial war. Montherlant later achieved a certain distinction as a novelist, poet, and dramatist, enough to win him election in 1960 to the citadel of French culture, the Académie française. His distinction also included admiration for the German war machine in 1940, a reputation for misogyny, and accusations of pederasty.

Somewhere between *Le Feu* and *Le Songe* is Colette's *Mitsou ou comment l'esprit vient aux filles (Mitsou)*, which is more interesting than either because of its ambiguity. By the Great War, Colette was both notable and notorious. Born Sidonie-Gabrielle Colette, in 1893 at age twenty she married the bisexual critic Henri Gauthier-Villars, who was a decade and a half older. She took his pen name, "Willy," for her first books, the *Claudine* series, naughty but charming accounts of girlhood and adolescence. After leaving Gauthier-Villars in 1906, she began a sensational series of affairs with both men, like the Italian Futurist poet Gabriele D'Annunzio, and women, like Moulin Rouge actress and aristocrat Mathilde de Morny, the Marquise de Belbeuf. In 1912, she married another aristocrat, Henri de Jouvenel, Baron des Ursins, editor of the popular newspaper *Le Matin*. When he was mobilized during the Great War, she opened a hospital on his Breton estate at Saint-Malo to rehabilitate wounded soldiers, for which she was made a member of the Légion d'honneur in 1920. The year before, she published *Mitsou*.[11]

At the Empyrée-Montmartre theater in 1917, Petite-Chose and Mitsou are the star performers in music hall revues. They have suffered not at all from the three years of fighting. Rather than devote spare time to knitting socks or making bandages, Petite-Chose makes her contribution to the war effort by offering sexual favors to soldiers on leave—"I open my arms and make them happy." Mitsou has a "petit ami," a lover more than twice her age whose wealth and attentions eliminate every concern but boredom. One evening, Petite-Chose bursts into Mitsou's dressing room seeking to hide her latest favorites, two young officers on leave. Mitsou is drawn to one of them, Robert, whom she calls the "Lieutenant in Blue" from his dress uniform. After he returns to the front, they begin a correspondence that transforms them both.[12]

Before Robert's letters, Mitsou's conception of the war is based entirely on the "brain stuffing" in the newspapers. Some of her roles are in costume dramas taken from Greek epics that exalt war as noble and glorious. They are a historical theme as patriotic propaganda and carry titles like *"L'Ame rouge de la victoire"* (The red soul of victory) and *"Le Lierre du champ de bataille"* (The ivy on the battlefield). She often carries a spear, sometimes a sword, and the flowers for the scenery and backdrop are always red roses. After reading Robert's account of the constant danger and the brutality of life at the front, Mitsou questions the impression she is conveying. The stage props begin to irritate her: she casts off her crown of laurels and trails her silver sword "like a broomstick." The roses she no longer associates with glory but with blood: "From now on, I want no more roles in red because it makes me sad." But for Robert, who remembers the roses from her dressing room, the color symbolizes a yearning passion for Mitsou, an escape from the realities of war. When she sends him a strip of "crimson velvet," he places it beside his cheek as he sleeps.[13]

Robert's letters confess his fear that the war has devoured the youth he might have had, "ripped us from our studies and turned us into men." Has he become "a poorly cultured fruit, ripe on one side, green on the other?" Recognizing how combat has coarsened him, he wonders whether he can ever "approach a woman without a sense of terror or a sense of cannibalism?" Compared to her older lover, what can he offer Mitsou? The war may eliminate any future and burdens his present. He curses the solitude that "fills you with dreams, trembling, cries you hold in check, emotions you suppress." For the past three years, he has been living "a life where either gesture or impassivity can take on the character of religious intensity, a life where one ends up believing in the significance of everything, even the significance of not loving."[14]

For Mitsou, the experience of the war has changed. By mid-1917, following the Nivelle offensive mutinies in April and May and the rise of defeatism, the French divide bitterly over fighting to the finish or seeking the best peace available. The extraordinary loss of men presses more and more women into service. Former acquaintances who are now nurses or telephone operators or clerks or whatever scorn her for remaining on the stage as a kept woman. Mitsou has no intention of changing her life, but she feels ashamed. When she is among other women now called "shirkers," doubts assail her: "These are the worst. After an hour with them, I ask myself, 'Am I like them— as mediocre, as lackluster, as contemptible?'" Robert's unrestrained infatuation deepens this guilt. He imagines her to be his "heroic passion" (*amour héroique*), as if she is playing a role in one of the epic dramas. She replies gently, "Some passages in your letters appear to take me for someone else." When he pays no heed, she warns him bluntly, "I am nothing extraordinary."[15]

Of course, these misconceptions collide when Robert finally has another leave, comes back to Paris, and searches out Mitsou's house. She answers the door, but he does not recognize her out of costume and theater makeup. Her simplicity in ordinary clothing disappoints, but the extravagance of her furnishings, gifts from her lover, offends. Staring at antique figurines, a brass chandelier, a gilt dressing table, he murmurs, "Obviously, burn everything!" Reality has spoiled his infatuation. The Mitsou he imagined is not the Mitsou sitting across from him. He considers leaving abruptly but then accepts her invitation for dinner and for bed. Afterward, he confesses to himself, "she has not made me laugh, not moved me to tears, not swept me up in waves of ravishing sensuality." He was hoping to find in her not just an escape from the present but an escape to the past. At night, his dreams are nightmares alternating with fantasies, "war and adolescence, both so close to him, mixing their memories of pooling black blood with summer houses in the country." When Robert has returned to his unit at the front, Mitsou sends him one last letter with the promise, "I am trying to become your illusion." The better word would have been "delusion."[16]

Colette divorced Jouvenel in 1924 after having a scandalous affair with her stepson. Eleven years later she married Maurice Goudeket, a Jewish pearl dealer seventeen years her junior. During World War II, she hid him from the Germans in her attic and wrote her most enduring work, *Gigi*, which was published in 1945. The Fourth Republic elevated her Légion d'honneur rank to grand officer in 1953, and when she died the following year, gave her a state funeral, the first in France for a woman.

No such honors came to Louis-Ferdinand-Auguste Destouches, who explored the longer-term impact from the Great War. He was born in 1894, the year before Montherlant, to a lower-middle-class family in Courbevoie, on the western edge of Paris. After completing primary school in 1905, he embarked upon a series of adventures. He worked odd jobs, spent a year each in Germany and England learning languages, and in 1912, three years before his required military service, joined the army. Not quite three months into the Great War, he suffered a severe wound to his right arm while on a volunteer mission, for which he received the Médaille militaire. After a medical discharge, he briefly represented a French export company in Cameroon. Following his return, he joined a project to suppress tuberculosis in Brittany and decided to study medicine. At the University of Rennes, he surmounted the educational barriers so rapidly that he completed his degree by 1924. Over the next three years, he traveled throughout Europe, back to Africa, and then to the United States, where he took a special interest in Henry Ford's assembly-line methods. Along the way, he left behind two wives and a child. Afterward, he practiced medicine in bedraggled parts of Paris and, under the name Louis-Ferdinand Céline, wrote *Voyage au bout de la nuit* (*Journey to the End of the Night*).

Rejecting traditional literary conventions and scorning any pretense of formal style, Céline adopted a raw, frenetic prose full of slang and vulgarities, mimicking the colloquial speech of the masses in the streets. He endowed this emotive style with a singular rhythm through punctuation that was as often suspension points as commas or periods. And he used it to tell stories, sometimes taken from his own unsettled life, portraying the world and mankind as corrupt, deceitful, malicious, brutal, and stupid. For him, the only expectation was suffering, the only release, death. When *Journey to the End of the Night* was published in 1932, its form and presentation generated such excitement that it became a serious contender for the Prix Goncourt, but its tone and bitter pessimism ensured that it did not win.[17]

Ferdinand Bardamu is Céline's guide on this journey through despair and menacing death. In the Great War, he faces the "hellish idiocy" of combat, wondering "how long could a fit of frenzy like this go on?" Perhaps love of country has been its origin, but once begun, the fighting is simply "a horde of vicious madmen who had suddenly become incapable of doing anything else as long as they lived but kill and be slit in half without knowing the reason why." To survive at the front, he and his fellow soldiers delude themselves, "in this suicide business ... you've got to pretend that life's going on as usual: that's the hardest part about it all, that damn lie." Sometimes, just one more hour without death "is miraculous enough." Wounded, Bardamu has leave in Paris during his recovery. He finds a city, a capital, "brain stuffed" on the propaganda of heroism and glory and nationalism, "flag worship" replacing "divine worship." With "no truth left in town," all he could do was "lie, copulate, and die. One wasn't allowed to do anything else."[18]

If not, then seize the moment: Bardamu takes an American woman as his mistress and concocts grandiose accounts of his bravery. One afternoon as they stroll near the Longchamp racecourse in the Bois de Boulogne, they happen on the remnants of a shooting gallery from a carnival long since closed down. Seeing it reminds him with great suddenness that he "had been shot at yesterday and would be shot at tomorrow." Overwrought, he cries out that everyone should scatter and take cover. Perhaps, he thinks, he should embrace insanity, for after all, "when one's in this world, surely the best thing one can do . . . is to get out of it?" He recalls his epiphany staring into the night before combat at dawn: "In this blackness, there was only one thing that was clear to me, which was—and it at least was very clear indeed—that the desire to kill was lurking within it, vast and multiform."[19]

Like Destouches, Bardamu is spared a return to the war by the severity of his wound, and after discharge he seeks refuge in Africa running a supply shop in the bush for the Pordurière Company. At first he considers himself fortunate to escape the "mad international shambles" of Europe, but he rapidly learns that in the colonies, the "whole of the white man's revolting nature is displayed in freedom from all constraints ... his real self as you saw it in war." He throws away his quinine tablets and welcomes malaria "so that the fever should hide life . . . as much as possible." Hallucinating, he imagines he is in America, where he works as an expert flea catcher, sorting them by country of origin and sex. To Bardamu, this delusion is no more absurd than the letter he has received from his mother imploring him to guard his health: "On the guillotine steps she would have scolded me for forgetting my muffler. She never missed a chance of making out that the world is a fine place and that she had done well to conceive me."[20]

Bardamu eventually does go to the United States, where he works in a Ford factory, but he returns to France after deciding—again like Destouches—that he should study medicine. Once a physician, he steps willingly into the darkness by establishing his practice at La Garenne-Rancy, a fictional working-class suburb of Paris. All around him he sees "nothing but the delirium of lies" spawned by the "malignant peace" after the Great War. Depravity, crime, corruption, dirty streets, dirty people, dirty world: "the night had come into her own." He resigns himself to this moral darkness because "that's the way the world goes, spinning in a night of peril and silence." His journey into the night has reached its end: "there was nobody but me ... a quite real Ferdinand who lacked what might make a man greater than his own trivial life, a love for the life of others."[21]

Céline enhanced his reputation with a second novel, *Mort à crédit* (*Death on the Installment Plan*) in 1936, but then he embraced a virulent anti-Semitism displayed in three abominable tracts, *Baga-telles pour un massacre* (*Trifles for a Massacre*) in 1937, *L'Ecole des cadavres* (*The School of Corpses*) in 1938, and *Les Beaux draps* (*The Fine Mess*) in 1941. He was an ardent supporter of the pro-German Vichy government, the "French State," and its principal leaders, Marshal Philippe Pétain and Pierre Laval. For a time, he was Laval's personal physician. After the Allied liberation of France, he escaped retribution by taking refuge first in Germany and then in Denmark. In 1950, the Fourth Republic convicted him in absentia for collaboration but imposed as punishment only the minor sentence of one year in prison and the meaningless designation "national disgrace." As in so many instances of famous collaborators, he received an amnesty and then returned to France in 1951. By his death ten years later, he had regained a measure of celebrity because the Beat Movement adopted him as a progenitor.

Through the vitiated world Céline portrayed, monsters stalked, as in Julien Green's *Léviathan* (*The Dark Journey*), which became a best seller in both France and the United States. For Green was an American born in Paris, his father a banker, his mother the daughter of a Confederate senator elected after Reconstruction to the House of Representatives. They were stern Protestants, and their household was repressive. Born in 1900, Green was the eighth and youngest child. When his mother died in 1914, he waited only two years to assert his independence, converting to Roman Catholicism, volunteering for the American ambulance corps on the Western Front, and when eligible for military service in 1918, accepting a commission in the French army as an artillery officer. After the Armistice, he studied at the University of Virginia and then returned to Paris determined on a literary career writing in French. By the time *The Dark Journey* was published in 1929, he had already written six novels.[22]

The French title—referring to Leviathan, the biblical sea monster destroyed by Yahweh—describes the wickedness of almost every character. The deepest pit of this hell is Mme Georges Lalonde's table d'hôte restaurant in the small town of Lorges, not far from Paris. She is a ponderous widow with a "gloomy and disapproving stare" who retains her all-male clientele by serving up both cheap fare and the young laundress from across the street. An orphan from Brittany, Angèle is eighteen years old and accommodating, available for a fee through Lalonde. They have an arrangement: Angèle keeps the gifts and money these men shower on her, and she reports their gossip and secrets to Lalonde, who thereby has them in her hands, "their little love affairs, their debts, their possessions." Her grip is insidious and tight. The most recent diner is Paul Guéret, a young tutor, unhappily married, who makes the fatal error of falling in love with Angèle. He has the "blighted and bitter look that one so often sees in those whose early years have been a perpetual struggle." His only pupil is André Grosgeorge, son of a wealthy bourgeois couple who casually despise each other and disdain their only child.[23]

Guéret lives with his wife, Marie, in nearby Chanteilles. Their wretched apartment is her workroom, where she sews alterations for a Paris dress shop. She tries to please her husband, but he has long since tired of her. He thinks himself a tortured figure, his youth robbed by disappointment, his marriage nothing but "pangs and recriminations." When he looks at Marie, all he sees is "a peasant girl . . . who wants to dress like a lady, without succeeding." He has "not got the right woman, I mean, solely, the woman whom nature destined for you," as Grosgeorge tells him one day after André's lessons. And neither has Grosgeorge, hence this unexpected familiarity between him and the tutor he regards as a servant. At nearly forty, Eva Grosgeorge is elegant and cold. At sixty, her husband is haughty and lascivious. With the arrogance of fortune and position, he confides in Guéret about Eva: "At the end of a month, she disgusted me, and yet she was beautiful." Then, he boasts of his affair with the girl who delivers the laundry.[24]

Of course, Grosgeorge's mistress is Angèle. She has "yielded to the men, . . . let herself go, from one to another." She knows her reputation, thinks it inevitable when one diner comments, "Angèle is not very austere." Lalonde gives her room and board and expects her compliance in return. When Angèle protests, "I suppose you don't know what they do with me? Where they take me?" Lalonde replies, "I'm not responsible for your behavior." For the first time, Angèle has regrets. She finds Guéret attractive, imagines running away with him, for his words are sweet, his caresses gentle. Does he know the truth about her, "that she had sold herself to others, to many others," and if so, "what would his voice be like then?" Indeed, he does know, "his eyes were opened and he knew she had belonged to everyone," and now "his heart seemed to him too small to hold all the hatred he felt for this one woman." Guéret waits to confront Angèle until he finds her alone along the road and then beats her senseless across the face with a branch. As he runs away, he attacks an old man he fears might be a witness. The old man dies, Angèle is left horribly scarred, and Guéret disappears. The police regard him as the prime suspect, but Angèle refuses to identify him, fearing that he will return to kill her and blaming herself for having enraged him.[25]

Eva Grosgeorge has no doubt that her son's tutor is guilty of this murder and grievous assault. She knows all about her husband and all about Angèle. "She had never lacked money or health, and nature had been generous to her," but she is profoundly unhappy. She detests her older and unfaithful husband who prefers slattern youth to mature grace. She despises their child who is "the living emblem of her servitude, . . . that order of things that had been imposed upon her without her consent." When André fails his lessons, she takes pleasure in beating him and hopes that "some fresh blunder would give her an opportunity for fresh punishment." From the moment she hires Guéret, she feels a kinship, guessing "immediately that they had many grudges and illusions in common" and that like her, years ago, "he probably did not see his mistakes until they were made, and did not know how to profit from them." When she notices him in Lorges a few months after the crimes, recognizing him despite the beard and disguise, she makes no effort to report him to the police and calls out that he should meet her.[26]

A fateful convocation of monsters attends. No longer of value to Lalonde, Angèle hopes that Grosgeorge will give her money to leave Lorges. She finds Eva Grosgeorge instead, who sends her away exulting, "After years of filthy debauch you have a debt to pay, my girl." Guéret is hiding nearby, sees the confrontation, and catches up to Angèle. He does not know about her scars and believes that she has refused to identify him out of love. When he proposes that they flee together, she is astounded—what would he say when he saw her face? Afterward, Guéret knocks on the Grosgeorge door, and Eva admits him. Because desperation whispers madness, she wants to believe that he has returned for her, not Angèle. But soon enough, she senses that she must not "fight over this man with a street-walker." She hides him in a vacant room only to come in later with the news that the police are on their way. He cries out at her, "You have only come here to laugh at my agony. You hate me, but your hatred is nothing compared to the hatred I have for you at this moment." Realizing that no one loves her, that no one can love her, she takes out a small revolver and fires at her abdomen. In agony, she begs for one more murder: "Finish me off. I don't want to live anymore." He refuses even to acknowledge her.[27]

Afterward, Guéret escapes before the police arrive and disappears into the underworld of Paris. Eva Grosgeorge recovers, her attempted suicide explained as shame that Guéret tried to rape her. Lalonde finds a new young girl to entice and keep her diners. The monsters survive—but not their prey, not their victim. Angèle sets out one night to escape Lorges. The weather is cold, and her clothes are not warm, but "some one will be waiting on the high road," maybe Guéret. The milk truck driver finds her alone and nearly frozen the next morning. Mercifully, as she dies, "the world was fading away like an evil dream."[28]

The characters in *The Dark Journey* are irretrievably lost, wallowing in their damnation. They destroy themselves through the suffering they inflict and endure. In their hopeless yet chosen fate, the novel bears the stamp of Green's particular Protestant upbringing. During the 1930s, he burnished his reputation with five more novels but gained even greater recognition for his journals, which recount both the intense struggles of his inner life and the literary world of Paris. After the German victory in 1940, he took refuge in the United States but made clear his passionate devotion to the French cause through almost daily broadcasts over the Voice of America. He returned to France following the Liberation and, in 1971, was elected to the Académie française, its first foreign member. A year later, President Georges Pompidou offered him French citizenship. Green declined, declaring that however much he lived as a Frenchman, he was born an American.

A second best seller in 1929, *David Golder*, introduced another monster, this one the creation of a Russian Jewish émigré, Irène Némirovsky, who was then only twenty-six years old. Némirovsky's father had been a wealthy financier in St. Petersburg, and the family fled the Bolshevik Revolution. Although they found safety in France, where they had spent luxurious holidays before the Great War, the family's financial situation was much reduced. After Némirovsky married a mid-level banker, Michel Epstein (another refugee from Russia), she sought additional income by writing about the milieu of her childhood. *David Golder* was her first novel and won instant acclaim for its portrayal of a ruthless but dying businessman confronting his past. A film version packed movie houses the following year.[29]

Almost every scene is in half-light, threatening the imminent coming of darkness. In an office overlooking the Eiffel Tower, David Golder meets with Simon Marcus, his partner for more than a quarter century in Golmar Petroleum. They discuss the Teisk oil fields concession under development by the Soviet Union in the Caucasus region. Golder reveals his deal with Tübingen Petroleum, a deal that cuts his partner out. Marcus is already strained by earlier losses, but when he pleads, "I'm really desperate for money, David, . . . let me make just a little?" Golder replies, "No!" That night, he receives a telephone call with the news that Marcus has shot himself in a brothel. Golder wonders, "Why kill yourself, at his age, over money like some little nobody?" But the question was already in his head—is death the answer?—because he has been contemplating mortality himself. He is sixty-eight years old, and he has stared in the mirror, seen "his drawn features, . . . the mottled bluish patches on his pale skin, and the two folds sunk into the thick flesh around his mouth like the drooping jowls on an old dog."[30]

After attending Marcus's funeral, Golder boards the night train for Biarritz, where he has a mansion and where his wife and daughter let his money run through their hands like sand through an hourglass. Alone in his sleeping compartment, he has pain in his chest that radiates down his left arm—angina or a heart attack. Death might be approaching, but he growls in defiance, "I have nothing to regret." By morning he is better, though exhausted. Arriving at his palatial house, he finds not only Gloria, his wife, but also Hoyos, her longtime lover; not only Joyce, his daughter, but Prince Alexis, a penniless Balkan royal attracted by her dowry; and finally Fischl, well-known for confidence schemes. Golder is "paying for that lot to eat, drink and get sloshed all night." Hoyos is a compliant gigolo, admitting, "I'd rather die than live to see the day when women stopped paying for me." Fischl has "a comical, vile, and slightly sinister air" and brags, "Austria, Russia, France. . . . I've been in prison in three countries. I hope that's the end of it now." Gloria, her fingers weighed down by diamonds, greets Golder, "Darling, I need some money." Joyce, eighteen years old, wearing too much makeup and too little dress, demands, "I want a Bugatti. I want to go to Spain with . . ." He knows she means Alexis. That night, he takes Joyce with him to the casino and gambles until dawn. At one point, he is down nearly a million francs (c. $700,000 in 2011) but then recoups it all and fifty thousand more ($37,228 in 2011). After handing his winnings to Joyce for the Bugatti, he faints from chest pains.[31]

Days later in his shuttered bedroom, Golder recovers slowly. When Gloria presses him to put the mansion and other property in her name, he angrily recalls her origins: "When I took you in, you were nothing but a penniless, miserable girl, remember? . . . And now, you're Gloria Golder! With gowns, jewels, houses, cars all paid for by me, by me, paid for with my health, with my life!" He has indeed made his plans. As long as he lives, he will provide for her, but at his death, "I've arranged things so that Joyce will get it all. And as for you? Not a penny. Not a cent. Nothing. Absolutely nothing." With a cruel laugh, she replies, "Your daughter! Are you sure about that? . . . Your daughter is not yours at all. She's Hoyos's daughter, you fool!" Golder is heartbroken and covers his face in shame: "To work all his life just to end up empty-handed, alone, and vulnerable." Embracing this fate, he refuses any longer to defend his endangered business empire. His competitors sense this weakness and drive down his shares on the market until he is bankrupt. The Biarritz mansion is sold and the Paris apartment stripped of decoration. Gloria asks him, "Are you satisfied, are you happy now?" "Yes," he tells her, before adding, "Go. I'm asking you to go."[32]

Golder has hidden money away and lives quietly in the dilapidated apartment. Slowly, his heart condition improves. He plays cards each evening with Soifer, an elderly miser who is worth millions of francs but lives in a single furnished room, walks on tiptoe to save shoe leather, and consumes only liquids to avoid buying dentures for his toothless mouth. Months pass, and suddenly Tübingen Petroleum contacts him with the news that the Teisk oil deal can be revived if he will be their representative in negotiations at Moscow. Any hesitations in Golder's mind about accepting disappear when Joyce knocks on his door to announce her plan to wed Fischl—for his fortune. "It's lucky he wants to marry me," she explains. "Otherwise, I would have just had to sleep with him, wouldn't I? Although that might have been better, easier at least, one night with him from time to time . . . but that's not what he wants, you see? The horrible old pig wants to get his money's worth!" She hopes that Golder will save her from this cynical sacrifice, but he erupts, "You're not my daughter. . . . You're Hoyos's daughter. . . . Let *him* protect you." Joyce breaks down completely, sobbing that Gloria will do nothing for her and that he is her last resort. Golder relents, wanting to believe, "Perhaps, after all, she *is* mine, who knows? And anyway, what does it matter, for God's sake, what difference does it make?" He promises to arrange a temporary allowance for her, thinking that once the Teisk deal is done, he will have the money to endow her properly.[33]

At Moscow, the negotiations require a tense eighteen weeks. By their end, Golder's health is ravaged. He heads south, to the Black Sea and a Greek ship that will take him to Constantinople. Overwhelming memories of leaving Russia half a century earlier flood his mind. On board, he meets a young man, hardly more than a boy, who reminds him of himself, bound for Paris, eager to seek his fortune. Golder tells him, "After that, you die, alone, like a dog, the same way you lived." For he is weak, hardly able to breathe, and then collapses to the deck. In extremis, he buys a promise from the young man, delivery of his papers to Tübingen in return for his wallet full of English pounds. As his life ends, Golder sees images flash before his eyes, of

Joyce, of Marcus, of his parents' shop, "lit up, on a dark street, a street from his childhood, a candle set behind an icy window, the night, snow falling," and he hears a voice calling, "David."[34]

So this monster dies at least partially redeemed. A significant reason for the sensation surrounding the publication of *David Golder* was that Némirovsky "did no favors to her own people": almost every character was a Jew, and they were all portrayed without sympathy. In fact, she based Golder and Gloria on her father and mother, merely describing what she had seen of a debased and corrupt society. By 1940, she published eleven more novels and many short stories, some superb, some dashed off simply to collect a royalty check as the Depression pinched hard. Anxious at the threat of war and the poison of anti-Semitism, she and her husband sought French citizenship, which was granted easily to their two daughters, born in France, but not to them because the Soviet Union's refusal to issue birth certificates for refugees snarled the bureaucracy. Desperate for some shield, the family converted to Catholicism and were baptized in February 1939. After the German victory, the Nazis paid no mind to such distinctions when rounding up Jews. Irène Némirovsky and Michel Epstein died in the gas chambers of Auschwitz.[35]

In 1932, three years after *The Dark Journey* and *David Golder* and the same year as *Journey to the End of the Night*, François Mauriac loosed yet more monsters in his *Le Noeud des vipères* (*Vipers' Tangle*). Némirovsky called it "a wonderful book.... the finest thing I've read in a long time"—perhaps because it made the Catholic bourgeoisie of Bordeaux appear as venomous as her Jewish businessmen. At forty-seven, Mauriac was almost a generation older than either Green or Némirovsky and already one of the grand masters of the French literary world. He was a devout Catholic who through his characters explored the effect of sin and anguish in the quest for divine grace, and never more so than in *Vipers' Tangle*, his sixth novel. The following year, he won election to the Académie française because of its influence.[36]

In an upstairs room at Calèse, his manor house deep in the Gironde countryside, a bedridden old man fills the pages of his journal. Like David Golder, Louis is sixty-eight, has a heart condition, and despises the family he has created. His own parents were peasants who saved every franc to make shrewd purchases of land until their wealth swelled from timber and vineyards. They sent him to law school, and their return on this investment was his brilliant career in the chancery courts of nearby Bordeaux. He attracted the attention of a proud bourgeois family, the Fondaudège, who were seeking a match for their daughter, Isabelle. Not yet twenty, a fragile beauty with a dowry of Suez Canal shares, she was irresistible to him. The sweet turned to bitter soon enough, and though they have three children, their marriage foundered on resentments. As a young man, Louis was a drudge who excelled at schoolwork but was awkward, shy, and overly sensitive, especially about his family's humble origins. His success as a barrister only masked these social failings, and he remains "one of Nature's wet blankets." Fleetingly, he believed that Isa, as everyone calls her, truly loved him, but then he discovered that she had briefly been engaged to an unsuitable rogue and that Louis was her parents' solution to this embarrassment. However distinguished he has become, to them he is but an arriviste with money. They are ostentatiously pious, the very definition of "right-thinkers," and deplore his "freethinking ways" when they are the origin of his scorn for religion. Now that he is old, he nurses his indignation: "All through my life I have made sacrifices, and the memory of them has poisoned my mind."[37]

Louis knows that "an old man lives only by virtue of what he possesses," and he possesses a great deal. An only child, he has inherited the farms, woodland, and vineyards from his parents. He has made a fortune at the bar, which he has invested in gilt-edged securities. By law he must pass on his real property to his family, but he plans to deny them the stocks and bonds. His journal will be an autobiographical justification to leave behind. Of Isa, "for thirty years I have been nothing to you but a machine for dealing out thousand-franc notes." Of Hubert and Geneviève, his son and daughter, "I know only too well what of myself I have bequeathed. . . . sharpness of temper, the exorbitant value which they attach to material things, and a certain violence of contempt." He hates them all, and unable to abide their presence anymore, he exiles himself in his room: "I am the owner of millions but am without so much as a glass of cold water to my name." He did love his younger daughter, Marie, but she died of typhus fever as a child. He did love Isa's nephew, Luc, but he died on the Western Front six months before the Armistice. Louis imagines with cruel pleasure the dismay and then the fury his wife and children will experience as they read the journal after his death: "I know my heart—it is a knot of vipers. They have almost squeezed the life out of it."[38]

One evening at Calèse, as if to live down to his expectations, Isa, Hubert, and Geneviève plot against him, weighing the chances of Isa's seeking a separation or of having his sanity questioned. They forget how easily the night air carries sound, and their voices drift up to his window. Louis is vindicated, "It was they who were the monsters, I who was the victim." By the time they finish, he revises his metaphor: "I had compared my heart to a knot of vipers. How wrong I had been! The knot of vipers was outside myself!" He devises a plan not only to cut them off but to do so defying every Fondaudège value. In 1909, he had taken on a rare criminal case, successfully defending a young schoolteacher charged with infanticide. After the trial, he took her as his mistress, and she became pregnant. Fearful of scandal, he moved her to Paris and has provided her and their son, Robert, a yearly allowance. Louis has not seen her since she left Bordeaux more than twenty years ago, has never seen Robert, but he now decides that they should have the securities. He gets up from his bed, takes the train to Paris, and meets them. She has aged badly, "this pale, flabby woman with the faded hair, this caricature of the girl I loved." He is a junior clerk, "a numbskull who . . . has shown himself incapable of passing even the simplest examination." Far worse, Robert is so terrified that the plan will involve him in a crime that he contacts Hubert with the details.[39]

While Louis is in Paris, Isa suffers a stroke and dies before he can return. Her death shakes him badly. He was not at her bedside because he was plotting against his family. This malice revives the accusation that he might be mentally incompetent, but Hubert and Geneviève hardly need to excoriate him. He admits his failure: "There was nothing left for me to do but curl up and turn my face to the wall." He decides to hand over everything to them, keeping only an annuity and Calèse for himself. He confesses, "I have been a monster of solitude and indifference. . . . I thought of my life and saw what it had been." Louis retreats to his room and his journal. Geneviève's daughter, Janine, comes to stay with him and seems to understand his torments. When he dies, Hubert finds the journal, and after reading it is horrified but admits that his father was more human and more complex than his wife or children ever understood. Janine goes further, insisting, "I am not trying to make him out a saint. I agree with you that he was a terrible, even at times a dreadful, man. That doesn't alter the fact that a great light shone upon him during those last days of his life."[40]

Unlike Lalonde, the Grosgeorges, and Guéret, and more so than Golder, Louis finds a modicum of grace, and perhaps a modicum is sufficient to save even a monster. This moral tone persisted throughout Mauriac's career. He condemned Francisco Franco's attack on the Spanish Republic, Benito Mussolini's invasion of Ethiopia, and above all, Adolf Hitler's persecution of German Jews. After France's defeat in 1940, he became an adamant supporter of Charles de Gaulle and the Free French. The following year, through a lapse in Nazi censorship, he published *La Pharisienne* (*The Woman of the Pharisees*), a novel that was widely viewed as an attack on the Vichy government under Pétain. He decried Nazi policies during the Occupation in *Le Cahier noir* (*The Black Notebook*), an extended essay that circulated beginning in 1943 under the pseudonym "Forez," and he insisted that Christians defend the values of their religion. The Germans knew full well that Mauriac was "Forez," and he had to go into hiding. By the time of the Liberation, he was the symbol of the intellectual Resistance. Under the Fourth Republic, he opposed continued French rule in Vietnam and denounced the use of torture in Algeria. He befriended Elie Wiesel, urging him to record his experience of the concentration camps—and thus the origin of *Night*. Almost in passing, Mauriac won the Nobel Prize for Literature in 1952.

If the role of grace and its acceptance are left ambiguous in *Vipers' Tangle*, they are certainly not so in *Journal d'un curé de campagne* (*The Diary of a Country Priest*), the masterpiece of Georges Bernanos. At the outbreak of the Great War, Mauriac was almost thirty years old and was mobilized as a male nurse. His service on the Eastern Front at Salonica was undistinguished. Three years younger, Bernanos wound up in a combat unit and received multiple wounds during the fighting at Verdun and along the Somme River. From his education at the hands of Jesuits he had a profound Catholic faith. From his wartime service he had a profound awareness of death. Their influence led to a fundamental conception: suffering leads to grace, and grace to the courage that endures human suffering. He worked as an insurance inspector to guarantee an income for his large family and wrote at every spare opportunity. When *The Diary of a Country Priest* appeared in 1936, it was his seventh novel.[41]

The curé of Ambricourt is young and inexperienced, his parish in the Pas de Calais near the Belgian border unruly and little observant. He feels unworthy and often unwell. At catechism classes the boys are rowdy and the girls flirtatious. The shopkeepers drive sharp bargains and resist any call for charity. The single aristocratic family remains remote and scornful in their château. Martin, the wizened curé in the neighboring parish of Torcy, makes light of these anxieties and upbraids him: "A true priest is never loved, get that into your head. . . . Try first to be respected and obeyed. What the Church needs is discipline." When the young curé protests that wickedness abides in Ambricourt, he hears in return, "A Christian people doesn't mean a lot of little goody-goodies. The Church has plenty of stamina, and isn't afraid of sin."[42]

This cynical tone offends, for the young curé has a tender conscience. Hoping for advice more spiritual, he seeks out his superior, the Dean of Blangermont, but finds him instead a prelate of supreme opportunism. The shopkeepers, the dean insists, must be coddled, not scolded. He remembers when they were the van of the anticlerical state, "almost entirely guided by an atheist or liberal Press." But now, with the Depression and the Popular Front, "they realize the time for such generous illusions is past, and the social order has no surer prop than our Holy Church." Perhaps these men are "greedy of gain, hard as nails in their dealings with the poor as with each other." But if they "were ever to take it into their heads to follow strict theological precepts on the subject of lawful profit, they would certainly end up in the bankruptcy court."[43]

The curé of Ambricourt finds no consolation when he turns to the local physician, Dr. Maxence Delbende, about the persistent pains in his stomach. Unsure of a diagnosis, Delbende recommends a specialist in Lille, the regional capital, and then turns the consultation into a discussion of religion. He mocks the church for comforting the rich while counseling patience to the poor. And of the poor: "I'll agree that it's the job of old fools like me to feed and clothe and look after them and keep them clean. But since they're really your responsibility I cannot forgive you sending them to us so dirty." Several days later, Delbende is found dead from a shotgun blast to the head. Local officials are quick to declare his death an accident, but the young curé suspects suicide. His fellow priest at Torcy braces him again, explaining that Delbende wanted to believe but could not, and even if he died a suicide, "Maxence . . . was a just man. God judges the just. Do you think I ever bothered my head much about fools, or mere knaves?"[44]

Is the curé of Ambricourt facing a spiritual trial, a test to determine whether his faith is zealous or merely accommodating? He recalls Martin's derision, that priests were once *"rulers. They could hold a whole country together, that sort could—with the mere lift of a chin. . . .* Nowadays the seminaries turn out little choirboys, little ragamuffins who think they're working harder than anybody because they never get anything done."* His dean is worried about him, and he is worried about himself. What is the tenor of his faith? The answer comes in the crucial episode of the novel. A family quarrel explodes within the family of the local count and countess. Their adolescent daughter, Chantal, threatens to run away and create scandal because they plan on sending her to a boarding school in England. Her father has been carrying on with Louise, the governess. Her mother does not care, but Chantal regards him as hers alone. Having heard out Chantal, alternately tearful and defiant, the young curé goes unbidden to the château.[45]

The countess receives him haughtily but then breaks down in hysteria. For so long, she has hidden the truth of the family and now reveals it during a scene of rare melodramatic power. Her second child, a son, died eleven years ago when only eighteen months old. The locket she wears around her neck contains a clipping of his hair. She blames God for his death and refuses any sacrament or even prayer. She resents her husband's frequent infidelity but, always before, he has conducted his affairs outside their walls. With Louise, he has broken the rules and upset Chantal, whose possessive attitude is intolerable. The countess has resolved to fire Louise and exile Chantal. The curé trembles with anger, "the folly of human beings seemed as nothing beside their stubborn malice, the sly help which under the eye of God himself they will give to all the powers of evil, of confusion and death." When he warns her sternly, "God will break you," she counters, "Break me! God's broken me already. What more can he do? He's taken my son. I no longer fear Him." He softens his tone and reaches toward her: "Hell is not to love anymore. As long as we remain in this life we can still deceive ourselves, think that we love by our own will, that we love independently of God. But we're like madmen stretching our hands to clasp the moon reflected in the water." The countess suddenly rips the locket from her neck and casts it into the fireplace, crying out, "Thy Kingdom Come," words she has been unable to utter since her son's death. Later that night, she suffers a heart attack and dies, surely in a state of grace.[46]

The curé of Ambricourt finally goes to Lille for a consultation with the specialist recommended by Delbende. The examination reveals that his stomach pains are from a malignant tumor far advanced. He thinks, "the Dean of Blangermont . . . was quite right to be uneasy about my future capabilities. Only I had no future, and we neither of us knew it." Of course, the future can be left aside because he has made the present matter. Not long after, he suffers a severe internal hemorrhage, and dying, reveals the reply Bernanos offers to a world where monsters roamed, "Does it matter? Grace is everywhere."[47]

This consolation was hard-won after years of internal struggle. As a young man, Bernanos fell under the spell of the Action française and its war against the ideals of the 1789 Revolution. His allegiance was sometimes tepid, more often fervid, as in the vitriolic and anti-Semitic 1931 essay *La Grande Peur des bien-pensants* (The great fear of conformist thinkers). A year later he broke with the Action française for good, but he did not shake himself free from reactionary opinions until the Spanish Civil War, which he witnessed in person on the Balearic island Majorca. His account, *Les Grands cimetières sous la lune* (The great cemeteries in the moonlight), published in 1938, blamed Franco for the atrocities and the hierarchy of the Catholic Church in Spain for failing to protest against them. Later that year came the Munich Conference, with the British and French capitulation before Hitler. "For Bernanos, France had been raped by hooligans as she slept. Munich was the miscarriage that followed." Despairing of the future, he moved his family to South America, where he had limited success running a ranch in Brazil. From this exile, he excoriated Pétain's "French State" and strongly supported de Gaulle's Free French.[48]

Bernanos exalted the courage to bear human suffering. Antoine de Saint-Exupéry exalted the courage to defy peril. Born in 1900, he was too young for the Great War. If the fighting had lasted even a few months longer, he would certainly have volunteered, like Montherlant, to fulfill the destiny of a son from an impoverished noble family reared at elite Jesuit schools. He failed the examination for the naval academy and instead received instruction as a pilot during his required military training in 1921 and 1922. Afterward, everything else was tedious, and he dedicated the rest of his life to flight. When he joined Aéropostale in 1926, the delivery of mail by aircraft was feasible for short distances, but any long-range route was inherently dangerous. Airplanes were still primitive in design, the engines and wings prone to failure under severe weather conditions. Navigation was primarily by maps and ground recognition, sometimes supplemented by radio or light beacon. To fly the airmail required bravery and self-discipline. The risk to life was part of the job and had nothing to do with being recklessly bold. Pilots shared a community of fate. The similarity to trench conditions on the Western Front was inevitable. Here was expiation for missing the Great War. He embraced the mystique of being a long-distance pilot, sangfroid joined to lyrical ideals, a secular religion of which he was "Saint-Ex."

His first routes took him from Toulouse, the headquarters for

Aéropostale, through the Pyrenees Mountains into Spain, then across North Africa, from Casablanca in Morocco to Dakar in Senegal. He became the master of flight across the trackless Sahara Desert. In 1929, he moved to South America, assuming direction of the Aeroposta airline in Argentina, pioneering flights through the Andes Mountains with his compatriot Henri Guillaumet. A year later in Buenos Aires, he met Consuelo Suncin, a beautiful and twice-widowed Salvadoran artist. He flew her above the city in ever more spectacular maneuvers until she agreed to be his wife. As she later recalled, their marriage was tempestuous, filled with "tears, champagne, lies, and infidelities," but it lasted. First in 1929 with *Courrier sud* (*Southern Mail*) and then in 1931 with *Vol de nuit* (*Night Flight*), he began writing about the awe of flight, capturing the danger and the risk and the disdain for fear. Coming back to France, he was a celebrity.[49]

At the end of December 1935, Saint-Exupéry and his navigator, André Prévot, took off in the Paris-to-Saigon air race (*raid*). After about twenty hours aloft, they crashed in the Libyan Desert more than a hundred miles west of Cairo. Both had survived many emergency landings forced by mechanical difficulties, but now they faced perilous conditions. Disoriented, dehydrated, and hallucinating, they wandered four days until by sheer chance a Bedouin caravan saved them. Undaunted, a year later they flew from Paris to Timbuktu in central Mali, some fifty-five hundred miles. Then, in February 1938, they began the New York–to–Tierra del Fuego race but crashed disastrously in Guatemala. Prévot escaped with a broken leg. Saint-Exupéry suffered eight fractures and nearly lost his right hand. By April he was well enough for a return to France. During a long convalescence, he had the leisure to consider the political and economic weakness that led to Munich. Recovery required steadfast courage—for him and for the nation. In this context, he wrote *Terre des hommes* (*Wind, Sand and Stars*).[50]

Saint-Exupéry insists that mankind is endowed with an essential virtue manifested at moments of profound consequence. As proof, he recounts Guillaumet's crash landing in January 1930 halfway down an Andean peak. His fellow pilot has flown the route ninety-two times before, but on this occasion a storm that drops fifteen feet of snow in forty-eight hours forces him down. For five days and four nights, through three mountain passes, he struggles to reach safety. To drive himself forward, he thinks, "If my wife still believes I am alive, she must believe that I am on my feet. The boys all think I am on my feet. They have faith in me." Although exhausted and freezing, he refuses to rest: "What saves a man is to take a step. Then another step. It is always the same step, but you have to take it." He has been given up for dead when a plane spots him and summons a rescue party. Resuscitated, his first words are, "I swear that what I went through, no animal would have gone through." For Saint-Exupéry, this sentence is "the noblest ever spoken, this sentence that defines man's place in the universe."[51]

The collective is heir to the individual. "Men travel side by side for years, each locked up in his own silence or exchanging those words which carry no weight—till danger comes. Then they stand shoulder to shoulder." Together, they discover within themselves resolution and endurance: "Only the unknown frightens men. But once a man has faced the unknown, that terror becomes the known." Duty is expected: "To be a man is, precisely, to be responsible." Evasion is reprehensible: "I once knew a young suicide. . . . I have no notion what literary temptation he had succumbed to when he drew on a pair of white gloves before the shot. But I remember having felt, on learning of this sorry show. . . . So! Behind that attractive face, beneath that skull which should have been a treasure chest, there had been nothing, nothing at all."[52]

When war came in the spring of 1940, Saint-Exupéry flew for the French air force during the disastrous campaign against Germany. France's defeat left him uncertain of his path: he refused to support Pétain's collaboration at Vichy, but he mistrusted de Gaulle. He and Consuelo escaped to the United States, where he wrote *Le Petit Prince* (*The Little Prince*), a book ostensibly for children but so filled with the essence of his wisdom that it is read by millions of all ages and assures his memory. He was also girding his conscience. On 29 November 1942, the *New York Times Magazine* published Saint-Exupéry's "Open Letter to Frenchmen Everywhere," urging a united response against Nazism. In 1943, he joined the Free French air force, first in Algeria and later in Corsica. Four years earlier in *Wind, Sand and Stars*, he had asked, "How does it happen that men are sometimes willing to die?" His answer was that courage requires sacrifice. By any standard but his own, he was too old and too decrepit from his many injuries to be flying combat missions. He flew his quota and demanded more, even though the Liberation of France was now certain. On 31 July 1944, his Lockheed P-38 Lightning went missing over the Mediterranean near Toulon. His body was never found. A week earlier, he had sent these brief lines to Consuelo: "Thank you for being my wife. If I am wounded, I will have someone to take care of me, if I am killed, I will have someone to wait for in eternity, and if I come back, I will have someone to come back to."[53]

CHAPTER 5

Edouard—The Hesitant

In the early morning hours of 7 February 1934, Edouard Daladier capitulated. He was prime minister of France, but a single night of violence broke his nerve and left him unwilling to remain in office. The critical hours began the previous afternoon when he faced a Chamber of Deputies in pandemonium. From the left came cries of "Provocateur!" and from the right, "Dictator!" The Communist deputies stood on their desks singing the "Internationale," while ragged groups in the center and right responded with the "Marseillaise." When some threw punches, the session was temporarily suspended. Eventually, near 10 p.m., Daladier won a vote of confidence, but by then he had far worse to confront. Directly across the Seine in the Place de la Concorde, about four thousand police and a thousand Gardes républicains (gendarmes assigned to security for Paris) struggled to control some fifteen thousand demonstrators who became a mob and their demonstration a riot. On the far side of the square, some set the Ministry of the Marine ablaze. On the near side, the most audacious tried to force their way onto the bridge that led to the Palais Bourbon, where the Chamber met. By midnight, the demonstrators had dispersed, but eighteen were dead and nearly fifteen hundred badly wounded. Accounts of this carnage—and predictions of worse to come—shook Daladier severely. When he proposed declaring a state of emergency and martial law, his advisors warned that the discipline of the army could not be assured. A report that looters had seized weapons from two armories and that menacing figures had knocked at his own home left him staggered. The following day, he resigned before even consulting his cabinet.[1]

The crisis that enveloped Daladier had begun six weeks earlier. Although the Great Depression came late to France, the nation was now tightly in its grip. Writing of turning fifty in 1931, novelist Roger Martin du Gard predicted, "The future appears laden with catastrophic events. Our . . . birthday will doubtless give us a chance to see the beginning of a vast social upheaval in Europe." How sad to be right. Unemployment in early 1931 was only 28,500, but by the end of the year it reached 248,100, and two years later 312,900. Industrial production had declined by 15 percent from 1931, exports by 39 percent, while business bankruptcies soared nearly 80 percent. Confidence in the economy plummeted, and fear of the future led consumers to hoard cash. Among postwar French political leaders, only Raymond Poincaré had a serious comprehension of fiscal policy, and he had retired in 1929 and was soon bedridden. Daladier himself admitted mystification. Hard feelings about the economy led rapidly to hard feelings about politics. Transforming them into rage required a catalyst, which took the form of a financial scandal interwoven with political corruption: the Stavisky affair, which first came to public notice right after Christmas 1933.[2]

Serge Alexandre Stavisky—he dropped his surname when he was in polite company—came to France at the age of fourteen from the Ukraine in 1900 with his father, who practiced dentistry in the Paris slums. By his early twenties, Stavisky was a minor player in the underworld of pimping, gambling, fraud, and petty theft. A brief prison term introduced him to past masters of these arts, and upon release he vowed to aim higher, with more sophisticated deceptions and more sophisticated partners. He became a specialist in pyramid schemes, shrewdly disappearing before their collapse and leaving little trace of his involvement. He used his ill-gotten gains to acquire newspapers, racehorses, nightclubs, an alluring mistress, and "friends" such as journalists, politicians, and police officials—to all of whom he purveyed the delights of the demimonde. Goodwill in high places was necessary, because hanging over Stavisky's head was trial for a charge of fraud dating from 1927. Such goodwill had an effect: by December 1933, this trial had been postponed no less than nineteen times. At that moment, he mishandled his current deception, having audaciously issued 239 million francs ($209 million in 2011) of bonds through the municipal pawnshop at Bayonne. The town's mayor was Joseph Garat, who sat in the Chamber of Deputies as a Radical. So did Albert Dalimier, who wrote letters recommending the purchase of these bonds by French insurance companies, but Dalimier was also minister for the colonies in the cabinet of Camille Chautemps, one of the great worthies of the Radical party, minister many times and prime minister twice. Worse, Chautemps was brother-in-law to Georges Pressard, head of the Paris prosecutorial office, responsible for Stavisky's trial and its postponements.[3]

Georges Clemenceau had been a Radical, but he left the party behind long before he departed the political stage in 1920. Radicals had been the far left when the Third Republic was founded, but the organization in 1905 of various factions to form a single Socialist party and then its split in 1920 to create a Communist party pushed the Radicals into the left center. As such, they became vital elements for the coalition cabinets that were the rule with so many political groupings. The Radicals' mind-set was ambiguous: recalling their origins, their hearts were on the left; aware that their voters were overwhelmingly lower middle class, their wallets were on the right. The exercise of politics requires money, and here lay their great weakness. Parties to the right attracted money from big business and the wealthy; parties to the left commanded union dues; the lesser bourgeoisie were tightfisted by nature and anyway had less to contribute. The Radicals drifted into the corruption that comes easily to political parties frequently in power or sharing it. They were, in a deadly piece of humor, like a radish: "red outside, white inside, and sitting in the middle of the butter-dish."[4]

A disturbing nexus of peculation and politics was already visible in the financial scandals of Marthe Hanau in 1928 and Albert Oustric in 1930, but these had occurred before the French economy collapsed. And they were small-time compared to Stavisky's sweep. Some of his confederates were rounded up quickly and revealed all they knew in hope of leniency. During the first week of January 1934, Paris newspapers published Dalimier's letters recommending the Bayonne bonds and revealed the nearly seven years of trial postponements. To prepare for such a time of calamity, Stavisky had won the favor of the Sûreté générale as their highest-level informant and courted the friendship of Jean Chiappe, once its director and since 1927 prefect of the Paris police. When he fled, he assumed that neither service would want to find him—because of the secrets he could reveal. Instead, on 8 January, Sûreté générale agents tracked him to Chamonix, where he was waiting permission to cross into Switzerland. They returned to Paris with his body and the story that he had committed suicide when they approached his chalet. The truth was that Stavisky did shoot himself but almost certainly would have survived his wound if the agents had not waited more than an hour while he bled to death. On 9 January, some Paris newspapers used the word "suicide," emphasizing the quotation marks. That same day, Chautemps offered up a sacrifice by dismissing Dalimier from the cabinet and then refused all further comment. Instead of dissipating, the storm of abuse intensified. What had begun as just one more scandal was now threatening the stability of the regime. At the end of the month, Chautemps resigned.

Angry demonstrations increasingly clogged Paris, men and sometimes women manifesting their anger at a government that not only could not govern but could not keep its hands out of the till. Hard times and the government's failure to lessen them made the political extremes more attractive, bringing them new and more ardent recruits. With the lessons learned from the Russian Bolshevik Revolution in November 1917 hardly a decade and a half old, the extreme left of French Communists were ever alert for what might be their moment of destiny. Disciplined, hierarchical, they had large numbers of the party faithful to send into the streets. With the lessons learned from the Italian Fascist coup d'état in October 1922 hardly a decade old, the extreme right of French Solidarity (Solidarité française), the Young Patriots (Jeunesses patriotes), and the Hawkers of the King (Camelots du roi) were at least as alert for what might be their own moment of destiny. Ill-disciplined and contentious, they each had a small but boisterous number of followers eager to make trouble. Somewhere between them lay the society of veterans, now become something more, led by the inspirational Colonel Count François de La Rocque de Sévérac. Their name, Fiery Cross (Croix de Feu), came from the medal for heroism, created in 1915, the Croix de Guerre; their symbol was that cross afire and surmounted by a skull. At the end of 1933, their ranks numbered some sixty thousand, men who demanded that government live up to the standard they themselves had set through service during the war. La Rocque and the Fiery Cross wanted a Third Republic more to their liking—Georges Clemenceau's wartime government was their model—not revolution or a coup d'état. They scorned extremism in all its forms, but by marching in the streets to demonstrate how they were fed up with its current leaders, they placed the regime in jeopardy by moral indictment.[5]

The circumstances required leadership to restore public confidence, but valor and virtue are always in short supply. The great men from before the war, during the war, and after the war—Clemenceau, Poincaré, and Aristide Briand—were dead or dying. Right of center, the only possibility was Clemenceau's onetime disciple André Tardieu, prime minister most recently from February to June 1932. Faced with rapid economic deterioration, he imposed budgetary reductions. Conditions only worsened, and his haughty arrogance cost him the respect he deserved for attempting unpopular measures. Among the Radicals untainted by links to Stavisky, the only possibility was Daladier, prime minister most recently from January to October 1933. He too adopted cutting the budget, with a similar lack of success, but his combative stubbornness was more palatable to a nation facing austerity. So Daladier it was. His initial impulse was to form a "national government," running from the moderate right of the Catholic Republican Federation (Fédération républicaine) to the moderate left of the Socialists. But when he made clear his definition of cleaning up the mess, only Radicals were willing to serve in his cabinet. For Daladier's solution had a distinctly partisan tone. He planned a legislative commission that would investigate the "Stavisky affair" but have no power to order searches, seizures, or arrests. Its report could be expected after many months. For the moment, he would demonstrate his resolution by acting against the judicial and police officials whose names were in the headlines, Pressard, Paris public prosecutor; Chiappe, Paris prefect of police; and Georges Thomé, director of the Sûreté générale. Instead, he demonstrated vacillation.

The summit of the French legal system is the Court of Final Appeal (Cour de Cassation). Every magistrate dreamed and schemed of being appointed to its long bench—a chief justice, three presiding justices, and forty-five associate justices. To remove Pressard from the public scrutiny of the prosecutor's office, Daladier proposed promoting him to associate justice on the Court of Final Appeal. For Chiappe, who had run the Paris police for almost seven years, the offer was greater and more distant, appointment as resident-general of Morocco, a position of power and independence—across the Mediterranean. Paris newspapers interpreted these rewards as purchasing silence. The disposition of Thomé excited scorn. Back in December, happily coincident with revelations of scandal, the Comédie Française had staged William Shakespeare's *Coriolanus*, in which a brave soldier is contrasted to contemptuous politicians. Radicals denounced such "fascist propaganda" at the temple of French culture. Because Thomé knew at least as many secrets as anyone else, he could not simply be dismissed and was named to head the "House of Molière" and its troupe of actors. Pressard at least knew the law. What Chiappe and Thomé knew of Morocco and classical drama, respectively, was uncertain.

Certain beyond doubt was the extent of Chiappe's influence. He had headed the Sûreté générale for thirty-three months between July 1924 and April 1927, the longest tenure since the Great War. According to Jean Belin (perhaps its most storied agent), Chiappe manipulated investigations to the benefit of his political friends and exploited reports of private indiscretions for blackmail. Léon Daudet, senior editor of *L'Action française*, denounced the Sûreté générale as an "association of evildoers" (*malfaiteurs*)—perhaps he had been a victim. From its headquarters on the Rue des Saussaies, Chiappe ascended to the Paris Prefecture of Police on the Ile de la Cité, where he ranked second only to the minister of the interior in the hierarchy of ensuring domestic order. He won the favor of the right-thinking and politically right-leaning bourgeoisie by making the streets safer: regulating automobile traffic, curbing open prostitution, and especially, breaking up demonstrations by the Communist party. His police broke up demonstrations by right-wing groups as well, but less brutally. He claimed to know "everyone," meaning anyone influential, and to no one's surprise, photographs of Chiappe with Stavisky were readily available for publication on newspaper front pages. For some combination of these sins, Chiappe had to go—to Morocco. But as the British historian Denis Brogan observed with the practiced cynicism of a witness, "if M. Chiappe was not to be trusted in Paris, he was not to be trusted in Rabat."[6]

On 3 February, when Daladier telephoned the prefecture with the dismissal and offer, Chiappe reacted with fury—eventually, according to Daladier, declaring that he would be "in the street" (*dans la rue*), a threat to lead demonstrations himself. Chiappe claimed his words were "broke and ruined" (*à la rue*). Misunderstanding was possible, for Paris telephones had notoriously bad reception, Chiappe spoke with a thick Corsican accent, and Daladier was overwrought. But supposition must be on Daladier's side, not only because Chiappe was wealthy and his wife wealthier still, but because Chiappe followed up the telephone call with a letter of stunning arrogance, which he released to the press: in leaving the prefecture, he would ask his top subordinates to stay on "no matter how keenly they feel the injustice done to their chief." To replace him, Daladier chose Adrien Bonnefoy-Sibour, prefect of the Seine-et-Oise, whom he did not know well, who had limited experience with the police, but who was a staunch Radical. In a crisis, political reliability is worth little without competence. After demonstrating his timidity on the night of 6 February, Bonnefoy-Sibour would last as Paris prefect merely a matter of weeks.

For 6 February was hard upon France and its beleaguered Republic. On 4 February, in his newspaper *La Liberté* Tardieu denounced the Daladier cabinet as "a coalition of horse-traders" (*cartel des maquignons*). Led by *L'Action française* and *Le Jour*, right-wing papers invited the masses to display their disgust at the regime's "general failure."

An old hand among the Radicals, Louis Malvy, whose experience during the Great War left him with both a past and a memory, warned that the treatment of Chiappe would have dire consequences. With him gone, rumors swirled of plots involving machine guns, artillery, and tanks, about insurrections to impose a dictatorship. Deputies anxiously avoided recognition as they slipped into the Palais Bourbon. By late afternoon, demonstrators filled the Place de la Concorde, some from the various right-wing leagues, more from La Rocque's Fiery Cross. To confront the armed police and the Gardes républicains, a small number of demonstrators concealed pistols in their pockets, some tied razor blades to the end of sticks to use against the horses, while many more gathered stones to throw or made pikes from the iron railings they had taken from around the trees. Tensions grew, amid the marching and the shouting, until at dusk the most rabid demonstrators charged the bridge, though the cordon of police was sufficient to prevent anyone from crossing. Gunfire broke out, with the attackers taking the worst. Whether he gave the order to shoot first or only in reply, Daladier's choice for minister of the interior, Eugène Frot, was responsible for permitting his men to use deadly force. And because he left all the details of maintaining order to Frot, the blame attached to Daladier as well. Smears of blood and the bodies of martyrs inflamed the hard core who mounted further assaults shouting "Killers! Murderers! [*Tueurs! Assassins!*]." Some broke into the Ministry of the Marine and set fires. Others lobbed stones from behind the walls of the Tuileries Garden. Around midnight with both sides exhausted, the police and Gardes républicains finally cleared the square. By then reports about the carnage had spread through Paris and provoked panic.[7]

Learning of the severity only after he had won his vote of confidence, Daladier huddled with Frot around 11 p.m. He issued a statement in which he accused the demonstrators of attempting to overthrow the government (*tentative à main armée contre la sûreté de l'Etat*) and pledged "to assure by all means the security of the population and the independence of the republican regime." Then, because the president of the Republic, Albert Lebrun, was prone to anxiety and even hysteria, Daladier had himself driven to the Elysée Palace to offer reassurances. Lebrun adjured him to "hold fast" (*tenir bon*). Finally, an hour or so later after 1 a.m., he convened a crisis team composed of Roger Genébrier (his personal assistant), Frot, Bonnefoy-Sibour, Eugène Penancier, minister of justice, Pierre Cot, minister for the air force, Charles Donat-Guigue, attorney general for the Paris region, and Jules Pailhe, solicitor general for the Court of Final Appeal. The two critical questions were how to strengthen the security forces and whether ordering preventive arrests might forestall further demonstrations. Frot and Cot called for the suspension of civil liberties through the declaration of a "state of siege" (*état de siège*), which would permit searches and seizures without a warrant, censorship of the press, and dissolution of the leagues. Donat-Guigue reminded them that by law a state of siege could be declared only if Paris was considered "a battleground" (*place de guerre*). Frot then demanded an investigation of the "plot to overthrow the state." Once again, Donat-Guigue rebuffed him, saying with scorn, "It is through imaginary conspiracies and the opening of premature inquiries that justice is discredited. Do not mix justice and politics." On both issues, Daladier sided with the Paris region attorney general against the interior minister under whose authority the demonstrations had become a riot. But Frot was not finished. He insisted that to maintain order, he would need reinforcement from the army—fifteen cavalry squads and even tanks. The new prefect of police, Bonnefoy-Sibour, exclaimed, "Their appearance would aggravate the tension!" Down to his trump card, Frot divulged that armed men had been seen at Daladier's home, where his two sons lay sleeping. At that news, the fortitude of the prime minister vanished.[8]

Shortly, the first newspapers appeared with the headline, "Civil War." Predictions of something similar came from the intelligence service of the French police, the Direction centrale des Renseignements généraux. Expecting the worst, Daladier did not believe himself the man to face it: "If I accepted from the outset the need to shoot men down, then I would not be accomplishing my duty as a republican." He wanted to resign but wanted to hear that he should resign. All morning that counsel was easy to find. Within his cabinet, Cot, Jean Mistler, minister of commerce, and Guy La Chambre, minister of the merchant marine, all of them his friends and like him regarded as "Young Turk" (*Jeune Turc*) Radicals, urged him to quit. So did two of the party's grand old men, Edouard Herriot, once Daladier's mentor, now his rival, and Fernand Bouisson, president of the Chamber. The president of the Senate, Jules Jeanneney, told him to remain at his post, but he had cut his political teeth working for Clemenceau. The only real surprise came from Léon Blum, the intellectual leader of the Socialists, who encouraged him to stay on—but refused to reinforce the cabinet's position by permitting his party to serve within it. By the early afternoon, Daladier returned to the Elysée Palace, some twelve hours since he left it the night before, a yawning chasm in political time. Lebrun had never sought prominence, had never been prime minister, had rarely been a minister. He was merely president of the Senate in May 1932, when a demented White Russian exile assassinated Paul Doumer, the president of the Republic. Given the highly partisan tone of politics, Lebrun's very lack of stature made him an easy choice by the senators and deputies as a compromise successor. Born to a peasant family, educated as an engineer before he entered politics, he was unworldly, diffident, and wept, his hands covering his face, without warning. Terrified by the predictions of uncontrollable violence, he suggested Daladier resign in the interest of his country, to prevent further disorder. The response was immediate.[9]

And the reaction was merciless. On the left, the Communist *L'Humanité* flayed the "regime of slime and blood. In the decomposition of the capitalist society, they parade their disgrace." The Socialist *Le Populaire* warned, "The riot has laid down its conditions, and democracy is dangerously menaced." Within the broad center, the moderately conservative *Le Figaro* decried "the incapacity that binds the Radicals together, the stubbornness of a party that is only a pathetic gang filing out like puppets in a circus: there is the origin and there are the men responsible for the blood that has been shed." On the right, *La Victoire* echoed the slogan heard late on the night of 6 February, "Lynch Daladier! [*Daladier au poteau!*]" and its editor, the pacifist-turned-ultra-nationalist Gustave Hervé, added, "Despite his expression of determination, he reminds me of the pathetic

Louis XVI." La Rocque's Fiery Cross plastered walls with a poster, "He massacred women and unarmed demonstrators!" Writing his memoirs much later, Daladier claimed that when he and La Rocque were together prisoners of the Germans in 1944, La Rocque told him that "the attempted seizure of power" was organized by the right-wing leagues and not by Chiappe. If true, here would be a confirmation of the threat Daladier was convinced existed and a justification for his unseemly haste in resigning. La Rocque died two years later leaving no confirmation of these words. Certainly, his Fiery Cross followers were never implicated in the violence of 6 February, and—at least at that moment—he himself remained a loyal defender of the Third Republic. Daladier's sympathetic biographer, Elisabeth du Réau, who alone has had complete access to Daladier's personal papers and files, emphatically rejects such an excuse: "Historians whether French or not who have studied this major political crisis have almost all refuted the thesis of a conspiracy." Instead, she concludes bluntly, "This abdication of responsibility should be interpreted as a first sign of the weakness in character for which he was later reproached."[10]

The reproaches did not come early. If, taking the heroic view espoused by Clemenceau, life is a series of difficulties to be mastered, Daladier began well indeed. Edouard was born on 18 June 1884 in Carpentras, an ancient town of southeastern France dating from Roman times. His father, Claude Daladier, a baker, had married his employer's daughter, Rose Mouriès, and in time took over the shop. They had two other children, an elder son, Gustave, and a daughter, Marie Madeleine Rose. Everyone in the family worked, and Edouard never forgot helping his father with deliveries—always to the back door at the houses of the well-to-do. Yet the French Revolution's legacy of egalitarianism and its ideal of meritocracy encouraged his ambition. After all, Michel Ney, Napoleon Bonaparte's greatest general, was born the son of a butcher, and Charles Garnier, architect of the Paris Opéra, was born the son of a blacksmith. So the son of a baker dreamed as he won prizes at the primary school the Third Republic made mandatory and free just before his birth, as he thrilled to the plots of Victor Hugo, as he prepared for examinations that could transform his destiny. And just as he imagined, he won a scholarship paying the costs of tuition and boarding to attend one of the elite state secondary schools. In the fall of 1896, at the age of twelve, he left Carpentras and his family for Lyon, more than a hundred miles away, and the Lycée Ampère. Almost immediately, he came under the influence of a florid and charismatic teacher, Edouard Herriot, who only a decade earlier had been a scholarship boy (*boursier*) himself. Here was the beginning of the "Two Edouards," for some two decades an alliance, then a decade and a half more a quarrel. Herriot taught Daladier history and politics—Radical party style. Daladier was a ready student, fascinated by the controversy of the Dreyfus affair, which had a special resonance in Carpentras, home since 1367 to France's oldest synagogue. In 1904, after eight years of courses in philosophy, history, and languages, Daladier attempted the competitive examination (*concours*) for admission to the Ecole normale supérieure in Paris, the summit of French liberal arts, but he failed because of weaknesses in Greek and Latin.

Rather than try again a year later, Daladier decided to remain at Lyon and continue his studies under Herriot's direction. In 1907 he completed the teaching diploma (*licence*) in history and geography and in 1909 passed the difficult comprehensive examination (*agrégation*) to qualify for lycée positions. Although his mother had died only days earlier, he won a special mention for the poise he exhibited during the oral segment. Daladier's first assignments were at Nîmes and Grenoble, conveniently within his own region because politics was trumping history in his life. With encouragement from Herriot and from the younger members of the Radical party in Carpentras, he ran for mayor in 1911 and won. He was only twenty-seven, and his sights were set on reaching Paris—and not as a student. In 1913, the critical national issue was whether to increase the term of required military service from two years to three. Most of the Radical party was opposed, including the deputy representing Carpentras, because the center-right, led by Raymond Poincaré from the presidential palace, was sponsoring it. By breaking ranks and supporting three-year service, Daladier attracted his first national attention. He cited history and national security in declaring that a great nation could never consider "peace at any price," for "slavery would be the worst affliction for France." When August 1914 brought war threatening that very fate, both Daladier brothers, the mayor and the baker, were mobilized at the outset. Their father had died the year before, leaving sister Marie to carry on, and to worry, alone—like so many women from farms and towns everywhere in a France suddenly stripped of men.[11]

Edouard Daladier served four and a half years as a combat infantryman in the trenches of the Western Front. He distinguished himself through his courage as a small-unit leader, winning three commendations, including the Croix de Guerre. His promotion from sergeant to lieutenant on 16 April 1917 cited his sangfroid, his energy, and his bravery. As if charmed, he had only minor injuries until the final German offensive in April and May 1918, when he received a dangerous wound to his left calf. Before 1938 and the threat of a new conflict, he rarely spoke of this frontline service, but the experience indelibly marked his view of national and foreign policy. Firsthand, he had come to know the power of the German war machine and how France had triumphed over it only through alliance with Great Britain and the United States. He sent letters home to his sister—but more often to his "soldier's pen pal" (*marraine de guerre*), Madeleine Laffont, the two forming a strong attachment through their correspondence. Her father was a wealthy Paris physician, and she was serious, lovely, but delicate. They married eight months after the Armistice in July 1919, almost as soon as Daladier was demobilized. For him, she represented the fulfillment of his escape from artisan origins. During his political speeches, he frequently declared that he "arose from the common people," but his choice of words— "Je suis *sorti* du peuple"—implied more a "deliverance."[12]

And those political speeches were not long in coming. November 1919 brought the first legislative elections since the eve of the war in 1914. The heavy favorite to win was a center-right coalition calling itself the National Bloc (Bloc national), which included many veterans. Running for the Chamber of Deputies to represent Carpentras as a Radical, Daladier risked being crushed between the National Bloc and a left energized by the Bolshevik takeover in Russia. But he too had the cachet of heroism under fire. He criticized the National Bloc for "narrowness of view" and the Socialists as "dangerous." Then he added, "I served my country and was wounded. The details are well known, but if I must still convince you, I can do so with more than words"—and showed off the scar on his leg. Already Daladier was adopting the persona for which he would become recognized. He deflected attention from his short stature by walking slowly, almost ponderously, and gesturing with great dignity. This sense of bearing combined with the rugged features of his face to imply solidity. Early on, he adopted dark double-breasted suits to affect a Napoleonic mien, chin tucked down, one hand in his jacket. Experienced as a lecturer from his lycée teaching, he excelled as a political orator, articulate, poised, able to explain complicated issues. He was a native son, a warrior returned, and at thirty-five, a young man of great promise. He won the seat and moved with Madeleine to Paris. In case he might become important, the ministry of education transferred his teaching appointment to the Lycée Condorcet, one of the oldest, founded in 1803, and one of the most prestigious.

The new Chamber of Deputies convened on 8 December 1919. The National Bloc had indeed won the election and commanded a strong majority. When so many of its veterans wore their sky-blue dress uniforms, journalists exclaimed they were viewing the Chamber of the Blue Horizon (*Chambre bleu horizon*). In the handing out of assignments, Daladier got a seat on the foreign affairs committee. His long study of history prepared him well for the analysis of international issues, and he spent many solitary hours in the Chamber's library using classified documents to prepare dossiers about the dramatic alterations of postwar Europe: the Bolshevik Revolution in Russia; the transformation of Austria-Hungary into smaller, and often Slavic, "successor states"; the collapse of the Ottoman Empire; and above all, the strictures placed on Germany by the Versailles Treaty. On 25 June 1920, after sitting silent for six months, Daladier offered an opinion before the Chamber of Deputies: "If France wants to maintain its freedom of action in Europe, if France wants to avoid becoming the brilliant second of some other power, France must be able to count on the Slavic world." When voices from the right accused him of being pro-Bolshevik, he responded quickly: "I am neither Bolshevik nor pro-Bolshevik. I do not favor dictatorship of the proletariat. I remain faithful to the spirit of the French Revolution, which was the first in the world to proclaim the principle of national sovereignty exercised by universal suffrage. But opinions aside, we must take account of events, and we must face up to realities."[13]

To alliances and alignments, Daladier now added a new preoccupation—military planning. He had first been drawn to it before the war by a controversial book, *L'Armée nouvelle* (The new army) by Jean Jaurès, leader of the Socialists, who argued for replacing France's traditional military establishment with a "nation in arms." Daladier had rejected this appeal for "citizen militias" as ludicrous, and confronting the highly trained German forces confirmed this judgment. But in the aftermath of the war's slaughter, in the hope for peace, and above all, in the absence of young Frenchmen, what kind of army, what size professional cadres, and what length of conscript service made sense? When the Chamber undertook that debate in March 1922, Daladier argued for minima: "The army in time of peace has for its exclusive task assuring the training of recruits and the security of mobilization." The Radical party adopted his position and, increasingly, adopted him as its bright new hope.[14]

The 1902 legislative elections marked the moment when Radicals became the dominant political party of the Third Republic. Left of the moderate conservatives and right of the Socialists, they were part of every cabinet including the "Sacred Union" national government created in August 1914 to confront the German invasion. The war and its consequences then deeply eroded the Radical position. Clemenceau was a Radical in name only, and the "defeatists" he arrested, above all Louis Malvy and Joseph Caillaux, were leaders of the party. The Socialists, who had been reliable election partners, broke apart in December 1920, an exultant majority calling themselves Communists and accepting direction from Moscow, a sour minority retaining the name Socialist and still lamenting the loss of Jaurès, assassinated by a right-wing fanatic on 31 July 1914, the day before Germany declared war. Assailed from the right as insufficiently nationalist and from the left as insufficiently internationalist, the Radicals were alone in the center when France was voting for the extremes—as the 1919 elections proved. To mount a comeback, they chose a new president, Edouard Herriot, lycée teacher turned politician. He naturally looked to his protégé Daladier as part of the recovery team. The National Bloc was riding high and was unpleasantly dismissive of overtures. The only alternative was to look left, and in late September 1922, both Edouards departed for the Soviet Union to see for themselves what Communists called the "Worker's Paradise."

Their moment was not propitious. Five months earlier, in April, while ostensibly discussing postwar economic recovery efforts with Great Britain and France at a conference in Genoa, German and Soviet representatives stole away to nearby Rapallo where they signed (openly) a bilateral trade agreement and (secretly) a memorandum by which the Soviet Union agreed to hide German weaponry outlawed by the Versailles Treaty. Here was grist for the mill of Poincaré, president of the Republic during the war and now prime minister, who regarded the Bolsheviks as duplicitous barbarians—for the separate peace they concluded with Germany in February 1918, which almost cost France the war; for their cold-blooded murder of Tsar Nicholas II and his family; and for their renunciation of bonds issued under Imperial Russia, which despoiled French investors of nearly 26 billion francs ($54.3 billion in 2011): 14 billion ($29.3 billion in 2011) in government obligations and 12 billion ($25 billion in 2011) in commercial. Poincaré refused any contact with the Bolsheviks, either official or unofficial, and preferred to believe their regime would be overthrown. Herriot thought negotiations might succeed, but Lenin was still recovering from a stroke suffered in May. He sent one of his lieutenants, Kamenev, who defended the Rapallo pact as a necessity for the Soviet Union to escape from its isolation and suggested France would do well to accept the Soviet regime without preconditions. A later meeting with Trotsky, Lenin's heir apparent, went no better.[15]

Upon their return, Herriot rapidly turned out a book that appeared before the end of the year, *La Russie nouvelle* (The new Russia), optimistically predicting—or at least, hoping—that the Soviet Union would be a revitalized Russia fundamentally different than when ruled by the tsars. Not many years later, he recognized that

Soviet Russia was different, but in a horrific way. Daladier's reaction came in a series of articles for the newspaper *Le Journal*, which read as if he were preparing a lecture on foreign policy: "The new [European] order, founded by the treaties, is still precarious; the uncertain peace must be reinforced. Is it possible to do so in neglecting the interests of Russia? To ignore the existence of 130 million people or to erect ramparts against them . . . is to aggravate existing conflicts and to prepare new ones. The laws of geography and history impose themselves on peoples no matter what their regime. . . . [Russia's leaders] are above all men of government, and no longer believing in the possibility of world revolution, they are thinking of alliances. Should we be indifferent about whether they look to Berlin or to Paris?"[16]

The trip by Herriot and Daladier to the Soviet Union provoked far less controversy in France than expected because, by the time they returned in late fall 1922, Poincaré was maneuvering for a showdown over reparations—meaning, their nonpayment. In April 1921, a commission established by the Treaty of Versailles had set 132 billion gold marks ($785 billion in 2011) as the amount owed by Germany to Great Britain, France, and Belgium for the damages of the war. From the outset, German leaders refused to pay the installments or paid only in part. Because the United States did not ratify the treaty, it made no effort to compel German compliance. Because Germany was a critical trade partner and reparation payments would hinder its economic recovery, and thus purchasing power, Great Britain limited its pressure. But France had every reason to want Germany hobbled and, owed 52 percent of the total, desperately needed reparations to restore its northern regions left devastated by the fighting. In December 1922, with Germany in default yet again, Poincaré announced his intention to occupy its heavily industrialized Ruhr Valley until the account was paid in full. Belgium and Italy sent supporting troops, but Great Britain, while not opposing France's decision, refused to participate. Shocked that its bluff had been called, Germany did everything possible to frustrate the Ruhr occupation, above all sending the mark into a hyperinflation that threatened calamity for the entire European economy. Most dangerous for Poincaré, the franc came under pressure on world currency markets, losing value against the pound and the dollar, when French imports were high and exports low because the rebuilding of vital industries remained incomplete. The only solution he found to shore up state finances was a highly unpopular 20 percent surcharge (*double décime*) on all taxes.[17]

Smelling political blood, the Radicals saw their chance in the legislative elections set for May 1924. They had opposed the Ruhr occupation as a dangerous gamble that threatened to alienate Great Britain, and they now claimed vindication. To prepare for the voting, Herriot commissioned the party's bright young men, especially Daladier, Emile Roche, Jean Montigny, and Jacques Kayser, to draw up an electoral program. They called themselves the "Young Turks," men defined by their war memories and thus the "generation of combat" (*génération de feu*). Although they wrote vaguely of "new solidarities at the heart of French society" in a manifesto called *Politique républicaine* (Republican politics), their principal contribution was to urge a strategic alliance with the Socialists. This Coalition of the Left (Cartel des Gauches) had little binding it together other than opposition to the National Bloc, but that knot was enough to win control of the Chamber. Of course, the coalition then began to unravel. Despite entreaties led by the Young Turks, the Socialists refused any seats in the cabinet itself, leaving Herriot to construct it entirely from among the Radicals, with Daladier becoming minister for the colonies.

The real action surrounded the budget. Since the Armistice, French financial policy had been borrowing to pay for reconstruction while awaiting reparations, an attitude summed up by the phrase "the Germans will pay." By the summer of 1924, France had withdrawn from the Ruhr, and the Dawes Plan, an American proposal for financial stabilization, was in effect, significantly lowering reparation installments in return for Germany's promise to cooperate. What, then, was the collateral for the billions of francs in bonds? Etienne Clémentel, the minister for finance, favored maintaining the new taxes Poincaré imposed—leaving him with the blame—while extending bond maturities and reducing their interest rates. Vincent Auriol, a Socialist and chairman of the Chamber's finance committee, demanded more, a levy on capital that the middle and upper classes denounced as Bolshevism come to France. Terrified by either alternative, investors went on strike, refusing to roll over their short-term bonds. The Bank of France, which since 1802 had the responsibility to regulate the amount of currency in circulation, adamantly refused to advance funds. After less than a year as premier, Herriot resigned in utter frustration. Despite his training as a historian, he had not the slightest comprehension of economic issues and threw up his hands in frustration when asked about them. During the next fifteen months, other Radicals sought to restore confidence, with limited success. The reassurance about financial policy that the bondholders required came only with the formation of a national government under Poincaré in July 1926.[18]

For Daladier, the exhilaration of winning the 1924 elections was followed by the disappointment of governing. His reward was charge of the colonies, hardly one of the power positions in the cabinet. Herriot had suddenly recognized him as a rival for control of the Radical party and preferred that he deal with hygiene or public order in Madagascar rather than critical national issues. Daladier fared only a little better in the succeeding Radical cabinets. For a month in the fall of 1925, he was minister of war and then, for nearly five months, minister of education. As a legacy from his days as an academic, Daladier rejected the convivial style adopted by most administrators and instead closeted himself alone in his office to work through the documents by himself. His habit of preparing massive dossiers became a compulsion, which he imposed on his assistants. When briefed, he took his own notes, interrogated at length, and was brutally critical when he suspected lack of preparation. Yet he could be disarming with a quiet humor. When Herriot resigned in April 1925, Daladier told one journalist that he was perfectly content: "Me, I'm not upset. My wife, my son, my pipe—that's what I call luxury." Madeleine had given birth to Jean in March 1922 and was pregnant again with Pierre, who would be born that August. Then tragedy: her health had always been fragile, and she was diagnosed with tuberculosis, still the most common cause of death in the Western world. She had to enter a sanatorium, and the two boys had to be kept under special watch for fear that they might have contracted the disease. Daladier's family was gone.[19]

When Poincaré returned as prime minister on 23 July 1926, he was less than a month short of his sixty-sixth birthday. Neither he nor the franc had any time to lose, and he quickly demonstrated a seriousness of purpose. His national union cabinet included the last remaining heroes from the war years, Briand and Louis Barthou, and it ran from the moderate right (Tardieu and Louis Marin, leader of the Republican Federation) to the moderate left (Herriot, Albert Sarraut, Henri Queuille, and Léon Perrier, all Radicals). A legislature terrified of a financial collapse like that of Germany's in 1923 hastened to do his bidding. He raised taxes, collected them more effectively, and imposed economies throughout the budget. He benefited from more willing German reparation payments under the Dawes Plan and the increasing income from industries now at full production after reconstruction. Most of all, his undoubted financial rectitude impressed investors—as they returned to the bond market, the franc stabilized. On 24 June 1928, after nearly two years of this rigor, he set its official rate at one-fifth the prewar value. He had saved something, almost certainly more than anyone else could have, but the "Poincaré franc" was symbolic of how severely the war and its aftermath had devastated France.

Nothing breeds resentment like success, in this case among some Radicals acutely conscious of their own failure. When Poincaré presented his cabinet, 50 of the 140 Radicals voting abstained despite the presence of four colleagues, including the party president, on the ministerial bench. Daladier led this rogue element. Did he truly reject Poincaré as the financial savior? Had he concluded that Herriot was blocking his rightful ascension? Was he in furious negation over the loss of his family? Or from naked political ambition could he bid to seize control of the Radical party himself? The new generation once called the Young Turks were a growing number and now took the name "Young Radicals" (*Jeunes radicaux*). Roche, Kayser, and Montigny remained principal figures, reinforced by Cot, Bertrand de Jouvenel, Gaston Bergery, and Pierre Mendès-France—with all of them acknowledging Daladier as the dominant figure. They attacked the Radicals serving in Poincaré's cabinet as "opportunists," pronouncing the word with the same opprobrium adopted by Clemenceau against

Jules Ferry in the 1880s. At the party's annual congress in November 1927, the principal issue was a proposal by Henry Franklin-Bouillon, a survivor of the war years, to shift the Radicals rightward by having them join with Tardieu in a "republican union" against the threat of collectivism, whether communist or socialist. Arguing instead for an alliance with the Socialists to block communism, Daladier rallied a majority against Franklin-Bouillon and then, in a surprise outcome, rode it to the party presidency. Which of the Edouards was now in charge?

The answer was in doubt for another year, but at the November 1928 party congress, Daladier and the Young Radicals narrowly passed a resolution requiring Herriot, Sarraut, Queuille, and Perrier to quit the national union cabinet or face expulsion. The effect of this *coup d'Angers* (shock from Angers), so-called from the town where the congress met, forced Poincaré to seek a majority further right and removed the Radical party from any governmental role. With Poincaré regarded by a great many in France as a national hero who had rescued the franc, such a maneuver appeared to make no sense unless the Young Radicals were indeed contemplating a revival of the longtime Radical slogan "no enemies to the left" (*pas d'ennemis à gauche*). Increasingly, journalists described Daladier as "the Bull of Vaucluse," the solid, sturdy, sometimes glowering appearance combined with a new audacity for charging into combat. The moderate conservatives at *Le Figaro* now saw him as a threat to be reviled: "his forehead low, hidden by hair, the chin of a boxer who proposes a fight but never accepts, his mouth hard, his eyes without sparkle, the fists of a knacker. . . . His genius is hatred, and he will not hesitate to throw the [Radical] party into the arms of revolutionaries if it would win him an election."[20]

The test of Daladier's strategy came during the fall of 1929. Ill health forced Poincaré's retirement in July. He was succeeded by Briand who, at sixty-seven, was only a year and a half younger. Before and during the war, Briand had been the great conciliator and since the Armistice had become the "Apostle of Peace." Negotiating the Locarno Pact in 1925, by which Germany accepted the borders in Western Europe as settled, won him the Nobel Peace Prize. He had a superb talent for ringing aspirations, and his speech welcoming Germany's entrance into the League of Nations was transcendent: "No more wars! No more brutal and bloody solutions to our differences. . . . Away with the rifles, the machine guns, the cannons! Make place for conciliation, for arbitration, for peace!" Almost exactly three years later, in 1929, he proposed a kind of European unity: "Among peoples so geographically grouped together there should be a 'federal linkage' [*lien fédéral*], granting them the right of contact and discussion, of acting in common and establishing solidarity, permitting them to confront together grave circumstances." Such a linkage might have lessened the beggar-my-neighbor tactics employed by all the European nations when the Great Depression descended upon the Western world, triggered by the New York stock market crash on 24 October. Briand realized he had nothing left but oratory and resigned to clear the way for a younger man with more energy. That definition eliminated all but two candidates, Tardieu from the moderate right and Daladier from the moderate left, and each hastened to organize supporters.[21]

To secure his position with the left and its embrace of Briand's internationalism, Daladier declared, "Europe must move toward federation. It is not a question of substituting a war of continents for the war of nations but of establishing necessary harmony." He made clear his embrace of "these vast economic accords leading to the lowering and then the abolition of tariffs." And if the Socialists would join him in forming a cabinet, he offered them four ministries—including the most important, war and finance. He added a pledge, as they desired, to cut military appropriations and to end as soon as possible the occupation of the Rhineland, which the Versailles Treaty had set at fifteen years. Daladier's counterpart among them was Marcel Déat, who likewise called for the creation of a united non-communist left. He almost carried his party with the argument that it might never have a better offer to share power. Almost—until the party's leader, Blum, retorted that while power might be shared, leadership could not be. When the Socialists declined, Daladier was lost, and Tardieu had a clear field.[22]

The rejection was a public humiliation. With his authority severely shaken, he ceded leadership of the Radicals back to Herriot in June 1930. But even as he appeared to slip backward, no other

French political leader was stepping much forward. After boasting in 1929 and 1930 that France would escape the worst of the Great Depression, Tardieu had no answers when its effects took hold in 1931. Neither did the onetime-Socialist-turned-centrist Pierre Laval. Elections turn on the economy, and the moderate conservatives who had ridden Poincaré's success to victory in 1928 rode Tardieu's and Laval's failure to defeat in 1932. For the first time since the mid-1920s, the Chamber of Deputies had a majority for the center-left. Leader of the Radicals, Herriot became prime minister again in June 1932, and he made a place for the other Edouard (the protégé who had revolted against his mentor), giving him public works. Daladier had little choice but to swallow his indignation. He had, besides, the personal grief of watching Madeleine slide ever further into the clutches of her disease until she died that autumn. Did he have the fortitude necessary for a recovery?

Clearly so, for at the end of the year, Daladier emerged from the ordeal of solitude freshly determined. With his sister, Marie, who came to Paris and kept house for him and the two boys (now returned to his care), he remade his family. With Joseph Paul-Boncour, an "independent socialist" who broke from the party in 1931, angry at Blum's antimilitarism and refusal to countenance serving in a Radical cabinet, Daladier remade his political career. Herriot had resigned in mid-December, diminished like Tardieu and Laval before him by his futility in the face of economic crisis. The obvious candidates for prime minister were running low, and because Paul-Boncour had a reputation for initiative, he became the next contender to enter the ring against France's ills. He respected Daladier's having sought the Socialist alliance, knew of his longtime interest in military planning, admired his war record, and so gave him the ministry of war. Profoundly appreciative, Daladier immersed himself in the files. His attention focused immediately on a series of blunt assessments from earlier in 1932 by General Maxime Weygand, army chief of staff and vice president of the supreme war council (Conseil supérieur de la guerre). Weygand warned in May, "The army has descended to the lowest level permitting the security of France in the current state of Europe"; in June, "Germany will seek to surprise our defenses through a sudden ground attack combined with aerial bombardments to weaken our morale and hinder our mobilization"; in December, "Even in the defensive, especially in the defensive, an army having neither the will nor the ability to maneuver is condemned to defeat; thus, in addition to its fortresses, the French system of defense must include large maneuver units." Daladier's principal military advisor, General Victor Bourret, called Weygand an alarmist and added in a report on 23 January 1933, "The axiom that a country must have the army of its policies must be completed by another, that a country must have the policies of its means." Seven days later, Adolf Hitler became chancellor of Germany.[23]

Almost simultaneously, Paul-Boncour resigned, having rapidly run out of initiatives. In essence by default, Daladier had a new chance to become prime minister. Once again, he offered to share power with the Socialists, and once again, negotiations broke down, this time with an added demand of cutting the military budget (Auriol, Blum's lieutenant, dismissed the news about Hitler). The best Daladier could get was a promise of their votes in the Chamber. He retained the war ministry for himself, gave Paul-Boncour the foreign ministry, and filled the rest with a combination of young (Cot) and seasoned (Sarraut, Chautemps, Queuille, Georges Bonnet) Radicals. Herriot was notably absent. The result was jury-rigged but good enough to win a majority on 1 February 1933: Daladier was prime minister at last. If the critical issue remained the economy, the problem of how to confront the potential threat from Germany added a confounding element. French economic theory argued for budgetary decreases to fight a depression, but the military loudly demanded budgetary increases to pay for expansion and rearmament. Dissatisfied after meeting with Daladier in mid-February, and alarmed by Paul-Boncour's trust in the League of Nations to preserve peace, Weygand complained to President Lebrun. The military's intelligence service (Deuxième Bureau) supported Weygand: "In brief, Germany will seek to regain its position of first place among the military powers of Europe." That admonition, the spur from Weygand, and the ascension of Hitler, all convinced Daladier that, whatever the political and economic costs, rearming could not be delayed. Indeed, General Maurice Gamelin, inspector general and second in command to Weygand, predicted this conversion, telling his fellow generals that this prime minister "loves the army profoundly while comprehending the issues of our profession quickly." The budget voted in April appropriated 400 million francs ($350 million in 2011) for artillery and 600 million francs ($525 million in 2011) for aircraft—virtually everything the military requested.[24]

For Daladier, carrying a bigger stick meant that he could also afford to speak quietly, in the manner preferred by Paul-Boncour and other internationalists. The World Disarmament Conference had been meeting at Geneva for more than a year, and in early March, Daladier told France's most respected newspaper, *Le Temps*, "For our part, we view arms control as the essential guarantee of peace." The following month, he initiated contacts with both Great Britain and the United States over possible cooperation on security measures, informed by his ambassadors that Prime Minister Ramsay MacDonald and President Franklin Roosevelt were increasingly worried about the power of Nazism. Because apprehension did not yet translate into action for them, however, the only remaining approach was to Germany directly. An opportunity came in August, when Fernand de Brinon, journalist, political hanger-on, and associate of Joachim von Ribbentrop, a foreign policy advisor to Hitler, proposed sounding out his German contacts—unofficially, of course. Brinon returned in September claiming that Hitler wanted nothing but to resolve all differences with France, disavowed absorbing the rump state of Austria (Anschluss), and had not the slightest desire for war with Poland. Anschluss was forbidden by the Versailles Treaty; Poland and France were linked by a treaty of guarantee. Distrusting Brinon, Daladier refused to pursue any separate accommodation with Germany. His instinct was validated when Hitler withdrew Germany from both the conference and from the League of Nations itself on 14 October 1933. Three days later, Daladier told the Chamber of Deputies, "We are neither deaf nor blind: if engagements of the future are to be respected, let us begin with the engagements of the past."[25]

Hanging fire over the cabinet were fiscal and economic decisions that could only divide the Radicals from the Socialists. Bonnet, as minister of finance, proposed that salaries of government workers be reduced by 6 percent. Blum objected, no longer dazzled by promises that sometime in the future—he could rightly complain how much like "opportunism" such talk was—the cabinet might propose reducing the workweek from forty-eight hours to forty and nationalizing the armaments makers. Without the votes of the Socialists, the Daladier cabinet no longer had a majority and resigned on 24 October. Sarraut took over for a month, keeping Daladier at the ministry of war, and then came Chautemps, who did not. The first news about the Stavisky affair broke five weeks later on 30 December. Why was Daladier called upon at the end of January 1934 to clean up the mess? He had not done well, but he had done better. A year earlier, *Le Petit Parisien*, the newspaper catering to the lower middle class whom Daladier so exemplified, wrote of him:

> He is the figure of the modern Jacobin, a man intransigent about the principles and laws that govern modern democracy. Powerfully built, his forehead prominent and heavy, his blue eyes lively, he presents an image of strength, of gravity, of concentrated energy that only increases when this orator speaks, borrowing from the ardor of Provence his fervor and his colorful expressions. Born among the common people, he raised himself up through his solid intelligence. In the midst of political melee, he is a man who has suffered for the last four years and who has sworn to save his country from falling back into upheaval. He excites the criticism of those who see in him only a hard, tough man ready to sacrifice all and anyone for the ideas of his party. They predict the blackest storms! The prime minister wants only the security of his country at a fair price. Is that not the best formula for a Europe unhinged, for a France impoverished?[26]

On 7 February 1934, no one, not even Daladier himself, could credit this image.

As the ultimate Olympian impresario, History sometimes permits a principal performer who has departed the stage a revival to confirm the judgment of his character. Georges Clemenceau returned as the government's goad in *L'Homme enchaîné* and then the redoubtable prime minister who led France to victory over Germany in the Great War. Edouard Daladier returned as the architect of the French army that would collapse under German assault and as the appeaser of Hitler at Munich. Each sought this reprise; perhaps Daladier should not have. Both cultivated a small coterie of faithful acolytes. Both had lost a wife and would find a substitute. Both were Radicals and belonged to the political left, but Clemenceau rejected the Socialists while Daladier coveted their embrace. Both defined themselves: Clemenceau the aggressive Tiger, Daladier the obstinate Bull. Did the contrast derive from their origins: Clemenceau the gentleman, Daladier the parvenu? Or from their character: Clemenceau confident and arrogant, Daladier aspiring but dubious? Clemenceau fought with alacrity; Daladier fought with reluctance.

Indeed, after the riots over the Stavisky affair, some bantered that the Bull of Vaucluse had the horns of a snail and observed that the more Daladier banged his fist on the table, the more likely he was to concede. Of course, Daladier and his allies defended his performance, claiming that he had prevented the overthrow of the Republic. Doing so pushed him and the Young Radicals further in the direction they were already going, toward Blum and the Socialists, who saw a French Mussolini at the head of every right-wing league. They had to stand together because no one else was standing with them. To inspire confidence in the wake of Daladier's resignation under fire, the grizzled veterans of France's political world demanded a national unity government, just as Poincaré had formed during the 1926 fiscal crisis. Gaston Doumergue—prime minister before the war as a centrist Radical, and from 1924 to 1931 president of the Republic—came out of retirement to lead this government and filled the ministries with a hero from the war, Marshal Philippe Pétain; the dying Poincaré's best friend, Barthou; conservatives, Marin and Tardieu; "older" Radicals, Herriot, Sarraut, and Queuille; but no Young Radicals, who were associated with Daladier; no Socialists, who refused to serve with centrists and conservatives; and no Communists, who were beyond the pale in thrall to Moscow.[27]

So unity was much less than national, and Doumergue proved to be much less than Poincaré redux, and unable to restore stability. He ordered investigations into the Stavisky affair and the 6 February riots but pursued them without vigor for fear of what might be found. More important, he had no solution to the continuing deterioration of the economy. The only innovation came from Barthou as minister of foreign affairs: to bind Poland, Czechoslovakia, Romania, Yugoslavia, and perhaps even the Soviet Union as an "iron ring" around Germany. Before Barthou could do more than begin, he was assassinated in October along with King Alexander I of Yugoslavia, and anyway, the Doumergue experiment ended a month later, having done little more than use up nine months. Government by moderate conservatives Pierre-Etienne Flandin and Laval from November 1934 to January 1936 filled another fourteen and proved that no ideas of any sort existed on the right side of the political spectrum. The French economy struggled, while Hitler announced a massive arms buildup for Germany, with his emphasis on an air force that would imperil Great Britain. Shifting government to the center under Sarraut brought worse on 7 March, when the German army entered the demilitarized zone of the Rhineland, the ultimate security guarantee of the Versailles Treaty. The following day, Sarraut declared loudly that he would never permit Strasbourg to be within range of German cannon fire. Two more days later, with the British unwilling to join in a military reply, he decided humiliation was better than acting alone.

Something had to change, and Daladier was far along with his version. He would remake his career—again—through a revitalized "no enemies to the left." Speaking at Beauvais and Orange in March 1935, he called for "defense of liberty" through a dissolution of the right-wing leagues, nationalization of credit as a solution to unemployment, enactment of the forty-hour workweek, and peace through mutual disarmament. On 24 May in the Radical party's newspaper *L'Oeuvre*, he proposed this program as the basis for a united left. The rules were in flux: from Moscow, from Joseph Stalin himself, came new orders for French Communists to seek allies against the spread of fascism. When their leader, Maurice Thorez, announced this position before the Chamber of Deputies on 29 May, he took up the theme of a left united around a program of public works, a forty-hour workweek without reduction in wages, and a levy on capital. During the next six weeks, Daladier, Blum, and Thorez plotted an alliance of the Radicals, Socialists, and Communists for the legislative elections less than a year away in April and May 1936. They announced it as the Popular Front (Front Populaire) on Bastille Day, 14 July 1935, before some three hundred thousand demonstrators at the Place de la Nation in eastern Paris. Herriot, still president of the Radicals, was aghast, insisting that these policies were "entirely unrealizable," threatening financial disorder and endangering national security. But he had served not only in the Doumergue cabinet but in the Flandin and Laval cabinets that followed—and what could they claim as accomplishments? Newly energized, Daladier then spent the next six months winning over the Radicals to the Popular Front. His election as party president in January 1936 demonstrated that, with only failures to choose among, the Radicals would back the leader who had failed less recently.[28]

Daladier saw the Popular Front as his return to power. The partners had agreed that whichever of them won the most seats would name the prime minister, and he wrongly assumed that the Radicals would outpace the Socialists and Communists easily. Instead, the election results in April and May 1936 left the Radicals behind the Socialists, meaning that Blum would become prime minister—the first Socialist and the first Jewish prime minister. Daladier's return to power meant his return to the ministry of war. Loyally, he assured the Radicals that "the program of the Popular Front should not trouble the legitimate interests of any citizen," but they took greater comfort in the decision of the Communists not to seek any cabinet ministries. Herriot maintained a stony silence. In June, a wave of illegal sit-down strikes swept the country, ultimately involving two million workers. Some of the Radicals in the cabinet favored using force to clear the factories, but Blum insisted on negotiating with the voters who had brought him to power. Within a week, the Popular Front majority approved the "Matignon agreements" by which French workers won the right to collective bargaining, wage increases, the forty-hour workweek, and two-week paid vacations. Conservatives warned that communism was next and began a campaign of opprobrium against Blum that quickly descended into anti-Semitism.[29]

Back at the war ministry, back with his dossiers, Daladier had to contemplate the disarray around him. He was not prime minister, and more than anyone else, he had made Blum prime minister by committing the Radicals to the Popular Front. He had campaigned for peace through mutual disarmament, but Germany in June 1936 was vastly more dangerous than Germany in 1934: witness the remilitarization of the Rhineland. He had campaigned for the forty-hour workweek, but Hitler had undertaken a rapid rearmament: how was France to catch up when Germans had a fifty-four-hour workweek? After Weygand's retirement in January 1935, Gamelin succeeded him as army chief of staff. In response to the German threat, both he and his deputy, General Alphonse Georges, urged massive new expenditures to mechanize infantry units and to construct more tanks. For half a decade and especially since his *Vers l'armée de métier* (*The Army of the Future*), Lieutenant-Colonel Charles de Gaulle had been arguing for such changes—to general ridicule and to the detriment of his career. De Gaulle conceived tanks and mechanized units as shock elements able to maneuver rapidly and independently across the battlefield; for Gamelin and Georges, they were merely hardened reinforcements for defensive purposes. Or more succinctly, de Gaulle saw the next war as offensive while Gamelin and Georges saw it as defensive. Although Daladier adopted the position of the army chiefs, the deployment of the new equipment could be altered later. What was vital at the moment was building them. Gamelin's proposal was for 14 billion francs ($12.9 billion in 2011) spread over four years to pay for 1,650 modern tanks by the end of 1937, and 3,200 by the end of 1940. The first problem was convincing Blum and his minister of finance, Auriol, to spend this extraordinary sum. The second was devising a means for the armaments industry to complete the work. Two other Radicals in the cabinet—Chautemps and Cot, both of whom had also revived their political fortunes after Stavisky and the riots—pushed hard for the appropriation, but they and Daladier could do nothing about the forty-hour workweek (which immediately became Blum's sacrosanct achievement) or about a new law in August 1936 that began the nationalization of some armaments works and turned government and industrialists into antagonists.[30]

France's system of alliances was a critical factor in devising a military strategy. What impressed Daladier most in reading reports from the military's intelligence service was the sense of French isolation. Since the construction of the Maginot Line of fortifications in the late 1920s and early 1930s, France's Eastern European allies, Poland and Czechoslovakia, had correctly questioned whether French forces would venture beyond these defensive bastions in any war with Germany. Their apprehensions increased at France's inaction in the face of Hitler's blatant violations of the Versailles Treaty, and the remilitarization of the Rhineland left their confidence in free fall. From the French perspective, German rearmament left Poland and Czechoslovakia qualitatively weaker and thus less able to serve as effective allies. The potential role of Soviet Russia was beyond calculation: the Bolsheviks had betrayed France during the Great War and, outside of Stalin's inner circle, were devouring their political and military elites through purge trials. Italy under Mussolini was laying waste to Abyssinia in the name of imperialism and had reacted to British and French criticism by moving closer to Germany. For France, Great Britain alone was left as a friend, but an ally that refused any security obligations in Eastern Europe and was currently preoccupied above all by an insistence on isolating the civil war in Spain through "nonintervention." Hitler and Mussolini were not so covertly aiding General Francisco Franco's Nationalists. France's Socialists and Communists wanted to help the Spanish Republicans. Blum agreed—but Daladier, with backing from the military leaders and from Alexis Léger, secretary general of the Quai d'Orsay, feared that doing so risked alienating the British. The result was the nonintervention pact signed by France, Great Britain, Germany, and Italy in August 1936. Germany, Italy, and the Soviet Union would then blatantly violate its provisions while Great Britain and France pretended not to notice. Daladier went further, warning urgently, "it would be blind not to see that intervention in Spain would trigger general war and the risk of leaving us alone against Germany and Italy."[31]

Never mind that here was one more capitulation, such blunt talk about war and foreign policy burnished Daladier's reputation as the "realist" within the Popular Front. He looked and sounded tough, a "strong man" (*homme fort*), especially in comparison to Blum and his foreign minister, Yvon Delbos, who looked like the intellectuals they were. Perhaps he could be—perhaps he already was—the Bull of Vaucluse after all. That was the impression, or at least the hope, among the Radicals and even among the moderate conservatives, who knew that no cabinet right of center could find a majority in the current Chamber. The reality for them was that someone from the left had to lead, and Daladier looked like the best bet. Wagering heavily on him was the new light of his life, the Marquise Jeanne de Crussol. Although starting from a higher plane, she was as much an arriviste as Daladier: daughter of a wealthy sardine canner in Brittany, she traded her dowry for marriage into the aristocracy and a title. She left her husband to his rural estates and established a political salon in Paris. Setting her sights on the widowed Daladier, she made him her own, and he could not have been more fortunate. Because she had married well, she provided him with new social connections. Because she had studied political science, economics, and foreign policy, she could be his secret confidante. Because she was discreet but utterly devoted, she became his emotional guide and stay. After its less than promising beginning, the Popular Front was nothing short of Daladier's personal and political resurrection.[32]

Dissenters remained, and their doubts were consistent. Jeanneney, president of the Senate and once an undersecretary to Clemenceau, described Daladier as a man "without a compass, torn among those he has consulted. Here is the origin of his taciturn nature, sometimes timid, sometimes abrupt: he senses the embarrassment of his irresolution." Pertinax (André Géraud), widely regarded as the most perceptive of French journalists covering national security issues, delivered a terrible indictment: "Clemenceau was convex, Daladier concave." And continued, "Of the Bull, he has the strong neck but certainly not the taste for charging at obstacles. . . . He is weak and vacillating." Guy de Girard de Charbonnières, then twenty years old and preparing for the diplomatic service, denounced this "abulia"—

the abnormal inability to make a decision. For Henri de Kérillis, the most independent conservative among the deputies, Daladier's record was "equivocation, hypocrisy, and deceit."[33]

But no critic was surprised when Daladier became prime minister again on 10 April 1938. He was the best of the possibilities because his last failure was now four years ago: trouble then threatened war from within; trouble now threatened war from without. For just over a year, June 1936 to June 1937, Blum had grappled with the critical problems facing France, the lingering economic depression, the rearmament of the military, the rising threat from Germany, and the decay of the alliance system. Giving him credit, he did press for enormous expenditures to rebuild the army—and even more important, the air force. He also withstood the anger of the center and the right for devaluing the Poincaré franc to make French exports more competitive and imports from anywhere else less appealing. His great failure of nerve was retaining the forty-hour workweek, the first achievement of the Popular Front, its symbol of social progress. Inevitably and predictably, the shortened workweek reduced productivity, and thus exports and armaments, so in turn limiting foreign policy and military options. In all, Blum did no worse than his predecessors, but the expectations aroused by the Popular Front made his failure seem worse. Chautemps took over as prime minister—who remembered the allegations about Stavisky now? A second devaluation accomplished little, and disappointment became endemic. Early in 1938, the foreign ministry and military intelligence warned that Hitler was plotting the annexation of Austria. In Great Britain, Anthony Eden resigned as foreign secretary because Neville Chamberlain, the prime minister, rejected standing firm against Germany in the name of collective security. Before the Chamber of Deputies, Flandin, once a prime minister himself, argued for France's "retrenchment" in Eastern Europe. Unwilling to confront this crisis, Chautemps asked that the legislature give him power to impose controls on the economy by decree, well aware that it would refuse, and then resigned on 10 March. Hitler sent his troops into Austria two days later. The despicable display of political cowardice by Chautemps changed nothing. Because Great Britain would not act, neither would France. To make certain that the decks were clear now for a Daladier cabinet, Blum was given one last chance to govern in the spirit of the Popular Front. When he renewed Chautemps's request for decree powers, he guaranteed his defeat. Daladier stood alone in the rubble.[34]

The critical decision for the new cabinet was how to confront the threat from Germany. Having absorbed Austria, Hitler immediately demanded the Sudetenland, the northwestern region of Czechoslovakia where ethnic Germans were 70 percent of the population. When creating Czechoslovakia in 1919 from the ruins of the Habsburg Empire, the Paris Peace Conference had included the Sudetenland to give the new multiethnic (Czech, Slovak, Ruthene, German, Hungarian, Polish) nation a defensible western border. To threaten Germany with potential war on two fronts, France had signed defensive alliances with Czechoslovakia, on 25 January 1924, and with Poland, on 19 February 1921, always assuming that they would be coming to the aid of France. Now, France might have to fight for Czechoslovakia, and France did not want to do so. As Charles de Gaulle once remarked, "Treaties are like roses and young girls—they last while they last." If Daladier planned to uphold French obligations in Eastern Europe, he needed a foreign minister firm and courageous. If he planned to "retrench," he needed a foreign minister supple and equivocating. Of lions, the best choice was Georges Mandel, once cupbearer to Clemenceau. Of weasels, the best choice was Bonnet, cupbearer to Chautemps. In choosing Bonnet, he tipped his hand.

During the five and a half months between the formation of his cabinet in early April and the Munich Conference at the end of September, Daladier and Bonnet pursued a consistent strategy. The best outcome would be for France and Great Britain to form a common front against Hitler and convince him to back down from his demands against Czechoslovakia. Barring such an unlikely outcome, France and Great Britain would pressure Czechoslovakia to make concessions acceptable to Hitler. If Czechoslovakia refused such concessions or Hitler found them unacceptable, France would defend Czechoslovakia if Great Britain agreed to do so as well. If Great Britain refused to do so, France would abandon Czechoslovakia to

Hitler. Put so bluntly, the diplomacy of 1938 becomes immediately comprehensible.

At the end of April, Daladier and Bonnet traveled to London for discussions with their counterparts, Chamberlain and Edward Lord Halifax. They heard a pessimistic assessment: Great Britain had no intention of forming a common front that might risk war; instead, France should pressure Czechoslovakia to make concessions. This rude welcome was followed by pomp, ceremony, and a night at Windsor Castle. Three weeks later when Czechoslovakia placed its forces on alert because it mistakenly suspected a sudden German attack, Halifax made clear that France could count on Great Britain's military support only if Germany attacked France without provocation and definitely not in defense of Czechoslovakia. Adding insult, if France were to fight for Czechoslovakia, Poland refused to promise assistance, and Belgium denied free passage to French troops. When Bonnet did not press the Czechs hard enough on concessions, the summer brought a British initiative, sending Walter Lord Runciman to suggest how Hitler might be satisfied. Even so, when the newly crowned King George VI and Queen Elizabeth made Paris their first foreign travel in mid-July, pageantry combined with fervent evocations of mutual sacrifice during the Great War. Of course, France and Great Britain were celebrating each other and their alliance to defend each other—Czechoslovakia was best forgotten.

Daladier and Bonnet had essentially given direction of France's foreign policy to Great Britain. But what if Daladier had been bold and challenged Chamberlain? Despite all the declarations dating back at least a decade and a half about refusing to act beyond the Rhine, Great Britain simply could not, almost certainly would not, acquiesce in a German defeat of France, because doing so would bring extreme peril. Daladier might well have told Chamberlain that France would look to its own interests, to defend Czechoslovakia or not, confident that Great Britain would have to follow France's lead. Bold and confident he was not. To the American ambassador, William C. Bullitt, Daladier worried that Anschluss had rendered Czechoslovakia's military position untenable, open to German attack from the north, west, and south. Bullitt agreed that France should find some means to escape its "moral commitment." In mid-August when Hitler mobilized his reserves and flaunted the German military with war games, Daladier refused the suggestion of calling up French reservists as a precaution. Two weeks later as Hitler strutted along new defensive works built in the remilitarized Rhineland, Daladier occupied himself with settling a dock strike in Marseille.[35]

Then suddenly, without his deserving it, Daladier got another chance. Hitler's tirades and threats at the Nazi party rally in Nuremberg terrified Chamberlain. Grasping for a counter, he had the British Foreign Office issue an "Authorized Declaration" late on 11 September 1938, explicitly warning that Germany could not attack Czechoslovakia "without fear of intervention by France and even Great Britain." A day and a half later, Mandel argued that Chamberlain's turn meant Hitler could still be stared down, but Daladier adamantly refused to take the logical step of ordering a mobilization. The chance was gone: the British correctly interpreted French inaction as demonstrating an unwillingness to fight. Chamberlain then flew to Germany on 15 September ready to deal. Hitler demanded the ethnically German portion of the Sudetenland but promised it was his last territorial ambition in Europe. When British and French leaders met three days later in London, Chamberlain insisted that Daladier accept Hitler's ultimatum and impose it on Edvard Beneš, the president of Czechoslovakia. After indignantly questioning Chamberlain's presumption, he slowly gave way and agreed. Afterward, with the French delegation, he fumed: "No, I am not proud. The Czechs are our allies, and we have obligations to them. What I have just done betrays them. . . . The truth is that France is in a serious state. I do not know whether you realize it, but that's the case. What can I do if I have no one behind me?" He directed the last line at Bonnet. Yet surely all of them had read the report from the Nuremberg rally by *Le Figaro*'s correspondent, "the Germans have become used to victories without battles." In Paris, Chautemps proved the point by saying, "It is honorable and indispensable to warn Beneš that if he refuses, he cannot count on us." When Beneš resisted, he was told bluntly by the French and British ambassadors in Prague that Czechoslovakia had to acquiesce or face Germany alone.[36]

Even this submission was insufficient, for when Chamberlain flew back to Germany on 22 September, he found that Hitler had raised his terms to include the entire Sudeten region and its immediate occupation by German troops. Angry at this betrayal and now fearful that Hitler threatened general war, Chamberlain returned home. British and French authorities now issued the orders to mobilize reserves and to prepare against air raids. Daladier praised the "sangfroid and resolution that the government expects of the nation." When he brought his delegation to London on 25 September for the second time in a week, he appeared to have imbibed the bitter acceptance shown by the French people during the preceding forty-eight hours. With Gamelin, he promised an offensive by one hundred infantry divisions within five days. And to Ambassador Bullitt, he was equally firm: "Hitler's last memorandum is not only the means for Germany to finish off Czechoslovakia but the expression of his determination to humiliate France and Great Britain. *Better to fight and die than to accept such abasement.* The war risks being long and painful, but whatever the final cost, France will triumph." A day later, on 27 September, the reality of what they were doing set in. That evening, Chamberlain delivered a radio address to the British people deploring, "It seems still more impossible that a quarrel which has already been settled in principle should be the subject of war." In Paris, Flandin, who had called for "retrenchment" from Eastern Europe in February, now had posters printed up proclaiming in bold letters to the French people, "*On Vous Trompe!*" (You are being deceived!). Daladier went on radio himself, insisting: "Negotiations continue. . . . As a veteran of the Great War, I need hardly say that the government over which I preside will neglect not a single possibility to maintain peace with honor."[37]

If "peace with honor" was not a possibility, would "peace" or "honor" matter more? The answer came quickly. Sensing that the democracies desired only a context in which to yield, Hitler had his ally Mussolini propose a conference of Germany, Italy, Great Britain, and France to begin on 29 September at Munich. The exclusion of Czechoslovakia made the outcome certain. Daladier attempted to coordinate strategy with Chamberlain the night before by telephone and at Munich the following morning after both arrived by air, but he was rebuffed. Once the conference began, Hitler's ultimatum of 22 September was the only basis of what were called negotiations. When Chamberlain made no objection, Daladier interjected that rather than participate in this "crime," he would "return to France." When no one else reacted to this threat, he sat listlessly, forgoing any contribution to the discussion. During an adjournment, he brooded, smoked, and drank beer. A final draft of the Munich "Agreement" dismembering Czechoslovakia was ready soon after midnight. Chamberlain and Daladier did not hesitate to sign. France's ambassador to Berlin, André François-Poncet, remarked acidly, "See how France treats the only allies who remained faithful to her."[38]

The following morning, Chamberlain gave an object lesson in betrayal by meeting privately with Hitler to sign a friendship pact that proclaimed, "We regard the agreement signed last night . . . as symbolic of the desire of our two peoples never to go to war with one another again." He deliberately failed to inform Daladier, who would learn of it only after returning to Paris. On that return flight, the French delegation was sullen and miserable, Léger recalled. Daladier was convinced that he would face a hostile reception on landing: he was bringing peace but not honor. Instead, he was mobbed by crowds bearing flowers, waving flags, and cheering "Harrah for Peace!" Before he disappeared into them, he had time to curse between his teeth, "*Les cons!* [God-damned fools!]" Bonnet was waiting with a chauffeured convertible for a ride in glory from Le Bourget airport to Paris. Well aware that "glory" was the last word that could be applied to Munich, Daladier sat hunched over in dejection.[39]

Chamberlain might claim upon his arrival in London that he had won "Peace in Our Time," but Daladier told Bullitt, who had become a confidant, that Munich was a catastrophic "diplomatic defeat" for France and Great Britain. War, he believed, was inescapable. Much had to be done beforehand, above all emergency measures to accelerate the French economy. He had first made the case nearly six weeks earlier in a speech broadcast by national radio on 21 August: "The strength of a nation, the guarantee of its independence, is maintained not only by the might of its armies but as much by the daily exertion in its factories, in all the work sites, by the stability of its currency and the state of its treasury. . . . France must go back to work. No other country in the world lets its industrial plant sit idle one or two days a week. As long as the international situation remains so delicate, a workweek of more than forty hours must be made possible." Now he needed someone presumptuous enough to disdain the symbol of the Popular Front and sufficiently skilled as an economist to implement such a policy. The obvious candidate was Paul Reynaud, a moderate conservative who made no secret of his ambition to attempt it. Although he and Daladier shared a cordial dislike for each other, and though his own titled mistress utterly despised Daladier's, national survival was in question. Given the ministry of finance on 31 October, Reynaud rapidly crafted a program to inspire investor confidence through drastic economies in everything but defense, to pay for rearmament through carefully targeted new taxes, and to increase production through mandatory overtime returning the workweek to forty-eight hours. When he announced its provisions, labor leaders howled that he was preparing a French fascism and announced a general strike for 30 November. Daladier reacted by threatening to dismiss any government and public service workers who were absent and strongly encouraged private employers to do the same. The general strike fizzled; the Bull of Vaucluse had finally charged—against other Frenchmen.[40]

During the next six months, Reynaud's policies raised productivity 14.9 percent while decreasing unemployment 6.4 percent. He had not ended the Depression, but he had made a beginning. Even so, catching up with Germany required more. Using Ambassador Bullitt as an intermediary, Daladier arranged for the talented young economist Jean Monnet's travel to the United States for a clandestine meeting with Roosevelt at Hyde Park. Together, they discussed the possibility of France's acquiring fighter and bomber aircraft from American manufacturers and paying for them through the cession to the United States of some French possessions in the Caribbean. On 28 March 1939, Guy La Chambre, minister for the air force, did place orders with Curtiss, Glenn Martin, and Douglas for more than five hundred planes. He acted too late. Because they were not ready by the outbreak of the war in September, the American Neutrality Act barred their delivery.[41]

In the aftermath of Munich, some around Paris used the French pronunciation of Chamberlain as a deadly pun: *"J'aime Berlin"* (I love Berlin). Daladier alleged that Chamberlain had led him into "an ambush, a trap" (*un traquenard, un piège*), but if so, he was a willing captive because he could have walked out of the conference at any moment. After the shame of abandoning Czechoslovakia, the German-British friendship pact left an especially bitter taste, with Daladier right to exclaim that France's most important security arrangement was in question. Neither he nor Bonnet could contrive any reply other than signing a friendship pact of France's own with Germany, however distasteful doing so might be. Distasteful it was, and disgraceful. The French government made no official statement about the atrocities of *Kristallnacht*, the "night of broken glass," 9–10 November, when Nazis destroyed 7,500 Jewish shops and 267 synagogues, using as their excuse the assassination of a diplomat at the German embassy in Paris by a Jewish refugee from Poland. Hitler insisted on sending Ribbentrop, now his foreign minister, to Paris in early December for the signing and on requiring that "non-Aryans" (meaning Jews) be barred from all the formalities. Quietly, Daladier complied, even though doing so meant excluding two of his cabinet ministers, one of them Mandel.[42]

To recover his dignity, Daladier had a gift from Mussolini in the Italian demand for Nice, Corsica, and Tunisia. Lacking any historical basis, the claims were ludicrous, and Fascist Italy had not the slightest possibility of winning them through military force. When Daladier announced that he would visit Corsica and Tunisia in early January, the Italian press made him all the more a hero by calling the French presence on "Italian Corsica" an "intolerable provocation." Celebrating New Year's Day, he set grandly to sea from Toulon aboard the battle cruiser *Foch*, accompanied by three destroyers. Not quite five years earlier, he had skulked out of the Elysée Palace after resigning at President Lebrun's request. He might well have asked himself what he had accomplished.[43]

CHAPTER 6

August 1939

In 1969, thirty years later, William L. Shirer described Paris during that last summer before World War II in *The Collapse of the Third Republic*. The 1789 Revolution and the storming of the Bastille were celebrating their sesquicentennial. Dressed by Schiaparelli, Maggy Rouff, Lanvin, and Robert Piguet, the women of high society were crazy for dancing, just as in the movie sensation *Toute la ville danse* (The whole town is dancing). The economy was a marvel: strikes and unemployment down, industrial production and the stock market up. Shirer remembered especially the gala soirée at the Polish Embassy in the Hôtel des Princes de Sagan that began on the night of 4 July and ended early the next morning. At its climax, the Polish ambassador, Jules Lukasziewicz, led a dozen dancers in a frenzied mazurka as more than a hundred onlookers, all privileged and powerful, clapped and stamped, the scene illuminated by the flames of Bengal torches. At least two of the guests were immune to the spell of this magic. Paul Reynaud, minister of finance and architect of the economic turnaround, told Pierre Lazareff, editor of *Paris-Soir*, "They are dancing on a volcano. For what is an eruption of Vesuvius compared to the cataclysm that is forming under our very feet?" And Georges Bonnet, the fearful minister of foreign affairs, would write in his memoirs: "This sumptuous fete marked for me the end of an epoch. I returned to the Quai d'Orsay, thinking about the wind of folly which was blowing all these carefree dancers towards a catastrophe without precedent."[1]

August 1939 began outwardly confident and carefree in Paris. Any hangover from the Munich Conference had been dispelled by the economic revival and by the newly confident policies of Prime Minister Edouard Daladier. Yes, at Munich on 30 September 1938, France and Great Britain had chosen "appeasement," permitting Adolf Hitler to despoil Czechoslovakia of its Sudetenland and more—for France, much the greater shame because a treaty of mutual assistance with Czechoslovakia was involved. And yes, both Great Britain, on 30 September, and France, on 6 December 1938, had signed friendship pacts with Germany—again, for France the greater shame because Nazi foreign minister Joachim von Ribbentrop was literally feted in Paris for the occasion. And finally, yes, on 15 March 1939, Hitler indeed violated his promises at Munich by destroying the remnant of Czechoslovakia. But in reaction, Great Britain and France shifted to "resistance," solidifying their alliance as two weeks later, on 31 March, they jointly issued a guarantee to Poland against German aggression and began serious staff talks about possible military steps. The Western democracies were reasserting themselves, recovering their nerve, and seeking to re-create the coalition that defeated Germany during the Great War two decades earlier by adding Russia (now, of course, the Soviet Union), opening those negotiations on 18 April 1939. Of lesser moment, but certainly not of less bravado, the effort by Benito Mussolini's Italy to extort French territory—the chant in the Italian legislature on 30 November 1938 was for "Tunisia! Corsica! Nice!"—had been well and truly rebuffed.

A contentious issue in the historiography of modern France is the degree to which the leaders of the Third Republic effectively confronted the challenges of the 1930s, above all the threat from Nazi Germany. The debate turns especially on the quality of the post-Munich revival. In his magisterial account of these years, *La Décadence, 1932–1939*, Jean-Baptiste Duroselle declared, "The French . . . were more and more attracted [*attiré*], the legend notwithstanding, to resisting Hitler." The conduct of French leaders in the last month before the war provides a measure of whether he was right.[2]

Immediately after the Munich Conference, hero aviator and writer Antoine de Saint-Exupéry captured the ambiguities of the moment in an interview for Lazareff's *Paris-Soir*: "We have chosen to save the peace. But in doing so, we have destroyed friends. . . . We have oscillated from one opinion to the other. When peace was threatened, we saw the shame of war. When war seemed to menace us, we felt the shame of peace." Half a year later in the summer of 1939, Saint-Exupéry elaborated on such experiences of peril in his new book, *Terre des hommes*: "I had found myself in the presence of a truth and had failed to recognize it. . . . I had thought myself lost, had touched the very bottom of despair; and then, when the spirit of renunciation had filled me, I had known peace . . . in such an hour a man feels that he has finally found himself and has become his own friend." This appeal was to the individual conscience. Surgeon-turned-litterateur Georges Duhamel aimed at the national conscience. His extended essay "Europe after the Crisis," published in eight segments by *Le Figaro* during November 1938, warned that, in cowering behind the Maginot Line, France was abandoning the "Descartes Line," that tradition of defending liberty and truth. The question after Munich was where best to defend Duhamel's Descartes Line.[3]

Traditional political division points were worthless as a guide. The Popular Front, which came to power in the 1936 elections claiming it would bar the way to fascism, had splintered into pieces. The Communist deputies stood unanimously against the Munich settlement. Their spokesman, Gabriel Péri, decried a ruling class that had bowed to Hitler and Mussolini. For the next nearly eleven months, the Communists would be the most united and strident voice against Germany. Every other political group was bitterly divided. The leader of the Socialist party, Léon Blum, rejoiced at France's reprieve from "a catastrophe beyond horror" but deplored how "the people of Czechoslovakia had to sacrifice their independence." At the party congress in December 1938, he narrowly won a vote backing a strong national defense. The Radicals, men of the center who had joined the Popular Front in 1936 and been sliding away ever since, were now running the government. Within the cabinet, Georges Bonnet, Camille Chautemps, Anatole de Monzie, Charles Pomaret, and Paul Marchandeau were adamant proponents of appeasement, while Jean Zay, Pierre Cot, and César Campinchi were just as much for resistance. Some leading Radical

deputies and senators like Joseph Caillaux and Jean Mistler were in
Bonnet's camp while others like Edouard Herriot and Joseph Paul-
Boncour were in Zay's. Among conservatives, a few in the center-
right Democratic Alliance (Alliance démocratique) followed Paul
Reynaud in demanding a new policy of firmness while more of them
sided with Pierre-Etienne Flandin, who sent a congratulatory telegram to Hitler after Munich. Further right, both the French Social
party (Parti social français) of Colonel François de la Rocque and
the Republican Federation and the far-right of the monarchist Action française claimed to be anti-German and pro-appeasement, but
Louis Marin, leader of the Republican Federation, warned that the
Munich settlement "confessed to the entire world that France was no
longer the nation of Foch and Clemenceau, of the Marne and of Verdun." The hardest of the hard-liners were lonely independent conservatives Georges Mandel, uncomfortable in the cabinet, and Henri de
Kérillis, who dared to exclaim, "If any one or more, from the Right or
the Left, wants to renounce partisan struggles and unite to remake
France, I am with them."[4]

On 3 October 1938, Daladier told American ambassador William C. Bullitt that Munich was an enormous "diplomatic defeat"
for France and Great Britain. Five days later, to voters in his home
district of Périgueux, foreign minister Bonnet insisted: "France's signature is sacred. Czechoslovakia was not invaded, was it?" Between
these two positions by the men most responsible for France's foreign
policy, where did the French people stand? Based on the first sam-
plings by the French Institute for Public Opinion (Institut français
d'opinion publique), founded in 1938 by Jean Stoetzel, they initially
sided with Bonnet but then moved toward Daladier. A poll taken less
than a month after Munich asked about the decisions made there and
found 57 percent approving, 37 percent disapproving, but 70 percent
agreed with the statement "France and England must henceforth resist any new demand by Hitler." Two factors above all handicap the
interpretation of this result: no comparable measure of sentiment
before Munich exists, and intensity of opinion is not tested. By July
1939, in response to the question of using "force" to defend Poland's
port at Danzig from seizure by Germany, 76 percent were in favor,

only 17 percent opposed. Other polls tracked the expectation of war. In August 1938, 78 percent believed "the Franco-English entente will maintain peace in Europe." Six months later in February 1939, 57 percent were convinced that France would end 1939 without having to cede any colonies. In April 1939, hard after Hitler seized the remainder of Czechoslovakia and Mussolini attacked Albania, only 47 percent thought that 1939 would end without war while 37 percent considered "war inescapable." In the final poll, July 1939, that 37 percent rose to 45 percent, "that we will have war in 1939."[5]

Certainly, Daladier was firmer. At the end of November 1938, he and Reynaud stood down a general strike called in opposition to new rules for the economy that effectively increased the workweek from forty hours—the formerly sacrosanct achievement of the Popular Front—to forty-eight. The futile resistance by labor leaders convinced the middle class that Communists deserved more scorn than fear. Industrial workers deserted the once militant, now ineffectual, General Confederation of Labor, reducing its ranks by almost one-third. Three weeks later, on 19 December 1938, before the Chamber of Deputies, Daladier responded to the Italian provocation of 30 November: the government would never yield "a single inch of French territory." At the beginning of 1939, he led a powerful naval squadron to Corsica and then Tunisia as a riposte to Mussolini. By March, in agreement with Reynaud and General Maurice Gamelin, commander in chief of French military forces, Daladier decided to commit 64.8 billion francs ($39.2 billion in 2011) to the next phase of rearmament. When legislators haggled over the appropriation, he used Hitler's seizure of rump Czechoslovakia to demand decree power for eight months. Shocked by this new brutality, the Chamber of Deputies assented 321 to 264, the Senate 268 to 17. A chastened General Confederation of Labor quickly issued a no-strike pledge based on the urgency of defense preparation. On 27 July 1939, using his power to rule by decree, Daladier prorogued the Chamber and the Senate, thereby eliminating the annoyance of "constitutional" criticism, and postponed national legislative elections from 1940 to 1942.[6]

A month before suspending the legislature, Daladier delivered a sensational speech before the Chamber of Deputies on 28 June, announcing that the Sûreté nationale (the Sûreté générale renamed) had penetrated both Nazi and Soviet espionage networks and was rounding up enemy spies, including some French citizens as well. "We are witnessing in our midst a singular act of propaganda, and it is now established beyond doubt that it emanates from abroad. The goal of these activities is to destroy the unity of France, to drive a wedge into the block of French energy in order to facilitate all kinds of sinister intrigues and maneuvers. . . . We are absolutely convinced that an attempt is being made to imprison France within a new web of intrigue." One prominent catch—certainly the most publicized— was Otto Abetz, a member of the Ribbentrop-*Dienststelle*, the German foreign minister's personal staff.[7]

Understanding Abetz requires starting with Jean Luchaire, a friend of Aristide Briand and Gustav Stresemann. As foreign ministers of France and Germany in the mid-to-late 1920s, they created the so-called Spirit of Locarno that implied Franco-German amity. Both were realistic enough, cynical enough, and old enough—Stresemann died in 1929, Briand in 1932—to doubt its lasting quality, especially after they were gone. Briand subsidized a newspaper edited by Luchaire in Paris, and Stresemann took Luchaire's wife as his mistress. One of the young Germans coming of age during this ruddy glow was Abetz, a Rhinelander from Baden-Württemberg born in 1903, a Francophile from childhood, and an art teacher by training. He formed the Sohlberg Circle to encourage cultural exchanges among German and French youth. Almost inevitably, he encountered Luchaire and married his assistant, Susanne de Bruyker. If Reinhard Heydrich, later to become Hitler's "governor" (*Reichsprotektor*) of Czechoslovakia, was the Ideal Type of "L'Allegro" Nazi, Abetz was the Ideal Type of "Il Penseroso" Nazi: tall, lean, reddish-blond hair, ice-blue eyes, deeply cultured, exquisitely mannered, and fluent in French. Although he joined the Nazi party only in 1937 when he applied to the German foreign service, he was a member of Ribbentrop's circle much earlier. His assignment, for which he was supremely prepared, was to charm his way through French society.[8]

In Paris, Abetz took up with a set of journalists whose pro-German sentiments led them to become pro-Nazi. Luchaire was the point of entry, leading to Paul Ferdonnet, director of the Agence Prima news service; Horace de Carbuccia, editor of *Gringoire*; and above all, Fernand de Brinon, whose interview with Hitler, published in *Le Matin* on 22 November 1933, was the first for any French newspaper. Abetz smoothly transformed his Sohlberg Circle into the France-Germany Committee (Comité France-Allemagne). Its funds, from Nazi coffers, paid for reciprocal visits of French and German war veterans to encourage a sense of camaraderie, paid for visits by French intellectuals to German universities and cultural events, paid for German editions of books by favored French authors, so welcome in such difficult economic times. With a sure sense of how sour times lead to sour feelings, he exploited the fears of communism and socialism among the people with wealth to defend. He warned that the only victor after a war between France and Germany would be the Godless Bolsheviks—and the Jews. Certain social circles embraced Abetz and this kind of thinking. He was welcome at the salons of Countess Hélène de Portes, the mistress of Paul Reynaud, and Odette Bonnet, wife of Georges Bonnet, where the politics were further right than in the cabinet.[9]

What was Abetz, and behind him, Ribbentrop, after? Rumor had it that he influenced the editorials and news coverage of three weeklies, *Gringoire, Candide,* and *Je Suis Partout,* and the daily *L'Action française.* But such ephemeral results could never justify his efforts and expense. The best guess at the real game is blackmail. Allegations—made and denied—held that Bonnet received payoffs in the early 1930s from Serge Alexandre Stavisky, whose illicit financial empire crashed in late 1933. Riots then briefly paralyzed the political process the following February, based on the widespread belief that prominent political figures had colluded with Stavisky before his fall and then covered up their involvement after his suspicious death. No politician of any party ever faced a formal investigation. Was there new evidence of Bonnet's participation? An agent for the Gestapo, Elizabeth Büttner—who had once worked as private secretary to Julius Streicher, editor of the notoriously anti-Semitic *Der Stürmer*—came to Paris in April 1938, just after Daladier named Bonnet his foreign minister. She claimed to be extorting Bonnet with canceled checks to him from Stavisky. Or perhaps the Gestapo was merely bluffing, content to diminish Bonnet through slander.

Abetz was the facilitator, the velvet touch of Nazi hell. By the late 1930s, he had discarded his wife and was escorting Baroness Greta Louise von Einem, who was presumed to be his mistress but was actually another Ribbentrop agent of influence. For his lover, Abetz had taken Luchaire's teenaged daughter, Corrine, who called herself an actress. He appears to have sensed that the Sûreté nationale was closing its net, because in May 1939 he shut down operations of the France-Germany Committee. A month later, at the end of June, he was in Paris for a party given by Carbuccia. After midnight when he returned to his room at the Hôtel d'Iéna, an officer from the Sûreté nationale awaited with an envelope. Abetz was told that he could either take the early plane to Berlin the following morning—a ticket was in the envelope—or be arrested and deported. Whichever his choice, he was no longer welcome in France and would not be permitted to return. Furious but anxious, he woke up the German ambassador, Count Johannes von Welczeck, with a telephone call to ask for instructions and was told to be on the flight. Perhaps Daladier's speech about arresting spies was more a final warning than anything else. Büttner fled Paris on 28 June after reading his words in the evening papers. Von Einem, always a Mata Hari–like figure, disappeared the following night after Carbuccia's party. Abetz's plane to Berlin left soon after dawn on 30 June. The authorities, whether Sûreté nationale or anyone else, did not stand in the way of their leaving. Worthy of note is that Luchaire, Ferdonnet, and Brinon would all be executed after World War II for collaboration with the Germans, and in Brinon's case, for war crimes.

Henri de Kérillis, angry independent conservative, had despised Abetz upon meeting him. Using his newspaper *L'Epoque*, he launched a diatribe against such Nazis and any French who would connive with them. Although safe in Germany, Abetz could not let accusations that he had bribed Parisian journalists go unanswered, and he threatened a suit for libel. Perhaps he had an argument, for Abetz may have merely arranged the transactions, with someone else the paymaster. At any rate, to clear his reputation, he had to return, and

from late July through early August, the German government peti-
tioned to have the designation persona non grata rescinded. When
Daladier and Bonnet received Ambassador Welczeck at the Quai
d'Orsay on 13 August 1939, they had good reason to refuse—without provocation. Thus, the French government claimed "no act of
espionage" by Abetz, but his "presence on French territory was not
desirable, and thus a new entry visa for him could not be provided."[10]

The "Abetz Case" uncovered intriguing fault lines. Beginning in early August, Maurice Pujo, a principal lieutenant of neo-royalist Charles
Maurras, used *L'Action française* to attack not Abetz but Kérillis. Because Kérillis claimed appeasers lacked the "guts" to face down Germany and because he dared praise the "nationalism" of French Communists for their willingness to do so, he had to be condemned as the
"dupe" of Bolsheviks and Jews. His warning that Hitler would destroy
"Judeo-Christian Civilization" meant that he was "Dreyfus de Kérillis," for "You have to be as ignorant as Kérillis not to recognize that
the Jewish contribution to Christian civilization has certainly not been
charity." And regarding his denunciation of Abetz, Kérillis was merely
a windup toy rabbit banging a drum: "Ce lapin mécanique . . . n'a que
des pattes pour jouer du tambour." Of course, Maurras and *L'Action
française* had supported the Munich Agreement, considered the position of the Communists a cynical plot to embroil France in a war
that could benefit only the Soviet Union, and knew well that many of
the French elite who found Abetz so agreeable were supporters of the
monarchist movement. The Communist response came from Lucien
Sampaix in the party newspaper, *L'Humanité*, of which he was the general secretary. Pretending that Kérillis did not exist, he aimed at "class
enemies," that French elite, the "upper crust" (*gratin*), which were, he
insisted, in "close relations with the Nazi spy." Any other explanation
was "simply for show" (*pour la frime*). "Would the traitors, would the
spies be punished?" And "who has protected the spy Otto Abetz?"
When the official government statement was released, *L'Humanité*
claimed that the sole reasons for denying any espionage was to protect
"*le gratin de Paris*."[11]

The Abetz story was played out by mid-August, supplanted by the
news of two deaths. One was already a kind of celebrity, at least to

the wealthy who could afford his creations. Late evening on 11 August, Jean Bugatti died in a fiery crash at the family's rural test road at Duppigheim, in Alsace. He was behind the wheel of a Bugatti Type 57-C tank-bodied racer, which Jean-Pierre Wimille had just driven to first place at the twenty-four hours of Le Mans competition. A man on a bicycle, identified as Joseph Merz and described as intoxicated, pushed his way through the track barrier. Swerving at high speed to avoid him, Bugatti crashed into a tree, the race car breaking in half and bursting into flames. He was thirty years old, the eldest son of automobile pioneer Ettore Bugatti, who established the family's manufacturing plant at nearby Dorlisheim. Together, they built the grandest and fastest touring cars of the day. Ettore was the mechanical genius of supercharged dual-overhead-camshaft in-line eight-cylinder engines mated to four-speed transmissions riding on independent suspension systems. Jean was the designer of luxurious, curvaceous, Art Deco–style coachwork, culminating in the Type 57 "Atalante" model. The brand would not recover after losing him.[12]

The other death, equally unexpected and two days earlier on 9 August, was of a banker, Fritz Mannheimer, director of Mendelssohn & Co.'s Amsterdam branch, hardly known outside financial circles but soon to become a symbol of current fears. That morning he left his office abruptly after concluding a telephone call, boarded the first train for France, traveled to his villa outside Paris at Vaucresson, where his wife awaited, and died soon after arriving. He was forty-eight years old and notoriously in bad health. Two months earlier, on 1 June, when he married Marie Annette Reiss, twenty-seven years younger, two injections from his personal physician were necessary to get him through the ceremony and reception. His best man was Paul Reynaud and the most honored guest, Edouard Daladier.

Born in 1890 to a German Jewish merchant family in Stuttgart, Mannheimer exploited the post–Great War chaos of Weimar Germany and Eastern Europe to make a fortune as a swashbuckling financier with the nickname "King of Flying Capital." Rumors that he worked for the central banks of Austria, Czechoslovakia, Poland, Hungary, Yugoslavia, and Romania were likely false. His twice refusing the presidency of the German Reichsbank was true. He concentrated his efforts on the Mendelssohn & Co. bank in Amsterdam and in 1936 became a citizen of the Netherlands. He was ostentatious: a mansion in Amsterdam, a country villa in the Dutch countryside, and a second villa at Vaucresson, a Rolls-Royce, many young mistresses. He was vulgar—ill-tempered, demanding, grasping, and cruel. He amassed an extraordinary collection of art: tapestries, Meissen porcelain, eighteenth-century furnishings, paintings by Rubens, Watteau, Fragonard, and Chardin. He was the last Jewish banker permitted to conduct business with the Third Reich. At the recommendation of Reynaud, he held the rank of commander in France's Légion d'honneur.[13]

Mannheimer collapsed soon after reaching Vaucresson. His physician, the renowned cardiologist Dr. Joseph Walser, was unable to prevent his losing consciousness later that afternoon and then dying at about 10 p.m. He told *Le Matin* that Mannheimer suffered from severe heart disease and had nearly died two years earlier during a trip to Egypt. He was grossly overweight, smoked cigars constantly, and disregarded all warnings about his health: "It is astonishing that medical science was able to prolong his life this long." No autopsy was performed, and in accordance with Jewish tradition, he was buried the following day.[14]

And then the questions began. Who was this man who had such wealth, such entrée—and were they related? Why had he left Amsterdam almost in flight? What of the anonymous report that he died not from a heart attack but from a gunshot? Was the hurried interment carried out to thwart any investigation? The questions gained greater urgency when Mendelssohn & Co. declared insolvency on 10 August and admitted that Mannheimer had acquired his art collection using "unlimited" bank credit. According to various informed sources, Mannheimer's bankruptcy arose from betting the wrong way on sovereign debt, the bonds issued by various nations. The Amsterdam tribunal took charge and declared a "provisional reprieve . . . for its payment operations." Reynaud's ministry of finance quickly issued a formal statement declaring that Mendelssohn & Co. had participated with other Dutch and Swiss banks in the conversion and consolidation of certain French bonds to lengthen the term and decrease the interest; because those operations were complete, the French government was in no manner affected by the bank's current failure. Legal filings did reveal an institution that was affected and significantly so—the Hague Investment Bank of Amsterdam, widely believed to be the conduit used by Joseph Goebbels to fund propaganda efforts beyond Germany's borders. Could that be a link to Abetz and Ribbentrop?[15]

The accusations came fast from the extremes. From "sudden death" and "bankruptcy," *L'Humanité* had no difficulty "refusing not to see a connection." That connection, its editors concluded, had to involve Reynaud, who was at both Mannheimer's wedding and his funeral. *L'Action française*—always quick to scent corruption among Republicans, even and especially among conservative ones like Reynaud—wondered first at the hasty burial and what it might conceal. When its senior editor, Léon Daudet, who was without peer among French journalists for his invective, took up the story on 18 August, the stakes went higher: "I say that little Paul Reynaud will one day explain before the High Court his subterranean bargains with Mannheimer." Reynaud was, in fact, so short of stature that he walked almost on tiptoe to give the appearance of being taller. On 20 August, Daudet had worse: "Mannheimer is a miserable Jewish crook, born in Germany, naturalized Dutch, who for several months has held in his hands the dishonest minister of our finances, Paul Reynaud. . . . Plutocratic democracy is a regime where either the minister of justice or the minister of finance is at the mercy and under the influence of riffraff financiers." Without warning, he thrust his knife deep into the Third Republican heart: But for decree laws and the proroguing of the legislature, Reynaud could be forced to answer for his actions through a parliamentary question (*interpellation*). Daudet had every right to ask, in a column entitled "The Foundering of Democracy" on 23 August, why Léon Blum and his Socialist party newspaper *Le Populaire* "were silent on the Mendelssohn affair and the case of little Reynaud."[16]

The cover of official communiqués and then official silence stifled what could have become the "Abetz Affair" and the "Mannheimer Affair." Both *L'Humanité* and *L'Action française* complained how a legislature elected but dismissed could offer no check on executive power. Traditional defenders of republican values like the moderate *Le Temps* and the moderate-conservative *Le Figaro* found no difficulty ignoring policies that they would have called "tyranny" if imposed by either Communists or royalists. *L'Humanité* argued that proroguing the legislature arose from Reynaud's fear of "the people's verdict" on his economic policies. Jacques Duclos, secretary of the French Communist party and a deputy, insisted, "the last word rests with universal suffrage." Emile Kahn, secretary general for the League of the Rights of Man and self-proclaimed guardian of the Third Republic, called it "a grave attaint to the regime." *L'Humanité* demanded "respect for the constitution." *L'Action française* claimed "the Chamber no longer exists" and described government under the decree laws as "undisclosed arrests, secret judicial investigations, debates closed to the public—such are the methods employed by the former knights of Justice and Truth." For Daudet, public indifference to the "Daladier coup" was proof that democracy had failed, and if so, why not restore the monarchy? Only a week earlier he had flayed the very legislative process he pretended to vindicate by listing the sins of its leaders: Jean-Louis Malvy, condemned by the High Court for betraying the interests of the nation at war, made president of the Chamber's finance commission; Joseph Caillaux, condemned by the High Court for commerce with the enemy in time of war, made president of the Senate's finance commission; Raoul Péret, minister of justice, implicated in the Oustric banking scandal; René Renoult, minister of justice, Albert Dalimier, minister of the colonies, and Camille Chautemps, minister many times and currently vice premier, all implicated in the Stavisky scandal; Albert Sarraut, minister of the interior, remiss in failing to prevent the assassination of Yugoslavia's King Alexander in October 1934.[17]

With serious discussion of issues blocked, the natural urge was toward farce. During the last few days of May and the first ten days of June, a foppish young man with a sketch pad haunted one second-floor gallery of the Louvre Museum. On 11 June he took advantage of a guard's distraction to take down from the wall the gallery's great treasure, Jean-Antoine Watteau's masterpiece *L'Indifférent* (known in

English as *The Casual Lover*). The painting was small enough to place under his jacket, and he walked out unchallenged. The Louvre offered a reward of 200,000 francs ($121,000 in 2011) for its return, nearly 7 percent of its 3 million francs ($1.8 million in 2011) appraised value. The police had no leads, and for two months the investigation generated not a single suspect.[18]

Then on 14 August, anonymous telephone tips to the authorities and the newspapers generated a frenzy around police headquarters, and pushing through the crowd strode the young fop, proudly bearing *L'Indifférent*. Superintendent Louis Roches, head of the Paris Police Special Brigade, hustled him into the office of Marius Marchat, the examining magistrate assigned to the case. Waiting within were three of the men with the greatest responsibility for preserving France's artistic heritage—Jacques Jaujard, deputy director of national museums; Carle Dreyfus, director of the Louvre; and Charles Sterling, curator of its paintings. After handing them *L'Indifférent* and shaking their hands, the clearly unrepentant thief began to explain himself. His name was Serge Bogousslavsky, called Bog, and he was an artist. He had "spirited away" (*subtilisé*) the painting to restore its "original beauty," which he alleged had been spoiled by inept restoration in 1869 and by the frame, which he thought "unsuitable." Jaujard, Dreyfus, and Sterling turned ashen-faced as Bog described burning the offending frame and then applying "certain retouchings" followed by a glaze made with alcohol. After the experts conducted a brief examination of the canvas and declared it "authentic," Bog was, to his evident surprise, arrested on the charge of grand larceny and taken directly to Santé Prison. Outside, reporters were crowding around Richard Desprès, who had accompanied Bogousslavsky and eagerly sought to be the narrator of this tale. He claimed to be Bog's longtime friend and took credit for urging the return of *L'Indifférent* when he learned, only a week earlier, about its theft. Slyly, he mentioned that Bog had written a memoir about the last three months and that it might be available for publication.

The Special Brigade rapidly established the facts of the case, which diverged significantly from the stories told by Bogousslavsky and Desprès. Bog was twenty-four years old, born in Paris to a naturalized

Russian family that had prospered in the fashion business. His father now disowned him, declared no interest in his fate, and insisted that his son had never studied art. Bog had a wife, Denise Nusillard, also twenty-four, who was a largely unknown comic actress. They were separated, and their two-year-old son, Philippe, lived exclusively with her. Also living with her was Desprès, whose definition of friendship did not preclude seducing Bog's wife after leaving his own. When Nusillard was summoned for a deposition, the press once again had an early alert. She posed prettily for photographs while telling the reporters to use her stage name, Nusia. Whatever Bohemian lives the characters in this drama led, the police established that Bog alone conceived and carried out the idea of stealing *L'Indifférent* and "improving" it. After extensive study, the curatorial staff at the Louvre officially declared that his retouching had caused "serious damage" (*des dommages fort importants*). Fortunately, he was confused about the glaze he used: if alcohol had indeed been in the mixture, the painting would have been ruined. Examining magistrate Marchat held Bogousslavsky at the Santé until trial, at which he was convicted and sentenced to five more years in prison. The situation for Desprès was ambiguous. He soon admitted lying in his original deposition. He had, in fact, known about the theft much earlier and encouraged Bog to write the memoir in hope of selling it as a sensation. He bought the more than two hundred handwritten pages and photographs of *L'Indifférent* before and after the retouching from his friend for 2,750 francs ($1,665.00 in 2011). He let Bog return the painting only after he had time to have the manuscript professionally typed. The publicity attracted the wife, Madeline, whom Desprès had abandoned, and she sued for divorce. Perhaps concluding that this torrent of humiliation was enough, Marchat demanded nothing from him beyond an abject public apology.[19]

The *L'Indifférent* affair wrapped up just as public attention turned decisively to the summer's main event, Hitler's latest assault on European stability. During the last four years, March had been his month of choice for action. On 9 March 1935, he announced the creation of the Luftwaffe, a powerful air force, and a week later on 16 March, the re-creation of the German Wehrmacht, an army of thirty-six divisions to be increased rapidly through conscription. On 7 March 1936, he denounced the Locarno Pact and reoccupied the demilitarized zone of the Rhineland. On 12 March 1938, he invaded Austria to effect Anschluss. On 15 March 1939, he occupied the remainder of Czechoslovakia, Bohemia, and Moravia, declaring them a German protectorate. In 1938, however, he waited until September to threaten an attack on Czechoslovakia and so gained the Sudetenland at the Munich Conference. Now, a year onward, he threatened to attack Poland. This time, French and British leaders, who had submitted in every previous instance, said "Assez!" and "Enough!"

The Munich capitulation and the German arrogance after was galling, the clumsy Italian effort at extortion infuriating, Hitler's seizing rump Czechoslovakia almost predictable. The prospect of war in the east and the north made securing the southern flank a necessity. Britain urged, and France agreed, to acknowledge General Francisco Franco as victor in the Spanish Civil War, despite his having won through substantial aid from Nazi and Fascist contingents. Official diplomatic recognition came on 28 February 1939, and to smooth relations, France sent as ambassador the overtly Catholic, profoundly conservative hero of Verdun, Marshal Philippe Pétain. If time and conditions had allowed a similar pacification of Italy's *Il Duce*, perhaps a means might have been found, but Mussolini had already made his decision, announced to the world in the 22 May Pact of Steel with Hitler.

On 31 March 1939, Prime Minister Neville Chamberlain, speaking for both France and his own Great Britain, issued a "guarantee" of Poland and Romania against German aggression. The true danger lay in Poland, where Ribbentrop had declared Hitler's demands: German annexation of the port city Danzig and an extraterritorial highway across the Polish Corridor linking Germany to its East Prussian provinces. Proud and disdainful of the danger, Poland's leaders resisted the idea of being "guaranteed"—especially because they knew that Britain and France wished to bring the Soviet Union into a revived Triple Alliance. Based on their experience since the partitions of Poland in the late eighteenth century, they considered oppression by Germans preferable to oppression by Russians, and the horrors perpetrated during the 1920 Russian-Polish War were fresh in their memory. In fact, the British and the French were reluctantly agreed that they could deter a German assault upon Poland only by aligning the Soviet Union with them. But exactly how—and with what effects? Since the middle 1930s, Stalin and his commissar for foreign affairs, Maksim Litvinov, had endorsed the idea of "collective security" so often proclaimed and so often abandoned by the Western democracies. When approached in mid-April, the Soviets demanded a formal treaty for their support, nothing less; and as proof of sincerity, a military convention had to precede any political agreement. The French were willing from the outset, but the British dithered. Daladier and his cabinet of Radicals and moderate conservatives did not like Communists but had worked with them during the Popular Front; Chamberlain and his cabinet from the Conservative party regarded Communists with true fear and loathing. More than three months passed (until 23 July) before an approval for military negotiations, and because the British preferred to send the delegation by ship, they did not arrive in Moscow until 11 August.[20]

By then, French leaders were increasingly apprehensive about a Soviet-German rapprochement. Robert Coulondre, then France's ambassador to Moscow, had reported soon after Munich a remark by Vladimir Potemkin, the assistant commissar for foreign affairs: "My poor friend, what have you done? For us, I see no other way out than a fourth partition of Poland." Three times between 1772 and 1795, Germans and Russians had divided Poland among them, and a fourth would leave France and Great Britain on the outside. Sources in Germany recruited by French intelligence warned of the same. On 4 May 1939, Litvinov, who had served since 1930 and been friendly toward the West, was abruptly replaced by Vyacheslav Molotov, a man without foreign policy experience but an absolute creature of Stalin. The French military attaché in Berlin, Captain Paul Stehlin, cultivated Wehrmacht general Karl Bodenschatz and in mid-May heard from him rumors about a new division of Poland. So did Coulondre, now the ambassador to Berlin. By the end of the month, Bonnet was seriously worried. When Daladier met on 31 July with General Joseph Doumenc, who was heading the French military delegation to the negotiations, he told him, "Get us an agreement at any price" (*Donnez-nous un accord à tout prix*).[21]

Moderate and conservative newspapers stiffened the mood. *Le Figaro* celebrated all things entente: Miss London and Miss Paris pose together at the New York World's Fair; George VI reviews 133 ships of the British fleet; Winston Churchill tours the Maginot Line; British and French air forces combine for training exercises. *Le Temps* and mass-circulation *Le Matin* were not far behind: more joint mock battles and photographs of Churchill. *Le Figaro*'s editorialists traditionally adopted a moral tone. Former diplomat Wladimir d'Ormesson, who had moved over from *Le Temps*, proclaimed: "we are conscious of defending not only our rights, our vital interests, but decency [*honnêteté*] itself, which is indispensable for European civilization. We shall defend them without fail." And: "Against these criminal collective menaces, Christian morality itself requires resistance. Neither France nor Great Britain will retreat before the frightful but ineluctable duty that is imposed on them." Novelist André Maurois wrote from rural Périgord, east of Bordeaux, where he found the peasants "ready for any sacrifice to save the independence of France." The extremes could not help picking fights. *L'Humanité*'s Péri, the most eloquent of the Communist deputies, called "the Anglo-French-Soviet pact" the barrier (*barrage*) against aggression while complaining that it was "still not signed." *L'Action française* replied that Stalin was seeking only advantage from the negotiations, "It is imprudent, even dangerous, to maintain the illusion among the French and British peoples that the participation of the Soviet Union in the 'front for peace' will assure their security."[22] By 20 August, that warning appeared prophetic as rumors ran wildly through Paris that discussions in Moscow were going badly. Both *Le Matin* and *Le Figaro* now prominently featured the pilgrimage for peace to Lourdes made by Jean Verdier, cardinal archbishop of Paris, and his exhortation: "God wishes to save us while obliging France to become again more so France." D'Ormesson enjoined "French calm." *Le Temps*, while calling into question "the fate of the world and the future of civilization," counseled, "We must prove, while waiting to learn whether disaster will strike, that we are stronger than the dictators; the democracies must be masters of themselves, dignified and composed."[23]

From the outset, the French and British negotiating position with the Soviet Union had been fatally handicapped by the recalcitrance of their Polish allies. At Moscow, defense commissar Marshal Kliment Voroshilov demanded to know whether Poland would accept the entry of Soviet troops to confront any German invasion. General Doumenc and the head of the British delegation, Admiral Sir Reginald Drax-Plumkett, temporized. They were well aware that the vital Polish leaders—Jósef Beck, foreign minister and de facto head of the government; Marshal Edward Smigly-Ridz, commander in chief; and General Waclaw Stachiewicz, army chief of staff—believed the Soviet Union's only interest was to restore the domination of Poland so long exercised by the tsars. Stachiewicz said bluntly, "I cannot believe that the Russians really want to fight the Germans. . . . If we allow them into our territory they would stay there." When Voroshilov suspended the discussions on 17 August 1939, any prospect of a revived Triple Alliance disappeared. Five days later, on 22 August, Ribbentrop arrived in Moscow to sign a German-Soviet non-aggression pact, a diplomatic term for the fourth partition of Poland.[24]

In Paris, the French government comprehended immediately that war was at hand. As the first steps toward mobilization, it recalled three classes of reservists and announced requisitions in the name of "national defense." Daladier prepared to address the nation through a radio broadcast scheduled for the evening of 25 August. Newspapers were stunned and reacted with outrage. For *Le Figaro*, "there are no words to condemn such an act." *Le Temps* on 25 August called the "Hitler-Stalin pact a serious blow to political morality." On 23 August, Léon Blum confessed in *Le Populaire*, "I can formulate no acceptable explanation. . . . Why have the Soviets played this double game?" On the same day, Charles Maurras could not resist exulting in the prescience of *L'Action française*, "the one daily paper in Paris that has never ceased saying *no* to any Russian alliance." When French Communists in *L'Humanité* on 22 August defended the pact as "a double proof that the Soviet Union wants and is able to live in peace with everyone and that its policy of firmness has obliged

Hitler to yield," the moderates shouted them down. For *Le Temps* on 24 and 25 August, the Communists had given measure of their "incredible bad faith and stupefying cynicism . . . and will be held as accomplices to aggression." But the deed was done: "the international tension reaches its most acute phase. . . . The fate of Europe and the whole civilized world is in play." *Le Figaro*'s d'Ormesson was somber: "The scenario takes shape. We begin the gravest hours."[25]

By coincidence during the preceding week, *Le Temps* had been running a three-part essay under the title "The Responsibilities of Marxism." All the traditional bourgeois fears of communism and bad memories of relations during the Popular Front animated the denunciations. The French tradition of liberalism and individualism, exemplified by the Declaration of the Rights of Man and the Citizen proclaimed by the Revolution in 1789, was under assault from totalitarian ideologies. Whether calling themselves Marxists or Fascists or National Socialists, their conception of society meant "the subjugation of the individual, the exaltation of the central government, the condemnation of economic liberalism, recourse to methods of repression, a closed economy, and identification of the dominant party with the state. . . . 'Totalitarianism' is not the brother of Marxism in the sense in which brotherhood evokes analogy, parallelism, or 'family likeness'; Totalitarianism is the son of Marxism in the strongest and clearest sense in which filiation evokes the relationship of cause and effect, of antecedent to consequent, of creation to creature." On 22 August, *Le Temps* wrote: "Before Marxism, the cause of liberal individualism . . . appeared definitively won; since Marxism, everything has been placed in doubt, and we must defend liberty against the followers of force and the apologists of violence, against the gainsayers of human rights, against the denigrators of law, against the high priests of materialism." All in all, not a bad summation of the situation at hand.[26]

For France had to don the sword and buckler of war. In his radio address, Daladier sought to lay harness on the national back.

> Every one of you understands that if by cowardice we permit one people in Europe after another to succumb, after having given our word; if we betray our ideals, if we misjudge our vital interest, we

would find ourselves without honor, without friends, without support, when these forces of European domination turn against us. . . . We French want to remain free. We want peace, but we cannot accept submitting ourselves to the demands of violence and to the reign of injustice. Frenchwomen and Frenchmen, I need not explain your duty. I know that you are resolved by every sacrifice to assure the safeguard of the nation."[27]

Daladier needed to rally national resolve because an element within his cabinet resisted the harness. Facing imminent war, Bonnet, Marchandeau, and Monzie argued that Polish concessions to Germany, a "new Munich," could save the peace. They preferred to believe that Hitler wanted only what he had been demanding, Danzig and passage through the Corridor, despite the implication of the Nazi-Soviet pact that Poland was to be destroyed. If further appeasement would suffice, why fight? Not four months earlier on 4 May, Marcel Déat, onetime Socialist and full-time appeaser, had contributed a notorious article to the left-wing daily *L'Oeuvre*, "Mourir pour Danzig?" (Die for Danzig?). His answer to this question was an unequivocal "No!" A day earlier, the *London Times* had editorialized, "Danzig is not worth a war." If only the Poles would give in, said the ministers of foreign affairs, justice, and public works, France would be spared—once again—from having to fulfill promises. They encouraged Daladier's own hesitations, sapping his resolve through fear and doubt. The result was an exchange of letters between Daladier and Hitler on 26 and 27 August. Writing as one Great War trench soldier to another in a style half-sentimental, half-despairing, Daladier sought some solution to maintain peace. Determined for war, Hitler merely increased his demands.[28]

This feckless correspondence aside, the chief "resisters" in the cabinet—Reynaud, Mandel, Campinchi, Zay, and Maurice Sarraut, ministers of finance, colonies, navy, education, and interior—carried Daladier with them. He authorized the recall of more reservists, bringing France closer to general mobilization. Resident foreigners were offered enlistment. Sarraut halted publication of the Communist newspapers *L'Humanité* and *Ce Soir* for their defense of the non-aggression pact and increased the police presence in Paris to prevent any hostile demonstrations. Reynaud met with representatives from Great Britain to freeze the value of the franc and pound against each other. Women and especially schoolchildren were urged to leave Paris while train service was not yet affected—as it would be severely, beginning 30 August. Telephone calls and telegraph messages to recipients beyond the borders came under new regulation. Notices announced the coming requisition of trucks, automobiles, horses, and bicycles. Restriction of illumination at night went into effect immediately. Paris grew dark and the streets quiet. Men and women lined up patiently for the distribution of gas masks. Workers heaped sand in front of buildings to use for extinguishing fires from expected aerial bombing. The Louvre and other museums began to pack away the most valuable items for storage in bank vaults. The stained-glass windows of Sainte-Chapelle and the cathedral of Chartres were taken down and hidden. The stock market held firm with sangfroid. Cardinal-Archbishop Verdier celebrated a mass for peace at Sacré-Coeur and in his sermon extolled the virtues of France: "National unity, flame of patriotism, noble French family, cheerful and organized work, trust of our friends, Christian faith." Chief Rabbi Julien Weill was more explicit: "My brothers, we need not exhort you to fulfill the duties that are incumbent on every Frenchman."[29]

Ganging up on French Communists was the new political game. The foreign affairs committee for the Chamber of Deputies met on 25 August. Its chairman was Jean Mistler, prominent eleven months earlier in his praise of the Munich settlement. According to L'Action française, Salomon Grunbach of the Socialist party, another defender of Munich, described the German-Soviet non-aggression pact as "a veritable treason." He was then supported by various other, now former, appeasers including Flandin, as well as by Kérillis and Jean Ybarnégaray, who had long warned of the Nazi menace. When the four Communist members of the committee, led by Péri, offered a defense of Soviet actions, onetime appeaser Gaston Riou, a Radical, howled at them: "Your party is the party of the enemy, the instrument of the enemy!" Ybarnégaray asked whether the Communists were "representatives of a party under orders from a foreigner, 'Stalin,' who has just committed one of the greatest crimes in history? Are you, yes or no, going to break with the Soviets or prove your absolute dependence on them? If you continue to associate yourselves with Stalin and Hitler, we shall no longer consider you members of the French family." Mistler proposed a resolution that was then passed over the dissenting votes of the four Communist deputies: "The committee considers that the pact called 'non-aggression,' far from diminishing the danger of war, has only increased it, but in no manner diminishes the will of France, loyal in its word, to resist all aggression and to defend the peace in honor and dignity with its allies." Shortly afterward, the Socialist party met to confirm the position of its committee members and to declare that the attitude of the Communists to the German-Soviet pact "rendered any further collective action with them impossible." Stéphane Lausanne, editor of *Le Matin*, wrote a personal and angry editorial on 26 August for his front page: "We behold an unprecedented spectacle where the organizers of treason defend it, glorify it, deify it. The men of Stalin, friends of Hitler, set him up, set themselves up, as arches of triumph. Let them who have charge of morale in this nation beware that tolerance risks becoming complicity."[30]

In *Le Figaro*, Jean Le Cour Grandmaison, conservative deputy and Catholic aristocrat, wrote almost as a knight of old: "If the worst comes, against the assembled banners of neo-paganism we shall fight, like our fathers before us, in the name of the Cross: By this sign we shall conquer." The converse came in *L'Action française*, where Charles Maurras, the self-appointed defender of French traditions and founder of integral nationalism, decried a war that he insisted would benefit only Communists and Jews. After Sarraut censored his column on 29 August, Maurras wrote, unrepentant, the following day: "we patriots call for and require peace. I would be happy, deliriously happy, to be shot for having uttered this truth." Maurras was not shot, and France did not have peace. Two more days later, at dawn, in the understated words of John Leslie Snell: "No Pole who has rubbed sleep from his eyes thinks the thunder in the west marks the passage of a late summer storm."[31]

The German attack on Poland began on 1 September at 4:45 a.m.; France declared war against Germany on 3 September at 5:00 p.m., sixty and one-quarter hours later, six hours after Great Britain. The long delay was forced when, for two days beginning 31 August, the dream that a conference hinted at by Mussolini might yet prevent war bewitched a majority of the cabinet. To his credit, Daladier rejected the idea out of hand, saying in disgust, "Should we dismember Poland and dishonor ourselves . . . only to have war anyway? The lesson of Munich is that Hitler's signature is worth nothing." Yet Daladier temporized. France acted only when a British declaration of war was certain. The cabinet convened the Chamber of Deputies and the Senate simultaneously on 2 September at 3:00 p.m. Daladier addressed the Chamber, and Chautemps, vice premier, the Senate. They asked not for a declaration of war but for the appropriation of 70 billion francs ($42.4 billion in 2011) "to confront the requirements of the international situation." The circumlocution was unnecessary. Everyone knew that war was imminent, and despite a few dissenting voices, the vote for this funding was declared unanimous in both houses. Even afterward, the cabinet delayed delivering to Germany a formal declaration of war until after—well after—the British had done so on 3 September.[32]

Jean-Baptiste Duroselle gave the title *La Décadence* to his account of French diplomacy in the 1930s, but as his assessment of the national mood when France embarked upon a second war with Germany in a quarter century (the third since 1870), he declared, "No matter what was said later, the French people were sad, certainly, but resolute." Eugen Weber, then fourteen years old and watching intently from Great Britain, came to a less sanguine conclusion when he prepared his study of the period, *The Hollow Years*, more than a half century later: "My own impression is close to that of the prefect of the Rhône in Lyons who, in September 1939, reported, 'something between resolution and resignation.' Much of the evidence bears him out, although it leans rather toward the latter term."[33]

In 1914 when the Chamber of Deputies voted a declaration of war against Germany, Albert de Mun, leader of the Catholic conservatives, rose from his seat and walked across the assembly to the far left where he embraced Edouard Vaillant, Communard and leader of the Socialist party since the assassination of Jean Jaurès four days earlier. In 1939, neither Le Cour Grandmaison nor his Communist counterpart Gabriel Péri so much as acknowledged each other. During the half decade before 1914, France experienced a nationalist revival that permitted its people to halt the German invasion at the Marne, fight the battle of the trenches, and survive losses almost beyond belief: approximately 1.3 million killed, 1.1 million left with permanent disabilities—on a per capita basis, the equivalent in the United States today of approximately 10 million and 8.5 million. In 1939, the recovery of nerve since Munich was equivocal. France began a token foray into German territory, then withdrew behind the Maginot Line when Poland's destruction appeared certain. Any willingness to fight in the fall of 1939 withered rapidly during the Phony War of the next half year. When the Germans launched their Blitzkrieg in May against Western Europe, France succumbed even faster than Poland. Although some units fought with bravery, surrender in others rivaled the Italian capitulation before the British in North Africa.[34]

During the Great War, France was closest to disaster in late 1917 and early 1918, when Russia had collapsed but American troops were yet to arrive. France was saved by Georges Clemenceau, who told the Chamber of Deputies on 8 March 1918: "Before Paris, I wage war! Behind Paris, I wage war! If we retreat to the Pyrenees, I shall continue to wage war, and I wage war until the last quarter hour, because the last quarter hour will be ours!" And then he did so. When France faced disaster in 1940, Philippe Pétain, a hero of the Great War, accepted an armistice with the Germans and then dismantled the Third Republic. His "French State" at Vichy provided the very definition of "collaboration," meaning Germany's lackey. Across the Channel, Winston Churchill, who took notes in the Chamber's gallery when Clemenceau spoke, borrowed his words on 4 June 1940 to rally a Great Britain nearly as defeatist as France: "We shall fight on the beaches, we shall fight on the landing grounds, we shall fight in the fields and in the streets, we shall fight in the hills, we shall never surrender." A week earlier he told his cabinet, "If this long island story of ours is to end at last, let it end only when each one of us lies choking in his own blood upon the ground."[35] No French political leader of this period was a Clemenceau or a Churchill.

Without question, France was profoundly wounded by the experience of the Great War and never recovered fully during the 1920s and 1930s. Even calling the prewar period *la Belle Epoque* (the "good old days") implied that the best times in France were gone. And thus, this France was not worth fighting for, if that fighting meant dying. The experience of German occupation and German pressure on Vichy soon enough changed minds. Irène Némirovsky, the Jewish Russian émigré who became a prominent novelist in the 1930s, fled from occupied Paris and, in the Burgundy countryside, wrote what became her posthumous masterpiece, *Suite française*. An entry in her notebook for 1942, not long before she was arrested and sent to die at Auschwitz, reads: "The French grew tired of the Republic as if she were an old wife. For them, the dictatorship was a brief affair, adultery. But they intended to cheat on their wife, not to kill her. Now they realize she's dead, their Republic, their freedom. They're mourning her."[36]

Another prominent novelist between the wars in France had proffered a lesson that might well have been admired but certainly went unlearned. André Malraux's *La Condition humaine* (*Man's Fate*) appeared in 1933. He demanded that his characters endow life with meaning through their actions and take responsibility not only for these actions but for inaction as well. Here was a heroic ethic of responsibility. Courage is moral strength, to be brave when there is much to suffer. French leaders in August 1939 lacked courage and failed the nation they led.[37]

NOTES

Throughout the book whenever I provided dollar values for francs, I adopted the following procedure. Using the table from the Institut national de la statistique et des études économiques: Pouvoir d'achat de l'euro et de franc (1 February 2011), available at www.insee.fr, I first converted francs to euros. Then, using the coefficient 1.36, I converted euros to dollars.

Chapter 1: July 1914

1. The historiography of World War I and its origins is massive, beginning with the old but still serviceable volumes in the Langer Series, first, Oron J. Hale, *The Great Illusion, 1900–1914* (New York: Harper and Row, 1971), then, Bernadotte E. Schmitt and Harold C. Vedeler, *The World in the Crucible, 1914–1919* (New York: Harper and Row, 1984), which are superb syntheses and have extensive bibliographies. A briefer and more popular introduction is Laurence Lafore, *The Long Fuse: An Interpretation of the Origins of World War I* (Philadelphia: J. P. Lippincott, 1965). For a summary of the scholarly debate, see Samuel R. Williamson, Jr., and Ernest R. May, "An Identity of Opinion: Historians and July 1914," *Journal of Modern History* 79 (June 2007): 335–87.

2. *L'Echo de Paris*, 12 January 1912. All translations from the original are mine unless the source note indicates a translator. See also Joseph Marie Auguste Caillaux, *Agadir* (Paris: A. Michel, 1919); André Tardieu, *Le Mystère d'Agadir* (Paris: Calmann-Lévy, 1912); Jean-Claude Allain, *Joseph Caillaux: Le défi victorieux, 1863–1914* (Paris: Imprimerie nationale, 1978), 364–401; Benjamin Franklin Martin, *Count Albert de Mun: Paladin of the Third Republic* (Chapel Hill: University of North Carolina Press, 1978), 241–58.

3. *L'Echo de Paris*, 4 November, 4 December 1912.

4. Benjamin Franklin Martin, *The Hypocrisy of Justice in the Belle Epoque* (Baton Rouge: Louisiana State University Press, 1984), 151–224; Edward Berenson, *The Trial of Madame Caillaux* (Berkeley and Los Angeles: University of California Press, 1992).

5. *Le Figaro*, 4–31 January, 1–3, 5–7, 9, 12–21, 23–27 February, 2–6, 8–13 March 1914.

6. *Le Figaro*, 17 March 1914.

7. *Journal Officiel*, Chambre des Députés, Débats parlementaires (hereinafter cited as J. O. C., Débats), 17 March, 3 April, 17 June 1914; Raymond Poincaré, *Au service de la France: Neuf années de souvenirs*, 11 vols. (Paris: Plon-Nourrit, 1926–74), 4:148.

8. There is a superb account in Edward Crankshaw, *The Fall of the House of Habsburg* (New York: Viking Press, 1963), 328–89.

9. *Le Temps*, 1, 2 (quote) July 1914; *L'Humanité*, 1 July 1914; *L'Action française*, 2 July 1914; *Le Figaro*, 1, 3, 6 July 1914; *Le Matin*, 6 July 1914.

10. *L'Action française*, 1, 9 July 1914; *Le Figaro*, 2, 5–7 July 1914; *L'Humanité*, 2, 5–8 July 1914; *Le Temps*, 2, 5–8 July 1914; *Le Matin*, 5, 10, 16–17 July 1914.

11. *L'Humanité*, 3 July 1914; *L'Action française*, 3, 9, 16, 19 July 1914; *Le Figaro*, 3, 5–6, 11, 13 July 1914; *Le Matin*, 11 July 1914; Jules Ferry, *Lettres de Jules Ferry, 1846–1893* (Paris: Calmann-Lévy, 1914); Paul Bourget, *Le Démon de midi* (Paris: Plon-Nourrit, 1914).

12. *Le Temps* and *Le Figaro*, 1–9 July 1914; *Le Matin*, 6–9 July 1914.

13. *Journal Officiel*, Sénat, Débats parlementaires (hereinafter cited as J. O. S., Débats), 13 July 1914 (Clemenceau); *L'Humanité*, 18 July 1914 (Jaurès); *Le Temps*, 18 July 1914 (Guesde). See also *L'Action française*, *Le Figaro*, *Le Matin*, 14–15 July 1914; *L'Humanité*, 14–20 July 1914; *Le Temps*, 15–20 July 1914.

14. *Le Figaro*, 17 July 1914; *Le Temps*, 21 July 1914; *Le Figaro*, 20 July 1914. See also *Le Figaro*, 19–24 July 1914; *Le Temps*, 18, 22–25 July 1914; *L'Action française*, 21–24 July 1914; *L'Humanité*, 21–24 July 1914; *Le Matin*, 19–24 July 1914.

15. This interpretation is based on John Keiger, *France and the Origins of the First World War* (London: Macmillan, 1983), and *Raymond Poincaré* (Cambridge: Cambridge University Press, 1997); Jean-Jacques Becker, *1914: Comment les Français sont entrés dans la guerre* (Paris: Presses de la Fondation national des sciences politiques, 1977). Stefan Schmidt, *Frankreichs Aussenpolitik in der Julikrise 1914: Ein Beitrag zur Geschichte des Ausbruchs des Ersten Weltkrieges* (Munich: Oldenbourg, 2009), argues that France pushed Russia to risk war over the Serbian crisis.

16. *L'Action française*, 7, 19 July 1914; *Le Figaro*, 22 May, 4–5, 11–12, 16–20 July 1914; *Le Temps*, 17–18 July 1914; *Le Matin*, 7 July 1914; Martin, *Hypocrisy of Justice*, 178–79.

17. Martin, *Hypocrisy of Justice*, 152, 175; *L'Action française*, 20 July 1914.

18. *L'Humanité*, *L'Action française*, *Le Figaro*, *Le Temps*, *Le Matin*, 21 July 1914.

19. *Le Figaro*, *Le Temps*, *Le Matin*, *L'Action française*, *L'Humanité*, 22 July 1914.

20. *L'Homme libre*, *Le Figaro*, 22 July 1914.

21. *Le Figaro*, *Le Temps*, *L'Humanité*, *Le Matin*, *L'Action française*, 23 July 1914.

22. *Le Figaro*, 24 July 1914.

23. *Le Figaro*, *Le Temps*, *L'Humanité*, *L'Action française*, *Le Matin*, 24 July 1914.

24. *Le Temps*, *Le Figaro*, *L'Humanité*, *Le Matin*, *L'Action française*, 25 July 1914.

25. *Le Figaro*, *L'Action française*, *Le Temps*, 26 July 1914.

26. *L'Action française*, 27 July 1914 (Bainville); *L'Humanité*, 26, 27 July 1914 (Jaurès); *Le Temps*, 27 July 1914 (Berlin). For the trial, see *Le Figaro*, *L'Action française*, *Le Matin*, *Le Temps*, *L'Humanité*, 26–27 July 1914. All five newspapers quoted Dr. Cunéo on 27 July.

27. *Le Figaro*, *Le Temps*, *Le Matin*, *L'Action française*, *L'Humanité*, 28 July 1914.

28. *Le Figaro* (Caillaux trial, Barrès), *L'Action française* (Caillaux trial, Bainville), *Le Temps* ("Sursam Corda"), *Le Matin*, *L'Humanité*, 29 July 1914.

29. Martin, *Hypocrisy of Justice*, 207; *Le Matin*, *Le Temps*, *L'Humanité*, *Le Figaro*, *L'Action française*, 30–31 July 1914.

30. *Le Figaro*, *Le Temps*, *L'Action française*, *Le Matin*, *L'Humanité*, 1 August 1914; *L'Echo de Paris*, 3 August 1914.

31. *L'Humanité*, *Le Figaro*, 3 August 1914; *L'Action française*, 4 August 1914.

32. J. O. S., Débats, J. O. C., Débats, 4 August 1914; *Le Matin*, *Le Figaro*, *L'Humanité*, *Le Temps*, *L'Action française*, 5 August 1914; Martin, *Count Albert de Mun*, 290.

Chapter 2: Georges—The Defiant

1. Georges Suarez, *Briand: Sa vie, son oeuvre, avec son journal et de nombreux documents inédits*, 6 vols. (Paris: Plon, 1938–52), 2:220; *Journal*

Officiel, Chambre des Députés, Débats parlementaires (hereinafter cited as J. O. C., Débats), 20 July 1909.

2. John Raymond Walser, *France's Search for a Battle Fleet: Naval Policy and Power, 1898–1914* (New York: Garland, 1992), 126–79.

3. J. O. C., Débats, 20 July 1909; Benjamin Franklin Martin, *Count Albert de Mun: Paladin of the Third Republic* (Chapel Hill: University of North Carolina Press, 1978), 219. See also Jean-Baptiste Duroselle, *Clemenceau* (Paris: Fayard, 1988), 368–75.

4. Duroselle, *Clemenceau,* 25–40, 35 (Clemenceau on his father), 67 (Scheurer-Kestner), 341 (Poincaré). Biographies of Clemenceau are many. See Duroselle, *Clemenceau,* for a full, intimate, and sympathetic account; David S. Newhall, *Clemenceau: A Life at War* (Lewiston, N.Y.: Edwin Mellen Press, 1991), the best in English; Gregor Dallas, *At the Heart of a Tiger: Clemenceau and His World* (New York: Carroll and Graf, 1993), for excellent context; Gaston Monnerville, *Clemenceau* (Paris: Fayard, 1968), and Philippe Erlanger, *Clemenceau* (Paris: Editions Bernard Grasset, 1968) for certain details.

5. Monnerville, *Clemenceau,* 31–44.

6. Duroselle, *Clemenceau,* 13–24; Dallas, *Heart of a Tiger,* 46–78.

7. Duroselle, *Clemenceau,* 80–91, 356 (Mary's letters), 357.

8. Dallas, *Heart of a Tiger,* 79–189, quotation from 102.

9. Duroselle, *Clemenceau,* 134–64, 164 (Clemenceau), 153 (Daudet); also Léon Daudet, *Devant la douleur* (Paris: Nouvelle histoire nationale, 1915), 175–76.

10. J. O. C., Débats, 30 July 1885, 8 May 1891, 22 November 1883, 18 February 1892.

11. John Patrick Tuer Bury and Robert Tombs, *Thiers, 1797–1877: A Political Life* (London: Allen and Unwin, 1986), 219 ("divides us least"); *Le Figaro,* 12 August 1881; J. O. C., Débats, 29 January 1891.

12. Duroselle, *Clemenceau,* 193–200, 368–75.

13. Duroselle, *Clemenceau,* 355–58; Dallas, *Heart of a Tiger,* 264–65, 302–3.

14. Duroselle, *Clemenceau,* 275 (Hertz); J. O. C., Débats, 20 December 1892.

15. *Le Figaro,* 23 December 1892. The duel with Poussargues was on 21 November 1871, the duel with Maurel on 15 December 1888.

16. Duroselle, *Clemenceau,* 291, 292, 293, 296–97; also Monnerville, *Clemenceau,* 175–210.

17. For the estimate of income, see Duroselle, *Clemenceau,* 311–17;

La Justice, 27 July 1894; for the Deschanel duel, see *Le Figaro,* 28 July 1894.

18. Duroselle, *Clemenceau,* 362–64; Theodore Zeldin, *France, 1848–1945,* 2 vols. (Oxford: Oxford University Press, 1973–77), 1:699–703; Georges Clemenceau, *Démosthènes* (Paris: Librairie Plon, 1926), translated by Charles Miner Thompson as *Demosthenes* (Boston: Houghton Mifflin, 1926), 150.

19. *La Justice,* 25 December 1894. For Clemenceau's mantra, see Joseph Caillaux, *Mes mémoires,* 3 vols. (Paris: Librairie Plon, 1942–47), 1:301; Benjamin Franklin Martin, "The Dreyfus Affair and the Corruption of the French Legal System," in *The Dreyfus Affair: Art, Truth, and Justice,* ed. Norman L. Kleeblatt (Berkeley and Los Angeles: University of California Press, 1987).

20. Duroselle, *Clemenceau,* 448.

21. *Journal Officiel,* Sénat, Débats parlementaires (hereinafter cited as J.O. S., Débats), 30 October 1902; Suarez, *Briand,* 1:439.

22. Wladimir d'Ormesson, *Qu'est-ce qu'un Français? Essai de psychologie politique: Clemenceau, Poincaré, Briand* (Paris: Editions Spes, 1934), 169; André Maurel, *Clemenceau* (Paris: Editions de la Nouvelle Revue Nationale, 1919), 29.

23. Suarez, *Briand,* 1:440, 2:99; Duroselle, *Clemenceau,* 509; J. O. C., Débats, 8 March 1907, 19 June 1906; Zeldin, *France,* 702 (Jaurès).

24. For Clemenceau to Radolin, see Monnerville, *Clemenceau,* 339, and Duroselle, *Clemenceau,* 533.

25. John McManners, *Church and State in France, 1870–1914* (New York: Harper and Row, 1972), 149; Berta Szeps Zuckerkandl, *Clemenceau, tel que je l'ai connu* (Algiers: Editions de la Revue Fontaine, 1944), 182–83. See also Benjamin Franklin Martin, *France and the Après Guerre, 1918–1924: Illusions and Disillusionment* (Baton Rouge: Louisiana State University Press, 1999), 59–61; Duroselle, *Clemenceau,* 546–54.

26. Maurice Paléologue, *Au Quai d'Orsay à la veille de la tourmente: Journal, 1913–1914* (Paris: Librairie Plon, 1947), 59–60, 139.

27. René Benjamin, *Clemenceau dans la retraite* (Paris: Librairie Plon, 1930), 139; *L'Homme libre,* 26 August 1914.

28. J. O. S., Débats, 22 July 1917; Raymond Poincaré, *Au service de la France: Neuf années de souvenirs,* 11 vols. (Paris: Plon-Nourrit, 1926–74), 9:321, 336.

29. Poincaré, *Au service de la France,* 9:367; *L'Homme libre,* 15 November 1917; J. O. S., Débats, 20 November 1917; Wythe Williams, *The Tiger of France: Conversations with Clemenceau* (New York: Duell, Sloan, and Pearce, 1949), 153; also Poincaré, *Au service de la France,* 9:382, 10:7–8.

30. J. O. C., Débats, 8 March 1918; Winston Churchill, *Great Contemporaries* (London: Thornton Butterworth, 1937), 310–11; J. O. C., Débats, 4 June 1918.

31. J. O. C., Débats, 20 November 1917. Benjamin Franklin Martin, *The Hypocrisy of Justice in the Belle Epoque* (Baton Rouge: Louisiana State University Press, 1984), 219.

32. J. O. S., Débats, 17 September 1918; J. O. C., Débats, 11 November 1918; Georges Wormser, *La République de Clemenceau* (Paris: Presses universitaires de France, 1961), 361.

33. Antony Lentin, *Lloyd George, Woodrow Wilson and the Guilt of Germany* (Baton Rouge: Louisiana State University Press, 1984), 108. For the economic devastation, see Alfred Sauvy, *Histoire économique de la France entre les deux guerres*, 3 vols. (Paris: Fayard, 1965–75), 1:19–27.

34. Poincaré, *Au service de la France*, 11:321; Jean Martet with Wilton Waldman, *Georges Clemenceau* (New York: Longmans, Green, 1930), 153 (handwriting); Duroselle, *Clemenceau*, 753 (fools).

35. J. O. C., Débats, 24–25 September 1919.

36. Martin, *France and the Après Guerre*, 53–56; Duroselle, *Clemenceau*, 251 (quote), 861–74.

37. Major General Sir Edward Louis Spears, *Assignment to Catastrophe*, 2 vols. (London: Heinemann, 1954), 1:157; Zeldin, *France*, 1:703–4; Duroselle, *Clemenceau*, 358–68. Michel Clemenceau's first wife was Ida Minchin, Madeleine Clemenceau's husband was Numa Jacquemaire, Thérèse Clemenceau's husband was Saint-André Louis Gatineau.

38. Duroselle, *Clemenceau*, 899; Benjamin, *Clemenceau dans la retraite*, 69–70. See also Dallas, *Heart of a Tiger*, 593–97; Duroselle, *Clemenceau*, 896–906.

39. Williams, *Tiger of France*, 143–44. See also *Le Figaro*, 23 June, 3 October 1921, 28–29 May 1922; Wormser, *La République de Clemenceau*, 448–62.

40. Martin, *France and the Après Guerre*, 156–57.

41. Duroselle, *Clemenceau*, 908 (quote); Georges Clemenceau, *Lettres à une amie, 1923–1929, édition établie et présentée par Pierre Brive* (Paris: Editions Gallimard, 1970). Pierre Brive was Pierre Baldensperger, her son.

42. Duroselle, *Clemenceau*, 894–95 (royalties); Clemenceau, *Démosthènes*, 39, 93, 158, 38; Georges Clemenceau, *Claude Monet: Les Nymphéas* (Paris: Librairie Plon, 1928). The permanent exhibition at the Orangerie opened on 17 May 1927; Georges Clemenceau, *Au soir de la pensée*, 2 vols. (Paris: Librairie Plon, 1927).

43. Raymond Recouly, *Le Mémorial de Foch* (Paris: Editions de France, 1929); Georges Clemenceau, *Grandeurs et misères d'une victoire* (Paris: Librairie Plon, 1929); Martin, *France and the Après Guerre*, 57 (funeral); James L. Stokesbury, *A Short History of World War I* (New York: Morrow, 1980), 323 (truce).

44. Gilbert Prouteau, *Le Dernier défi de Georges Clemenceau* (Paris: France-Empire, 1979), 41 (quote); Williams, *Tiger of France*, 10.

45. Newhall, *Clemenceau*, 506–7; Duroselle, *Clemenceau*, 950–52; Dallas, *Heart of a Tiger*, 597; Clemenceau, *Grandeurs et misères d'une victoire*, iii.

Chapter 3: The Thibaults

1. For these issues, see Eugen Weber, *Peasants into Frenchmen: The Modernization of Rural France, 1870–1914* (Stanford: Stanford University Press, 1976), and "The Secret World of Jean Barois: Notes on the Portrait of an Age," in *The Origins of Modern Consciousness*, ed. John Weiss (Detroit: Wayne State University Press, 1965), 79–109, 199–202 (88 , Léon Bloy quoted); Henry Stuart Hughes, *Consciousness and Society: The Reorientation of European Social Thought, 1890–1930* (New York: Alfred A. Knopf, 1958).

2. Roger Martin du Gard (hereafter cited as MdG for correspondence), *Jean Barois* (Paris: Librairie Gallimard, 1913), translated by Stuart Gilbert as *Jean Barois* (New York: Viking Press, 1949), 112–13, 290.

3. Roger Martin du Gard, *Correspondance générale*, ed. Maurice Rieuneau, Jean-Claude Airal, et al., 10 vols. (Paris: Librairie Gallimard, 1980–2006), MdG to René Lalou, 25 February 1937, 7:43. For brief biographical details and analysis of his work, see Denis Boak, *Roger Martin du Gard* (Oxford: Clarendon Press, 1963); David L. Schalk, *Roger Martin du Gard: The Novelist and History* (Ithaca, N.Y.: Cornell University Press, 1967).

4. MdG, *Jean Barois*, 10, 17, 52, 95, 103.

5. MdG, *Jean Barois*, 115, 235, 269. For the Dreyfus affair, see Jean-Denis Bredin, *L'Affaire* (Paris: Julliard, 1983), translated by Jeffrey Mehlman as *The Affair: The Case of Alfred Dreyfus* (New York: George Braziller, 1986); Ruth Harris, *Dreyfus: Politics, Emotion, and the Scandal of the Century* (New York: Henry Holt, 2010).

6. MdG, *Jean Barois*, 272, 252, 255, 279, 287.

7. MdG, *Jean Barois*, 307, 313, 317, 333, 334, 335, 336.

8. MdG, *Jean Barois*, 352–53, 354-55, 356, 357.

9. MdG, *Correspondance générale*, MdG to Pierre Rain, 9 July 1913,

1:309 (quoting Gide); to Marcel Hébert, 3 November 1914, 2:34–35 ("savagery"); to Maurice Ray, 7 January 1915, 2:43 ("Catholic" newspapers), 8 December 1914, 2:37 (Valmont).

10. MdG, *Correspondance générale*, MdG to Maurice Ray, 11 April 1915, 2:61 (near miss), 24 April 1915, 2:63–64 ("haunts"); to Marcel Hébert, 31 August 1915, 2:76 (Foucault), 16 October 1915, 2:86 (Bourget); André Fernet to MdG, 13 April 1916, 2:285–86; MdG to Fernet, 27 April 1916, 2:129–30. See also Paul Bourget, *Le Sens de la mort* (Paris: Plon-Nourrit, 1915).

11. MdG, *Correspondance générale*, MdG to Maurice Ray, 5 August 1916, 2:157 ("massacre"); to Pierre Rain, 17 December 1916, 2:164 (predicting defeat); to Henriette Charasson, 20 December 1916, 2:167 ("destiny"); to Maurice Ray, 29 March 1917, 2:176 ("misery"), 14 June 1917, 2:183 (bankruptcy, mutinies), 1 August 1917, 2:191 (Hélène).

12. MdG, *Correspondance générale*, MdG to Maurice Ray, 24 November 1917, 2:205 (French exhaustion); to Yvonne de Coppet, 24 December 1917, 2:210 (close friends, "scalp dance"); to Maurice Ray, 19 October 1918, 2:247 ("collapse").

13. MdG, *Correspondance générale*, MdG to Ferdinand Verdier, 16 May 1920, 3:70 ("forty years"); to Georges Duhamel, 2 June 1920, 3:74 ("joyously"); to Ferdinand Verdier, 23 September 1920, 3:85–86 (delays); to Félix Sartiaux, 3 February 1921, 3:107–8 ("wedding"); to Georges Duhamel, 28 March 1921, 3:117 ("air").

14. MdG, *Correspondance générale*, MdG to Gaston Gallimard, 28 July 1921, 3:127 ("new war"); to Ferdinand Verdier, 11 September 1921, 3:136 (progress); to Jean Schlumberger, 28 January 1922, 3:150 (progress); to Gaston Gallimard, 28 July 1921, 3:127 ("eight times"); Romain Rolland to MdG, 10 June 1922, 3:468; MdG to Ferdinand Verdier, 31 August 1922, 3:177 ("presumption").

15. MdG, *Correspondance générale*, MdG to Ferdinand Verdier, 15 February 1922, 3:152–53 ("new war"); to Michel Alexandre, 20 December 1923, 3:265 (Poincaré); to Lt. Col. Emile Mayer, 11 May 1924, 3:295 (politics), 5 July 1924, 3:304 (Poincaré); to Berthe Lemarié, 11 September 1923, 3:244 ("excess").

16. MdG, *Correspondance générale*, MdG to Georges Duhamel, 12 October 1922, 3:187 ("started"); to Ferdinand Verdier, 23 May 1923, 3:223 ("reckless"); to Berthe Lemarié, 6 April 1924, 3:289 (parents' health), 30 September 1924, 3:333 ("ghastly"); to Lt. Col. Emile Mayer, 31 December 1924, 3:345 ("ulcers"), 15 January 1925, 3:347 ("Mama"), 7 May 1925, 3:379,

("disequilibrium"); to Jean de Lacretelle, 10 September 1924, 3:325 ("impossible"); to Jean-Richard Bloch, 26 February 1925, 3:352 ("standstill"); to Ferdinand Verdier, 9 March 1925, 3:360 ("breath"); to Gaston Gallimard, 19 May 1925, 3:382 (apologies).

17. MdG, *Correspondance générale*, MdG to Ferdinand Verdier, 18 October 1925, 3:427–28 ("future"); to Robert de Traz, 22 December 1925, 3:446 ("donkeys"); to Ferdinand Verdier, 9 April 1927, 4:151–52 ("intellectual").

18. MdG, *Correspondance générale*, MdG to Lt. Col. Emile Mayer, 10 November 1925, 3:437 ("refuge, good life"); to Lucien Maury, 22 January 1927, 4:127 (snow); to Lt. Col. Emile Mayer, 14 February 1928, 4:274 ("Thibauderie"); to Jean Paulhan, 6 November 1927, 4:229 (royalties); to Lt. Col. Emile Mayer, 10 September 1926, 4:84 (drawer); to Ferdinand Verdier, 10 September 1926, 4:85 (never worn); to Jean Schlumberger, 25 January 1927, 4:129 ("utopian"); to Pierre Rain, 10 February 1928, 4:269 (Christiane).

19. MdG, *Correspondance générale*, MdG to Ferdinand Verdier, 7 February 1926, 4:27 ("twenty years"), 20 November 1926, 4:113 ("bullet"), 18 January 1927, 4:126 ("depths"); to Jean Fernet, 24 March 1927, 4:145 (aging).

20. MdG, *Correspondance générale*, MdG to Henri Ghéon, 5 April 1928, 4:312 (question); Ghéon to MdG, 13 July 1928, 4:567–69 (answer); MdG to Ghéon, 16 July 1928, 4:357 ("exactly"); to Robert de Traz, 20 November 1928, 4:405 (drafts); to Lt. Col. Emile Mayer, 12 November 1928, 4:396 ("death and suffering"); to Félix Sartiaux, 27 November 1928, 4:406 ("fragility").

21. Roger Martin du Gard, *Les Thibault* (parts 1–6) (Paris: Librairie Gallimard, 1922, 1923, 1928, 1929), translated by Stuart Gilbert as *The Thibaults* (New York: Viking Press, 1939), 20, 8, 97.

22. MdG, *The Thibaults*, 110, 112, 167.

23. MdG, *The Thibaults*, 189, 191, 238.

24. MdG, *The Thibaults*, 263, 334, 341.

25. MdG, *The Thibaults*, 404, 419, 455, 456.

26. MdG, *The Thibaults*, 585.

27. MdG, *The Thibaults*, 602, 618.

28. MdG, *The Thibaults*, 734, 780, 791, 869, 870.

29. MdG, *Correspondance générale*, MdG to Ferdinand Verdier, 30 May 1929, 4:450 (religion and morality); Jean-Richard Bloch to MdG, 14 June 1929, 4:581 (evolution of *Les Thibault*); MdG to Bloch, 16 June 1929, 4:454 (reaction to criticism).

30. MdG, *Correspondance générale*, MdG to Jean Schlumberger, 2 December 1929, 4:515 ("passion"); to Maurice Martin du Gard, undated

[December 1929], 4:517 ("worthy"); to Georges Duhamel, 12 December 1929, 5:525–26 ("grieving"); to Ferdinand Verdier, 17 December 1929, 4:531 ("only child").

31. MdG, *Correspondance générale*, MdG to Emilie Noulet, 16 January 1930, 5:11 ("family"); to Henri Ghéon, 29 January 1930, 5:15 ("shattered"); to Lt. Col. Emile Mayer, 30 January 1930, 5:18 (phlebitis), 28 April 1930, 5:47 (pulmonary congestion); to Ferdinand Verdier, 24 August 1930, 5:100 ("loose bonds"); to Marthe Lamy, 19 October 1932, 5:479–80 (Hélène on Coppet); to Jean Schlumberger, 25 April 1933, 6:66 (Coppet); to Lt. Col. Emile Mayer, 21 March 1933, 6:50 (Daniel).

32. MdG, *Correspondance générale*, MdG to Georges Duhamel, 7 January 1931, 5:147 (accident); to Noël Margaritis, 9 January 1931, 5:149 (clinic); to Jean Paulhan, 5 February 1931, 5:167 (phlebitis); to Gilles Margaritis, 9 April 1931, 5:216 ("idiots"); to Lucien Maury, 10 April 1931, 5:217 (pleura); to Jean Schlumberger, 15 July 1931, 5:274 (tumor); to Jean-Richard Bloch, 2 August 1931, 5:278 ("terrible fear"); to Georges Duhamel, 25 June 1932, 5:435 ("beaming"); to Marthe Lamy, 19 October 1932, 5:479–80 ("bad state").

33. MdG, *Correspondance générale*, MdG to Lt. Col. Emile Mayer, 29 April 1932, 5:401–2 ("revenue"); to Jean Schlumberger, 27 May 1932, 5:415–17 ("material existence," "Impossible to sell"); to Georges Duhamel, 25 June 1932, 5:435 (better times).

34. MdG, *Correspondance générale*, MdG to Jean-Richard Bloch, 21 December 1932, 5:492 ("salvation"); to Lucien Maury, 5 December 1930, 5:133 (initial plans); to Félix Bertaux, 3 April 1932, 5:388 (new approach); to Gaston Gallimard, 20 June 1932, 5:546 (renewed work); to Pascal Copeau, 25 February 1933, 6:36 ("re-energized"); to Jean Fernet, 9 November 1934, 6:315 (Hélène's cooking); to Lt. Col. Emile Mayer, 17 July 1933, 6:100 ("not valiant"); to Marthe Lamy, 21 July 1935, 6:401 ("stamina"); to Lt. Col. Emile Mayer, 21 March 1933, 6:50 (birth of Daniel, 19 March 1933); to Marcel Lallemand, 11 November 1935, 6:441 (birth of Anne-Véronique, 9 November 1935); to Mme. Bergmann (daughter of Lt. Col. Emile Mayer), 8 February 1933, 6:20 ("suburb").

35. MdG, *Correspondance générale*, MdG to Eugène Dabit, 30 July 1933, 6:101, 652 (screenplay); to Jean-Richard Bloch, 2 October 1933, 6:136 (screenplay); to Jean Schlumberger, 24 August 1933, 6:117 (mortgage), 14 March 1934, 6:223 ("that point"); to Berthe Lemarié, 11 June 1935, 6:383–84 (painting by Johan Barthold Jongkind), 6 July 1935, 6:393 (frantic), 11 July 1935, 6:395–96 (accepts low offer), 28 September 1935, 6:428–29 (painting by Giuseppe Palizzi); to Jean Schlumberger, beginning of October 1935,

6:431 (insomnia, indebtedness), 27 December 1935, 6:456–57 (completes *L'Eté 1914*).

36. MdG, *Correspondance générale*, MdG to Florent Margaritis, 19 March 1932, 5:378 (German traits); to Lt. Col. Emile Mayer, 19 March 1932, 5:379 (Hitler followers); to Wladimir d'Ormesson, 30 October 1933, 6:149 (*Le Temps* columns), 5 November 1933, 6:158–59 (*Mein Kampf*), 27 November 1933, 6:170; to Lucien Maury, 15 February 1934, 6:202 (demonstrations); to Jules Froment, 18 February 1934, 6:203 (adventure). See also Wladimir d'Ormesson, *La Confiance dans l'Allemagne?* (Paris: Gallimard, 1928).

37. MdG, *Correspondance générale*, MdG to Lt. Col. Emile Mayer, 13 May 1935, 6:376 (interwar policies); to Marcel Lallemand, 3 June 1935, 6:383 ("Germanism and Slavism"); to Maurice Martin du Gard, 25 August 1935, 6:419 (Mussolini); to Emilie Noulet, 4 September 1935, 6:425 ("imposters").

38. MdG, *Correspondance générale*, MdG to Lt. Col. Emile Mayer, 16 March 1936, 6:490 (Rhineland); to Simon and Dorothy Bussy, 8 August 1936, 6:554 (Spanish Civil War); to Lt. Col. Emile Mayer, 14 August 1935, 6:414 ("capitalism"), 9 May 1936, 6:510–11 (Communist party), 13 August 1936, 6:559 (Communists and war); to Marcel Lallemand, 9 September 1936, 6:567 (anything but war).

39. Roger Martin du Gard, *Les Thibault* (part 7 and epilogue) (Paris: Librairie Gallimard, 1936, 1940), translated by Stuart Gilbert as *Summer 1914* (New York: Viking Press, 1940), 26, 69–70, 75.

40. MdG, *Summer 1914*, 114, 144, 157.

41. MdG, *Summer 1914*, 259, 312, 342, 352.

42. MdG, *Summer 1914*, 360, 493, 506.

43. MdG, *Summer 1914*, 511–12, 522, 524, 526, 532, 534.

44. MdG, *Summer 1914*, 576, 607.

45. MdG, *Summer 1914*, 659–60, 670.

46. MdG, *Summer 1914*, 678, 703, 718, 756.

47. MdG, *Correspondance générale*, Raymond Aron to MdG, 25 December 1936, 6:724 (*L'Eté 1914*); to Lt. Col. Emile Mayer, 13 November 1937, 7:188 (Nobel Prize); to Gaston Gallimard, 14 November 1937, 7:189 ("presumptuous"); to Per Hallstrom, permanent secretary to the Royal Academy of Sweden, 16 November 1937, 7:196–97 ("Armistice").

48. MdG, *Correspondance générale*, MdG to Lt. Col. Emile Mayer, 31 December 1937, 7:224 ("fairy story"); to Henri de Saussine, 1 January 1938, 7:225 ("terrifying"); to Berthe Lemarié, 13 January 1938, 7:233 (Vienna); to Alphonse Delubac, 23 March 1938, 7:258 ("tour"); to Emilie Noulet, 2 April 1938, 7:264 ("world is insane"); to Jean Rostand, 14 May 1938, 7:279 (coda).

49. MdG, *Correspondance générale*, MdG to Jules and Lise Romains, 25 May 1938, 7:284 (bulldog, "end of the year"); to Anne Heurgon-Desjardins, 16 June 1938, 7:305 ("application"); to Edy Debray, 31 August 1938, 7:325 ("solace"); to Marcel Lallemand, 3 September 1938, 7:329 ("July 1914"), 12 September 1938, 7:331 ("Summer 1938"); to Jean Blanzat, 29 September 1938, 7:336 ("danger averted"), 8 October 1938, 7:338–39 (Munich).

50. MdG, *Correspondance générale*, MdG to Jacques de Lacretelle, 25 January 1937, 7:24 ("confidante"); to Félix Sartiaux, 16 January 1939, 7:387 (Hélène's sister and father); to Elisabeth Herbart, 6 February 1939, 7:398 (Literary Guild); to Félix Bertaux, 6 May 1939, 7:423 (Czechoslovakia and Albania); to Marcel Lallemand, 12 May 1939, 7:425 ("anguish"); to Gaston Gallimard, 23 May 1939, 7:429 (*Epilogue*); to Jean Schlumberger, 5 June 1939, 7:433 ("whole and complete").

51. MdG, *Summer 1914*, 785, 789.

52. MdG, *Summer 1914*, 844, 845, 875.

53. MdG, *Summer 1914*, 901, 902, 918.

54. MdG, *Summer 1914*, 954, 922, 931, 995.

55. MdG, *Summer 1914*, 929, 986–87, 1004, 1008.

56. MdG, *Correspondance générale*, MdG to Jean Schlumberger, 31 August 1939, 7:481 (war crisis); to Noël Margaritis, 5 October 1939, 7:488 (war, censorship, decisions); to Jean Schlumberger, 17 October 1939, 7:489 (plans to return); to Gaston Gallimard, 25 December 1939, 7:498–501 (arrival).

Chapter 4: Shifting Ground

1. For these statistics, see Benjamin Franklin Martin, *France and the Après Guerre, 1918–1924: Illusions and Disillusionment* (Baton Rouge: Louisiana State University Press, 1999), 16–20; Alfred Sauvy, *Histoire économique de la France entre les deux guerres*, 3 vols. (Paris: Fayard, 1965–75), 1:21–27, 169–72.

2. For an introduction to these issues, see Siân Reynolds, *France between the Wars: Gender and Politics* (London: Routledge, 1996); Mary Louise Roberts, *Civilization without Sexes: Reconstructing Gender in Postwar France, 1917–1927* (Chicago: University of Chicago Press, 1995); Gérard Noiriel, *The French Melting Pot: Immigration, Citizenship, and National Identity* (Minneapolis: University of Minnesota Press, 1996); Romy Golan, *Modernity and Nostalgia: Art and Politics in France between the Wars* (New Haven: Yale University Press, 1995). The last sentence is a paraphrase from *Hamlet* I.v.166–67, in *The Complete Works of William Shakespeare* (Garden City, N.Y.: Garden City Books, 1936), 743.

3. Frank Field, *Three French Writers and the Great War: Studies in the Rise of Communism and Fascism* (Cambridge: Cambridge University Press, 1975); Henri Barbusse, *Le Feu: Journal d'une escouade* (Paris: Ernest Flammarion, 1916), translated by Fitzwater Wray as *Under Fire: The Story of a Squad* (New York: E. P. Dutton, 1917), 17, 14, 36, 32.

4. Barbusse, *Under Fire*, 48, 153, 82, 205.

5. Barbusse, *Under Fire*, 114, 313, 130–31, 275.

6. Barbusse, *Under Fire*, 338, 342, 343, 344, 345.

7. Lucille Frackman Becker, *Henry de Montherlant: A Critical Biography* (Carbondale: Southern Illinois University Press, 1970); Henry de Montherlant, *Le Songe* (Paris: Editions Bernard Grasset, 1922).

8. Montherlant, *Le Songe*, 8, 12, 25, 23, 26, 22.

9. Montherlant, *Le Songe*, 40, 44–45, 125, 126, 258.

10. Montherlant, *Le Songe*, 150–51, 294, 296.

11. See Judith Thurman, *Secrets of the Flesh: A Life of Colette* (New York: Ballantine Books, 1999); Patricia Tilburg, *Colette's Republic: Work, Gender, and Popular Culture in France, 1870–1914* (New York: Berghahn, 2009).

12. Colette [Sidonie-Gabrielle Colette], *Mitsou ou comment l'esprit vient aux filles* (Paris: Arthème Fayard, 1919), 48.

13. Colette, *Mitsou*, 29, 62, 68.

14. Colette, *Mitsou*, 67, 68, 67, 60–61, 111.

15. Colette, *Mitsou*, 65, 52, 63.

16. Colette, *Mitsou*, 79, 110, 98, 122.

17. Patrick McCarthy, *Céline: A Biography* (New York: Viking Press, 1975); Louis-Ferdinand Céline [Louis-Ferdinand-Auguste Destouches], *Voyage au bout de la nuit* (Paris: Editions Denoël et Steele, 1932), translated by John H. P. Marks as *Journey to the End of the Night* (Boston: Little, Brown, 1934).

18. Céline, *Journey to the End of the Night*, 9, 11, 30, 31, 36, 66, 50.

19. Céline, *Journey to the End of the Night*, 55, 56, 19.

20. Céline, *Journey to the End of the Night*, 108, 110, 174, 172.

21. Céline, *Journey to the End of the Night*, 363, 68, 316, 323, 501.

22. Jean Touzot, *Julien Green* (Paris: Klincksieck, 1997); Jean-Eric Green, *Album Julien Green* (Paris: Editions Gallimard, 1998); Julien Green, *Léviathan* (Paris: Librairie Plon, 1929), translated by Vyvyan Holland as *The Dark Journey* (New York: Harper & Brothers, 1929).

23. Green, *The Dark Journey*, 18, 28, 4.

24. Green, *The Dark Journey*, 41, 44, 77, 78.

25. Green, *The Dark Journey,* 106–7, 130, 94, 120–21, 137, 138.

26. Green, *The Dark Journey,* 210, 213–14, 213, 215.

27. Green, *The Dark Journey,* 272, 350, 367, 367.

28. Green, *The Dark Journey,* 375, 376.

29. Olivier Philipponnat and Patrick Lienhardt, *La Vie d'Irène Némirovsky* (Paris: Editions Grasset et Fasquelle and Editions Denöel, 2007), translated by Euan Cameron as *The Life of Irène Némirovsky, 1903–1942* (New York: Alfred A. Knopf, 2010); Irène Némirovsky, *David Golder* (Paris: Editions Bernard Grasset, 1929), translated by Sandra Smith as *David Golder* (New York: Alfred A. Knopf, 2008).

30. Némirovsky, *David Golder,* 6, 14, 11, 8.

31. Némirovsky, *David Golder,* 25, 30, 80, 30, 31, 39, 44.

32. Némirovsky, *David Golder,* 85, 87, 88, 89–90, 99, 101.

33. Némirovsky, *David Golder,* 116, 117, 119.

34. Némirovsky, *David Golder,* 136, 142.

35. Philipponnat and Lienhardt, *The Life of Irène Némirovsky,* 151.

36. Jean-Luc Barré, *François Mauriac, biographie intime, 1885–1970,* 2 vols. (Paris: Fayard, 2009–2010); François Mauriac, *Le Noeud des vipères* (Paris: Editions Bernard Grasset, 1932), translated by Gerard Hopkins as *Vipers' Tangle* (New York: Carroll & Graf, 1987); Philipponnat and Lienhardt, *The Life of Irène Némirovsky,* 192.

37. Mauriac, *Vipers' Tangle,* 25, 14.

38. Mauriac, *Vipers' Tangle,* 42, 32, 108, 106, 114.

39. Mauriac, *Vipers' Tangle,* 129, 137, 119, 118.

40. Mauriac, *Vipers' Tangle,* 158, 185–86, 207.

41. Georges Bernanos, *Journal d'un curé de campagne* (Paris: Librairie Plon, 1936), translated by Pamela Morris as *The Diary of a Country Priest* (New York: Carroll & Graf, 1983); Pierre Gille, *Bernanos et l'angoisse: Etude de l'oeuvre romanesque* (Nancy: Presses universitaires de Nancy, 1984).

42. Bernanos, *The Diary of a Country Priest,* 11–12, 18.

43. Bernanos, *The Diary of a Country Priest,* 65, 65, 66, 67.

44. Bernanos, *The Diary of a Country Priest,* 81, 117.

45. Bernanos, *The Diary of a Country Priest,* 9.

46. Bernanos, *The Diary of a Country Priest,* 158, 162, 162, 171, 172.

47. Bernanos, *The Diary of a Country Priest,* 291, 298.

48. Eugen Weber, *The Hollow Years: France in the 1930s* (New York: W. W. Norton, 1994), 176.

49. Consuelo de Saint-Exupéry, *Mémoires de la rose* (Paris: Editions

Plon, 2000), translated by Esther Allen as *The Tale of the Rose* (New York: Random House, 2001), 202. See also Stacy Schiff, *Saint-Exupéry: A Biography* (New York: Da Capo Press, 1994).

50. Antoine de Saint-Exupéry, *Terre des hommes* (Paris: Editions Gallimard, 1939), translated by Lewis Galantière as *Wind, Sand and Stars* (New York: Harcourt, 1992); also Geneviève Le Hir, *Saint-Exupéry ou la force des images* (Paris: Imago, 2002).

51. Saint-Exupéry, *Wind, Sand and Stars*, 35, 38, 32, 38.

52. Saint-Exupéry, *Wind, Sand and Stars*, 29, 39, 39, 40.

53. *New York Times Magazine*, 29 November 1942; Saint-Exupéry, *Wind, Sand and Stars*, 176; Saint-Exupéry, *The Tale of the Rose*, viii.

Chapter 5: Edouard—The Hesitant

1. For Daladier, see the remarkable biography by Elisabeth du Réau, *Edouard Daladier, 1884–1970* (Paris: Librairie Arthème Fayard, 1993), based on her much longer *thèse d'état*, and René Rémond and Janine Bourdin, eds., *Edouard Daladier, chef de gouvernement, avril 1938–septembre 1939* (Paris: Presses de la Fondation nationale des sciences politiques, 1977).

2. Roger Martin du Gard, *Correspondance générale*, ed. Maurice Rieuneau, Jean-Claude Airal, et al., 10 vols. (Paris: Librairie Gallimard, 1980–2006); Martin du Gard to Félix Sartiaux, 22 June 1931, 6:260–61. See also Alfred Sauvy, *Histoire économique de la France entre les deux guerres,* 3 vols. (Paris: Fayard, 1965–1975), 2:15–76, 488–89, 506, 528, 554, 562–63, 577; Peter J. Larmour, *The French Radical Party in the 1930s* (Stanford: Stanford University Press, 1964), 71.

3. Paul F. Jankowski, *Stavisky: Confidence Man in the Republic of Virtue* (Ithaca, N.Y.: Cornell University Press, 2002); Benjamin Franklin Martin, *The Hypocrisy of Justice in the Belle Epoque* (Baton Rouge: Louisiana State University Press, 1984), 225–28.

4. John Michael Wallace-Hadrill and John McManners, eds., *France: Government and Society* (London: Methuen and Co., 1957), 227. The image explained: "red," the color of revolution; "white," the color of conservatism; "butter," an analogy for corruption.

5. Piers Brendon, *The Dark Valley: A Panorama of the 1930s* (New York: Alfred A. Knopf, 2000), 167–71; Benjamin Franklin Martin, *France in 1938* (Baton Rouge: Louisiana State University Press, 2005), 31–33. In general, Sean Kennedy, *Reconciling France against Democracy: The Croix de Feu and the*

Parti Social Français, 1927–1945 (Montreal: McGill-Queens University Press, 2007); Robert Soucy, *French Fascism: The Second Wave, 1933–1939* (New Haven: Yale University Press, 1997); Jessica Wardhaugh, *In Pursuit of the People: Political Culture in France, 1934–39* (Basingstoke, U.K.: Palgrave Macmillan, 2009); and Samuel Kalman, *The Extreme Right in Interwar France: The Faisceaux and the Croix de Feu* (Burlington, Vt.: Ashgate Publishing, 2008), all portray La Rocque and the Croix de Feu more negatively than I have done.

6. Denis William Brogan, *The Development of Modern France (1870–1939)* (London: Hamish Hamilton, 1940), 657. See also Benjamin Franklin Martin, *Crime and Criminal Justice under the Third Republic: The Shame of Marianne* (Baton Rouge: Louisiana State University Press, 1990), 97; Jean Belin, *Trente ans de Sûreté nationale* (Paris: Bibliothèque France-Soir, 1950), 167–69; Léon Daudet, *La Police politique: Ses moyens et ses crimes* (Paris: Denoël et Steele, 1934), 69–70.

7. *La Liberté*, 4 February 1934; *L'Action française*, 3–4 February 1934; *Le Jour*, 5 February 1934.

8. Réau, *Edouard Daladier*, 121–33 (quotations from 127, 128, 129).

9. Réau, *Edouard Daladier*, 131–33 (quotation from 133). See also *Le Matin* and *Le Figaro*, 7 February 1934.

10. *L'Humanité*, *Le Populaire*, *Le Figaro*, *La Victoire*, 8 February 1934; Réau, *Edouard Daladier*, 134–36 (quotation from 136); Edouard Daladier, *Journal de captivité, 1940–1945* (Paris: Calmann-Lévy, 1991), 272.

11. Réau, *Edouard Daladier*, 15–27 (quotation from 27). See also Jean-Jacques Becker, *Les Français dans la grande guerre* (Paris: Robert Laffont, 1980).

12. Alexander Werth, *France and Munich, before and after the Surrender* (London: Hamish Hamilton, 1939), 137–38.

13. *Journal Officiel*, Chambre des Députés, Débats parlementaires (hereinafter cited as J. O. C., Débats), 25 June 1920.

14. J. O. C., Débats, 15 March 1922.

15. Benjamin Franklin Martin, *France and the Après Guerre, 1918–1924: Illusions and Disillusionment* (Baton Rouge: Louisiana State University Press, 1999), 23–25, 124–31. The full names of the Bolshevik leaders are Vladimir Ilyich Ulyanov (alias Lenin), Lev Borisovich Kamenev, and Lev Davidovich Bronshtein (alias Leon Trotsky).

16. Edouard Herriot, *La Russie nouvelle* (Paris: J. Ferenczi et fils, 1922); *Le Journal*, 19 (Daladier quotation), 26 October, 2 November 1922.

17. Martin, *France and the Après Guerre*, 159–66.

18. Larmour, *French Radical Party*, 74; Martin, *France in 1938*, 21–25.

19. Réau, *Edouard Daladier*, 56–62 (quotation from 62).

20. *Le Figaro*, 4 November 1928. See also Réau, *Edouard Daladier*, 69–74. For all these developments, see the superb account in Brogan, *Development of Modern France*, 581–622, 635–50.

21. *Le Matin*, 11 September 1926, 6 September 1929, for Briand's speeches at Geneva on 10 September 1926 and 5 September 1929.

22. *Le Matin*, 25 October 1929; Joel Colton, *Léon Blum: Humanist in Politics* (New York: Alfred A. Knopf, 1966), 75–77.

23. Réau, *Edouard Daladier*, 92, 93 (Weygand), 94 (Bourret); see also Maxime Weygand, *Mémoires: Mirages et réalités*, 2 vols. (Paris: Flammarion, 1957), 2:387.

24. Colton, *Léon Blum*, 80–88, for the negotiations with the Socialists; Réau, *Edouard Daladier*, 104 (Gamelin), 105 (intelligence service); see also Maurice Gustave Gamelin, *Servir*, 3 vols. (Paris: Librairie Plon, 1946), 2:79, 88–92.

25. *Le Temps*, 3 March 1933; *Le Matin*, 18 October 1933; J. O. C., Débats, 17 October 1933; also Réau, *Edouard Daladier*, 99–115.

26. René Mazedier in *Le Petit Parisien*, 31 January 1933.

27. Eugen Weber, *The Hollow Years: France in the 1930s* (New York: W. W. Norton, 1994), 134; Brendon, *The Dark Valley*, 167.

28. *Le Matin*, 23, 30 March 1935; *L'Oeuvre*, 24 May 1935; J. O. C., Débats, 29 May 1935; Edouard Herriot, *D'une guerre à l'autre*, 2 vols. (Paris: Flammarion, 1948), 2:429.

29. *L'Oeuvre*, 16 May 1936 (Daladier); *L'Humanité*, 11, 15 May 1936 (Communist position); Colton, *Léon Blum*, 129–59.

30. Charles de Gaulle, *Vers l'armée de métier* (Paris: Berger-Levrault, 1934); Charles de Gaulle, *Lettres, notes et carnets, 1919–1940*, 2 vols. (Paris: Plon, 1980), 2:407–8, 411; Gamelin, *Servir*, 2:240–46; Robert Jacomet, *L'Armement de la France, 1936–1939* (Paris: Lajeunesse, 1945), 217–18.

31. Réau, *Edouard Daladier*, 196.

32. Martin, *France in 1938*, 92–93. A clever but cruel pun described the elevation in social standing of Jeanne de Crussol based on the pronunciation of her married name: "la sardine qui s'est crue sole" (the sardine that took itself for a sole).

33. Jules Jeanneney, *Journal politique* (Paris: Armand Colin, 1972), 19; Charles Joseph André Géraud [Pertinax], *Les Fossoyeurs: Défaite militaire de la France, armistice, contre-révolution*, 2 vols. (New York: La Maison française, 1943), 1:113; Guy de Girard de Charbonnières, *La Plus évitable de*

toutes les guerres: Un témoin raconte (Paris: Albatros, 1985), 113; *L'Epoque,* 13 April 1938.

34. Colton, *Léon Blum,* 160–307; J. O. C., Débats, 26 February 1938.

35. Telford Taylor, *Munich: The Price of Peace* (New York: Doubleday, 1979), 507–19 (quotation from 519); Martin, *France in 1938,* 146–48.

36. *London Times* and *Le Matin,* 12 September 1938; Girard de Charbonnières, *La Plus évitable,* 159–60 (Daladier); *Le Figaro,* 9 September 1938; Jean Zay, *Carnets secrets* (Paris: Les Editions de France, 1942), 6 (Chautemps).

37. *Le Matin,* 25 September 1938; *London Times,* 28 September 1938; J. O. C., Débats, 25 February 1938 ("retrenchment"); Werth, *France and Munich,* 301 (posters); *Le Matin,* 28 September 1938. See also Orville H. Bullitt, *For the President, Personal and Secret: Correspondence between Franklin D. Roosevelt and William C. Bullitt* (London: Deutsch, 1973), 290–91.

38. Lacaze, *La France et Munich: Etude d'un processus décisionnel en matières de la relations internationales* (Berne: Peter Lang, 1992), 255 ("crime"); Réau, *Edouard Daladier,* 278 ("return to France"); Taylor, *Munich,* 48 (François-Poncet); Martin, *France in 1938,* 173–77.

39. Taylor, *Munich,* 59–64 (quotation from 62); Etienne de Crouy Chanel, *Alexis Léger, l'autre visage de Saint-John Perse* (Paris: Picollec, 1989), 235; Martin, *France in 1938,* 177 ("fools").

40. John McVickar Haight, *American Aid to France, 1938–1940* (New York: Atheneum, 1970), 13 (Bullitt); *Le Matin,* 22 August 1938 (Daladier speech); Martin, *France in 1938,* 202–10.

41. Sauvy, *Histoire économique,* 2:528, 555; Réau, *Edouard Daladier,* 345–47.

42. Réau, *Edouard Daladier,* 287 ("*un traquenard*"); for the Ribbentrop visit, Martin, *France in 1938,* 194–95, 199–202; *Le Matin,* 7–8 December 1938, and especially *Le Figaro,* 7–8 December 1938, exercised because of the presence with Ribbentrop of Joseph Caillaux.

43. *Le Matin,* 1, 12 (quotations from Italian press) December 1938, 2 January 1939.

Chapter 6: August 1939

1. William L. Shirer, *The Collapse of the Third Republic: An Inquiry into the Fall of France in 1940* (New York: Simon and Schuster, 1969), 436–38; Pierre Lazareff, *De Munich à Vichy* (New York: Brentano's, 1944), 125; Georges Bonnet, *Défense de la paix,* 2 vols. (Geneva: Bibliothèque du Cheval ailé, 1946–48), 2:258–59.

2. Jean-Baptiste Duroselle, *Politique étrangère de la France: La Décadence, 1932–1939* (Paris: Imprimerie nationale, 1979), 364. The traditional interpretation of France in the 1930s as a nation decadent, discouraged, and defeatist began with the personal testimony of Marc Bloch, *L'Etrange défaite: Témoignage écrit en 1940* (Paris: Paris Franc-Tireur, 1946), and Charles de Gaulle, *Mémoires de guerre*, 3 vols. (Paris: Librairie Plon, 1954–59). In the same vein came the meditations of French philosophers such as Jacques Maritain, *A travers le désastre* (New York: Editions de la Maison française, 1941), and Raymond Aron, *De l'armistice à l'insurrection nationale* (Paris: Editions Gallimard, 1945). Then came the work of French historians writing of "international relations": Pierre Renouvin, *Histoire des relations internationales: Les crises du XXe siècle* (Paris: Hachette, 1957–58), vols. 7–8; Maurice Baumont, *La Faillite de la paix (1918–1939)*, 2 vols. (Paris: Presses universitaires de France, 1945–46); Duroselle, *La Décadence*. To various degrees and in various ways, this interpretation has been furthered by later historians, both inside France—such as Serge Bernstein, *La France des années trente* (Paris: Armand Colin, 1988); Pierre Laborie, *L'Opinion française sous Vichy: Les Français et la crise d'identité nationale, 1936–1944* (Paris: Seuil, 2001); and François-Georges Dreyfus, *1919–1939: L'Engrenage* (Paris: Editions de Fallois, 2002)—and outside France—such as Anthony Adamthwaite, *France and the Coming of the Second World War* (London: Cass, 1977); Williamson Murray, *The Change in the European Balance of Power, 1938–1939: The Path to Ruin* (Princeton: Princeton University Press, 1984); Piotr Wandycz, *The Twilight of French Eastern Alliances, 1926–1936* (Princeton: Princeton University Press, 1988); Nicole Jordan, *The Popular Front and Central Europe: The Dilemmas of French Impotence, 1918–1940* (Cambridge: Cambridge University Press, 1992); Eugen Weber, *The Hollow Years: France in the 1930s* (New York: W. W. Norton, 1994); Richard Francis Crane, *A French Conscience in Prague: Louis Eugène Faucher and the Abandonment of Czechoslovakia* (Boulder, Colo.: East European Monographs, 1997); Michael Carley, *1939: The Alliance that Never Was* (Chicago: I. R. Dee, 1999); Benjamin Franklin Martin, *France in 1938* (Baton Rouge: Louisiana State University Press, 2005); and Raphaële Ulrich-Pier, *René Massigli (1888–1988): Une vie de diplomate* (Berne: Peter Lang, 2006). A counter—sometimes termed "revisionist"—argument is that France played a bad hand (the effects of the Great War, demographic and economic inferiority to Germany, insoluble diplomatic contradictions) reasonably well and by the end of the 1930s had reached a *redressement psychologique*, defined as preparation, however reluctant, to face the third war with Germany in seventy

years, only twenty years since the last one. The first expression of this argument came from Arnold Wolfers, *Britain and France between the Two World Wars: Conflicting Strategies of Peace from Versailles to World War II* (New York: Harcourt, Brace, 1940), even as the fighting began. It was elaborated by John C. Cairns, in "Along the Road Back to France 1940," *American Historical Review* 64 (June 1959): 583–603, and "A Nation of Shopkeepers in Search of a Suitable France," *American Historical Review* 79 (June 1974): 710–43, and also by Geoffrey Warner, in *Pierre Laval and the Eclipse of France* (New York: Macmillan, 1969).

Revisionism became full-throated in several works by Robert J. Young—*In Command of France: French Foreign Policy and Military Planning* (Cambridge, Mass.: Harvard University Press, 1978), *France and the Origins of the Second World War* (New York: St. Martin's Press, 1996), and *Marketing Marianne: French Propaganda in America, 1900–1940* (New Brunswick, N.J.: Rutgers University Press, 2004)—and in Jean-Pierre Azèma, *De Munich à la libération* (Paris: Seuil, 1979); Henry Dutailly, *Les Problèmes de l'armée de terre française, 1933–1939* (Paris: Imprimerie nationale, 1980); Robert Frank[enstein], *Le Prix du réarmament français, 1935–1939* (Paris: Publications de la Sorbonne, 1982) and *La Hantise du déclin: La France, 1920–1960: Finances, défense et identité nationale* (Paris: Belin, 1994); Jean-Louis Crémieux-Brilhac, *Les Français de l'an 40*, 2 vols. (Paris: Editions Gallimard, 1990); Martin Alexander, *The Republic in Danger: General Maurice Gamelin and the Politics of French Defense, 1933–1940* (Cambridge: Cambridge University Press, 1992); Martin Thomas, *Britain, France and Appeasement: Anglo-French Relations in the Popular Front Era* (Oxford: Peter Berg, 1996); Eugenia Kiesling, *Arming against Hitler: France and the Limits of Military Planning* (Lawrence: University Press of Kansas, 1996); Elizabeth Kier, *Imagining War: French and British Military Doctrine between the Wars* (Princeton: Princeton University Press, 1997); Peter Jackson, *France and the Nazi Menace: Intelligence and Policy-Making, 1933–1939* (New York: Oxford University Press, 2000); and a tendentious historiographical essay, "Post-War Politics and the Historiography of French Strategy and Diplomacy before the Second World War," *History Compass* 4 (September 2006): 870–905. Somewhat less full-throated in revisionism are the works by Elisabeth du Réau, *Edouard Daladier, 1880–1970* (Paris: Librairie Plon, 1970); Julian Jackson, *France: The Dark Years* (Oxford: Oxford University Press, 2001), and *The Fall of France: The Nazi Invasion of 1940* (Oxford: Oxford University Press, 2003); Ernest May, *Strange Victory: Hitler's Conquest of France* (New York: Hill and Wang, 2000); and Talbot Imlay,

Facing the Second World War: Strategy, Politics and Economics in Britain and France, 1938–1940 (Oxford: Oxford University Press, 2003).

3. *Paris-Soir*, 2 October 1938, quoted in Réau, *Edouard Daladier*, 254–55; Antoine de Saint-Exupéry, *Terre des hommes* (Paris: Editions Gallimard, 1939), translated by Lewis Galantière as *Wind, Sand and Stars* (New York: Harcourt, 1992), 174; *Le Figaro*, 3, 5, 7, 9, 12, 15, 18, 22 November 1938. 4. *Journal Officiel*, Chambre des Députés, Débats parlementaires (hereinafter cited as J. O. C., Débats), 2 October 1938. The vote at the Socialist party congress was 4,322 votes in favor of Blum's resolution to support national defense "totally and without reservation"; 2,837 for a competing resolution by Paul Faure, "The victory of peace is possible only if one does not believe in the inevitability of war"; and 1,014 abstentions; see *Le Populaire*, 27 December 1938.

5. John McVickar Haight, *American Aid to France, 1938–1940* (New York: Atheneum, 1970), 13 (Daladier); *Le Petit Parisien*, 9 October 1938 (Bonnet); Christel Peyrefitte, "Les Premiers sondages d'opinion," in *Edouard Daladier, chef de gouvernement: avril 1938–septembre 1939*, ed. René Rémond and Janine Bourdin (Paris: Presses de la Fondation nationale des sciences politiques, 1977), 265–74 (quotations from 270, 271, 272).

6. Martin, *France in 1938*, 203–13; J. O. C., Débats, 19 December 1938; May, *Strange Victory*, 188–91; Réau, *Edouard Daladier*, 315–16; Pierre Hoff, *Les Programmes d'armement de 1919 à 1939* (Paris: Service historique de l'armée de terre, 1982), 216. The votes for decree power were on 18 March 1939.

7. J. O. C., Débats, 28 June 1938.

8. Reinhard Tristan Eugen Heydrich was born in 1904, a year after Abetz. That Adolf Hitler regarded Heydrich as his most worthy successor is a sufficient characterization; see Robert Gerwarth, *Hitler's Hangman: The Life of Heydrich* (New Haven: Yale University Press, 2011).

9. Information in this and the next two paragraphs is taken from Alfred Kupferman, "Diplomatie parallèle et guerre psychologique: le rôle de la Ribbentrop-Dienststelle dans les tentatives d'action sur l'opinion française, 1934–1939," *Relations internationales* 3 (July 1975): 72–95; Pierre Lazareff with David Partridge, *Deadline: The Behind-the-Scenes Story of the Last Decade in France* (New York: Random House, 1942), 225–26; Adamthwaite, *Coming of the Second World War*, 332; Dietrich Orlow, *The Lure of Fascism in Western Europe: German Nazis, Dutch and French Fascists, 1933–1939* (New York: Palgrave-Macmillan, 2009), 21–22, 33–34, 46–47, 49, 71–75, 132; Otto Abetz, *Histoire d'une politique franco-allemande (1930–1950): Mémoires d'un ambassadeur* (Paris: Librairie Stock, 1953).

10. *L'Epoque*, 23 July–16 August 1939. *Le Figaro* and *Le Matin* reported the refusal of a new visa on 14 August 1939; see also Carmen Callil, *Bad Faith: A Forgotten History of Family, Fatherhood, and Vichy France* (New York: Alfred A. Knopf, 2006), 181.

11. Quotations are from *L'Action française*, 10, 15 August 1939; *L'Humanité*, 4, 10, 11, 15 August 1939. See also *L'Action française*, 3, 4, 9 August 1939; *L'Humanité*, 5, 6, 9, 14 August 1939.

12. Jean Bugatti was born Gianoberto Maria Carlo Bugatti. His death was reported in *Le Matin* and *Le Figaro*, 13 August 1939.

13. Biographical details from *New York Times*, 11 August 1939, and *Time*, 21 August 1939.

14. *Le Matin*, 12 August 1939, quoting Walser.

15. *New York Times*, 14 August 1939; *Le Matin*, 12 August 1939. See also *Le Matin*, 13 August 1939; *L'Action française*, 22 August 1939.

16. *L'Humanité*, 12, 13, 21 August 1939; *L'Action française*, 18, 20, 23 August 1939. See also *L'Action française*, 12, 14, 24 August 1939.

17. *L'Humanité*, 2 ("verdict"), 3, 4 (Duclos), 5 (Kahn), 6 ("respect"), 14, 15 August 1939; *L'Action française*, 3 (sins of the leaders), 7 ("Justice and Truth"), 9 ("Chamber"), 11 (restore the monarchy) August 1939.

18. The painting was twenty-five by nineteen centimeters, that is, ten by seven inches.

19. *Le Matin* (and every other French daily), 15–20, 23 August 1939.

20. A sure guide is Duroselle, *La Décadence*, 396–428.

21. Robert Coulondre, *De Staline à Hitler: Souvenirs de deux ambassades, 1936–1939* (Paris: Hachette, 1950), 169 (Third Partition), 181, 270–75; André Beaufre, *Le drame de 1940* (Paris: Librairie Plon, 1965), 124 (Daladier). See also [Captain] Paul Stehlin, *Témoignage pour l'histoire* (Paris: Robert Laffont, 1964), 147, 151–52, 375–79; Duroselle, *La Décadence*, 429–31.

22. *Le Figaro*, 14, 19, 17 (Maurois) August 1939; *L'Humanité*, 1 August 1939; *L'Action française*, 3 August 1939. Maurois was elected to the Académie française in 1938; d'Ormesson in 1956.

23. *Le Matin*, 21 August 1939 (Lourdes); *Le Figaro*, 21 August 1939 (Lourdes, d'Ormesson); *Le Temps*, 20 August 1939. See also *Le Figaro*, 1, 10, 16, 20 August 1939; *Le Temps*, 11 August 1939; *Le Matin*, 18 August 1939; *L'Action française*, 15, 18 August 1939.

24. Duroselle, *La Décadence*, 432–35 (quotation from 435).

25. *Le Figaro*, 24 ("defense"), 25 August; *Le Temps*, 25 August; *Le Populaire*, 23 August; *L'Action française*, 23 August; *L'Humanité*, 22 August; *Le Temps*, 24, 25 August; *Le Figaro*, 25 August 1939. See also *Le Figaro*, 22,

23 August; *Le Temps*, 22, 23 August; *L'Action française*, 22, 24, 25 August; *L'Humanité*, 23, 24, 25 August 1939.

26. *Le Temps*, 15, 17, 22 August 1939.

27. The Paris newspapers published Daladier's speech in its entirety, 26 August 1939.

28. *L'Oeuvre*, 4 May 1939; *London Times*, 3 May 1939; Duroselle, *La Décadence*, 475–79.

29. *Le Figaro*, 29 August 1939, quoting Verdier and Weill; see also *Le Temps*, *Le Figaro*, and *Le Matin*, with striking photographs, 26, 27, 28, 29, 30, 31 August 1939.

30. *L'Action française*, 26 August 1939; *Le Temps*, 27 August 1939 (Riou; Socialist party reaction); *L'Action française*, 26 August 1939 (Grunbach; Ybarnégaray; committee resolution); *Le Matin*, 26 August 1939.

31. *Le Figaro*, 29 August 1939; *L'Action française*, 30 August 1939 (also 26–29, 31 August); John Leslie Snell, *Illusion and Necessity: The Diplomacy of Global War, 1939–1945* (Boston: Houghton Mifflin, 1963), 1.

32. Duroselle, *La Décadence*, 479–93 (Daladier quoted 481); J. O. C., *Débats*, 2 September 1939; *Journal Officiel*, Sénat, Débats parlementaires, 2 September 1939.

33. Duroselle, *La Décadence*, 493; Weber, *Hollow Years*, 262.

34. Benjamin Franklin Martin, *Count Albert de Mun: Paladin of the Third Republic* (Chapel Hill: University of North Carolina Press, 1978), 290; Shirer, *Collapse of the Third Republic*, 519–802; Weber, *Hollow Years*, 281–87.

35. J. O. C., *Débats*, 8 March 1918; Max Hastings, *Winston's War: Churchill, 1940–1945* (New York: Alfred A. Knopf, 2010), 41.

36. Irène Némirovsky, *Suite française* (Paris: Denoël, 2004), translated by Sandra Smith as *Suite française* (New York: Alfred A. Knopf, 2006), 344. Stéphane Audoin-Rouzeau and Annette Becker, *14–18, retrouver la guerre* (Paris: Editions Gallimard, 2000); Benjamin Franklin Martin, *France and the Après Guerre, 1918–1924: Illusions and Disillusionment* (Baton Rouge: Louisiana State University Press, 1999).

37. André Malraux, *La Condition humaine* (Paris: Editions Gallimard, 1933).

INDEX

Journey to the End of the Night,
123; *Le Feu,* 116
Paléologue, Maurice, Agadir Crisis,
15; warning of war, 21; mentioned 61
Paris Peace Conference, discussed,
67, 68
Paris Stock Market. *See* Bourse, the
Paul-Boncour, Joseph, prime minister 1932, 165
Pelletan, Camille, 40, 41, 47
Pétain, Philippe, Marshal: ambassador to Spain, 198; compared
to Clemenceau, 207; mentioned,
139, 141, 169
Poincaré, Raymond: 1901 politics,
58, 61; 85; prime minister 1912,
15–16; president 1913–20,
16–17, 154; editorials against
Caillaux, 17; visit to Russia in
1914, 26, 33, 36; declaration of
war, 38; Paris Peace Conference,
67; prime minister 1922–24,
144; on Soviet Union, 158; occupation of Ruhr Valley, 159; prime
minster 1926–29, 162, 163;
d'Ormesson on, 58; Clemenceau
on, 71, Martin du Gard on, 85
Poland, German demands on, 198;
partitions of, 199; distrust of
Soviet Union, 201–2; German
invasion of, 206
Popular Front (*Front Popuaire*),
101, 171
Pressard, Georges, 145, 148
Proust, Marcel, 81

Reinach, Joseph, 48–49
Reparations, 159

Reynaud, Paul: economic policy,
181; on July 1939 celebrations,
183; Mannheimer affair, 193–94;
as minister of finance, 203
Ribbentrop, Joachim von, 167, 198;
visit to Paris, 182, 184; Abetz
affair, 187, 189

Sacred Union: Barrès on spirit of, 35;
French response to, 37; Clem-
enceau's abstinence from, 61
Saint-Exupéry, Antoine de, 139–40,
141–42
Sarraut, Albert, on German remilitarization, 170; condemned by
L'Action française, 195; minister
of interior, 203, 205; mentioned,
162, 163, 166, 168, 169
Scheurer-Kestner, Auguste, 41–43,
47
Smith, Edward "Gunboat," boxing
match 1914, 24
Songe, Le, discussed, 117–18
Spanish Civil War: Bernanos on,
139; mentioned, 173, 198
Stavisky affair: discussed, 144–46;
Communist demonstrations following, 146; Daladier's investigation of, 147; political aftermath,
169; mentioned, 100, 168

Tardieu, André, 58, 149, 162, 169
Temps, Le: assassination of Archduke Franz Ferdinand, 23;
military expansion, 26; French-
Russian alliance, 26; Austro-
Hungarian ultimatum, 33; assassination of Jaurès, 37; "Letters
from America," Clemenceau, 43;

Lightning Source UK Ltd.
Milton Keynes UK
UKHW012227121222
413820UK00003B/180